IBM PC AS LANGUAGE

A Guide for Programmers

Leo J. Scanlon

Robert J. Brady Co.
A Prentice-Hall Publishing and
Communications Company
Bowie, MD 20715
Scholars Book Co., Ltd.
Taipei, Taiwan

IBM PC Assembly Language: A Guide for Programmers
Copyright © 1983 by Robert J. Brady Company.

Library of Congress Cataloging in Publication Data

Scanlon, Leo J., 1941–
    IBM PC assembly language.

    1. IBM Personal Computer—Programming.   2. Assembler
language (Computer program language)   I. Title.
II. Title: I.B.M. P.C. assembly language.
QA76.8.I259483   1983   001.64'2   83-3848
ISBN 0-89303-241-7

" Reprinted in Taiwan by The Scholars

Book Co., Ltd. by Special Agreement

With Prentice-Hall International Book Co."

有著作權◇不准翻印

台內著字第　　　號

IBM PC Assembly Language: A Guide for Programmers

原著者：Scanlon, Leo J.,

發行人：楊　鏡　秋

發行所：儒　林　圖　書　有　限　公　司

　　　　台 北 市 重 慶 南 路 一 段　111 號

　　　　電話：3140111 郵撥帳戶：106792 號

行 政 院 新 聞 局 局 版 台 業 字 第 1492 號

印刷所：吉　豐　印　製　會　限　公　司

　　　　板橋市三民路 2 段正隆巷 46 弄 7 號

中　華　民　國　73　年　　　月　　　版

實價 NT $

Contents

Preface

This book puts the full power of the IBM Personal Computer at your fingertips. The speed and efficiency of *assembly language* are the keys to this power—power largely unavailable through high-level languages such as BASIC.

There's nothing wrong with using BASIC if you're programming operations that don't require a great deal of speed. But if you're writing a program in which a lot of things are going on at the same time, such as moving several objects around on the screen in a game program, you'll find that BASIC can't do the job. Objects may mysteriously disappear or move in a jerky fashion. Obviously, BASIC just breaks down under the work load.

BASIC and most other high-level languages are also unsuited for communicating with attached equipment in "real time." Moreover, programs you write with these languages take up a lot of memory, and maybe you don't have a great deal of memory in your computer. For these and other problems, you might consider writing your programs in assembly language.

Even if assembly language *is* your likely choice, you may be wondering whether you have enough background to learn assembly language programming. You *do* if you have done some programming of *any* kind. If you know BASIC or some other high-level language, that's fine. If you have developed programs in an assembly language, that's even better. For the benefit of former high-level language users, the book has two starting points.

If you've never programmed in assembly language, start with Chapter 0, which gives you a "crash course" in the *binary* and *hexadecimal* numbering systems. Otherwise, if you already know what these terms mean and understand how to use them, proceed directly to Chapter 1.

The Contents of This Book

In Chapter 1, we introduce the 8088 microprocessor—the Personal Computer's "brain"— and discuss its role in the system.

Chapter 2 discusses assemblers in general, then describes two typical assemblers, the IBM *Small Assembler* and *MACRO Assembler*. (Although the book uses these two assemblers for illustration, the general principles apply to any other IBM-compatible assembler you might own.) Chapter 2 also tells you how to enter a program into the computer and how to execute (run) it. A simple example program is also included.

Chapter 3 describes the instruction set of the 8088 microprocessor, the commands you use to communicate with your Personal Computer. *This book treats the 8088 instructions in functional groups, rather than alphabetically.* That is, we group add with subtract, multiply with divide, and so on. Through this approach you not only get to *understand* what the instructions do, but you also appreciate how they fit together.

In Chapter 4 you learn how to combine instructions to perform extended math operations that the microprocessor's instruction set doesn't provide directly. Chapter 5 covers operations on lists and tables.

The IBM Personal Computer has a built-in operating system called the *BIOS* (for Basic I/O System) that regulates the equipment in the system. It does everything necessary for the microprocessor to "talk" to the keyboard, display screen, and other peripherals. In doing so, BIOS serves as the PC's "chief administrative officer." BIOS contains many useful features that can save you hours of programming time in your own applications. Chapter 6 shows you how to take advantage of them.

In Chapters 7 and 8 you learn how to develop programs that display simple graphic shapes on the screen and generate sounds (and eventually *music!*) through the computer's built-in speaker.

The book provides four appendices for your convenience. Appendix A has tables that help you convert hexadecimal numbers to decimal, or vice versa. Appendix B summarizes the ASCII character set. Appendices C and D summarize the 8088 microprocessor's instruction set in alphabetical order, and show how long the 8088 takes to execute each instruction, how many bytes each instruction occupies in memory, and which status flags it affects.

Study Exercises

Most chapters conclude with a set of questions and programming exercises. Some of these test your understanding of the material in the chapter, others are meant to extend your knowledge of the material into additional, related topics.

What You Need With This Book

To use this book, you need an IBM Personal Computer with an attached display unit and a mass storage device, either disk or cassette. You also need an *8088 assembler* software package.

This book describes two assemblers offered by IBM, the Small Assembler and the MACRO Assembler, but the general principles are readily adaptable to any other IBM-compatible assembler you might have. At this writing, all assemblers for the Personal Computer come on floppy disk drive. One drive is adequate, but two drives make your job a lot easier. Of course, with disk you also need a *Disk Operating System* (*DOS*) software package.

Supplementary Reference Books

This book is designed to complement the manuals that come with the IBM Personal Computer, so you probably won't need any other reference books. However, every serious Personal Computer user should have a copy of the IBM *Technical Reference* manual, which is an invaluable source for technical information. Among other things, the *Technical Reference* manual contains a complete and fully-documented listing of the Personal Computer's built-in operating program, called the *Basic I/O System* (*BIOS*).

Further, if you are designing add-on hardware for the Personal Computer, or just wish to have the full details on the chips in the system, you may want to get one or more of the following reference documents:

- *iAPX 86,88 User's Manual* and Numeric Supplement
- *iAPX 88 Book*
- *iAPX 88/10 Data Sheet*

To order, contact Intel Corporation, Literature Dept., 3065 Bowers Ave., Santa Clara, CA 95051.

May you have as much satisfaction developing assembly language programs as I had writing this book.

Leo J. Scanlon

LIMITS OF LIABILITY AND DISCLAIMER OF WARRANTY

The author and publisher of this book have used their best efforts in preparing this book and the programs contained in it. These efforts include the development, research, and testing of the theories and programs to determine their effectiveness. The author and publisher make no warranty of any kind, expressed or implied, with regard to these programs or the documentation contained in this book. The author and publisher shall not be liable in any event for incidental or consequential damages in connection with, or arising out of, the furnishing, performance, or use of these programs.

This book is dedicated to my sons, Roger and Ryan, whose generation will perform "miracles" in the 21st century.

0

A Crash Course in Computer Numbering Systems

Unless you are visiting from another planet, you've probably spent your entire life counting things using decimal numbers. Decimal is a *base 10* numbering system, which means it has 10 digits—0 through 9.

Human beings are quite comfortable with the decimal system (probably because we have ten fingers and ten toes), but computers are not. Instead, computers are designed around the base 2, or *binary*, numbering system, which consists of only two digits, 0 and 1. Hence, to communicate with the computer at its own level (as you do when you program with assembly language), you must be familiar with binary numbering. In addition to binary numbering, assembly language programmers also use other numbering systems—primarily base 16 (hexadecimal)—to represent combinations of binary digits, so you must be familiar with these systems as well.

This chapter is a "crash course" in computer numbering systems, for readers who have no previous exposure to them. That's why we call it Chapter 0. If you already understand binary and hexadecimal numbering, feel free to skip this chapter and begin at Chapter 1.

0.1 The Binary Numbering System

In a computer, all program instructions and data are stored in the computer's *memory*. Memory is comprised of a vast number of electrical components. These components act like light switches in that they have only two possible settings: "On" and "Off." Still, with only these two settings, combinations of memory components can represent numbers of any size. How? Read on.

The On and Off settings of memory components correspond to the two digits of the *binary numbering system,* the fundamental system for computers. Having only two digits, 1 (On) and 0 (Off), the binary numbering system is a *base 2* system. (Again, this contrasts with the standard decimal numbering system, which has 10 digits—0 through 9—making it a *base 10* system.)

The switch-like components of memory are called "bits," short for *binary digits.* By convention, a bit that is On has the value 1 and a bit that is Off has the value 0. This appears to be woefully limiting, until you consider that a decimal digit (no, it's not called a "det") can only range from 0 to 9. Just as you combine decimal digits to form numbers larger than 9, you combine binary digits to form numbers larger than 1.

As you know, to represent a decimal number larger than 9 requires another digit, a "tens position" digit. Likewise, to represent a decimal number larger than 99 requires a "hundreds position" digit, and so on. Each decimal digit you add has a *weight* of 10 times the digit to its immediate right.

For example, you can represent the decimal number 324 as

$$(3 \times 100) + (2 \times 10) + (4 \times 1)$$

or as

$$(3 \times 10^2) + (2 \times 10^1) + (4 \times 10^0)$$

So, in more mathematical terms, each decimal digit is a power of 10 greater than the preceding digit.

A similar rule applies to the binary numbering system. In this system, *each binary digit is a power of two greater than the preceding binary digit.* The rightmost bit has a weight of 2^0 (decimal 1), the next bit to the left has a weight of 2^1 (decimal 2), and so on. For example, the binary number 101 has a decimal value of five, because

$$101_2 = (1 \times 2^2) + (0 \times 2^1) + (1 \times 2^0)$$
$$= (1 \times 4) + (0 \times 2) + (1 \times 1)$$
$$= 5_{10}$$

Do you now understand how binary numbers are constructed? To find the value of any given bit position, you double the weight of the preceding bit position. Thus, the first eight binary weights are 1, 2, 4, 8, 16, 32, 64, and 128. Figure 0-1 summarizes these weights.

7	6	5	4	3	2	1	0	BIT POSITION
2^7	2^6	2^5	2^4	2^3	2^2	2^1	2^0	POWER OF TWO
128	64	32	16	8	4	2	1	DECIMAL VALUE

Figure 0-1. Weights of eight binary digits.

To convert a decimal value to binary, you make a series of simple subtractions. Each subtraction gives you the value of a single binary digit (or bit).

To begin, subtract the largest possible binary weight from the decimal value and enter a 1 in that bit position. Then subtract the next largest possible binary weight from the result and enter a 1 in *that* bit position. Continue until the result is zero. Enter a 0 in any bit position whose weight cannot be subtracted from the current decimal value.

For example, to convert decimal 50 to binary:

```
   50
 - 32      Bit position 5=1
   18
 - 16      Bit position 4=1
    2
 -  2      Bit position 1=1
    0
```

Entering a 0 in the other bit positions (Bits 3, 2 and 0) yields a final result of 110010.

To verify that the binary equivalent of decimal 50 is indeed 110010, add the decimal weights of the "1" positions:

```
   32    (Bit 5)
   16    (Bit 4)
 +  2    (Bit 1)
   50
```

Eight Bits Make a Byte

The Apple II and III, the Commodore PET/CBM, the Radio Shack TRS-80, and many other popular microcomputers are designed around an eight-bit *microprocessor.* Eight-bit microprocessors are so named because they process eight bits of information in a single operation. To process more than eight bits requires them to perform two or more separate operations.

In computer nomenclature, an eight-bit unit of information is called a *byte.* With eight bits, a byte can represent decimal values from 0 (binary 00000000) to 255 (binary 11111111).

Because a byte is the fundamental unit of processing, microcomputers are described in terms of the number of bytes (rather than bits) contained in their memories. Further, microcomputer manufacturers generally construct memory in blocks of 1,024 bytes. This particular quantity reflects the binary orientation of computers in that it represents 2^{10} bytes.

The value 1,024 has a standard abbreviation; it is referred to by the letter *K*. Hence, an advertisement for a computer that has a "48K memory" tells you this product has a storage capacity of 48 x 1,024 (or 49,152) bytes.

Adding Binary Numbers

You add binary numbers the same way you add decimal numbers: by propagating any carry from one column to the next. For example, if you add the decimal values 7 and 9, you must carry a 1 into the "tens" column to produce the correct result (16). Similarly, if you add the *binary* values 1 and 1, you must carry a 1 into the "twos" column to produce the correct result (10).

The addition gets slightly more complicated if you are adding multi-bit numbers (as you normally are), and have to include a carry from a previous column. To illustrate, this operation:

```
  1011
+   11
  1110
```

involves two carries. The addition of the rightmost column (1 + 1) produces a result of 0 and a carry into the second column. With the carry, the addition of the second column (1 + 1 + 1), produces a result of 1 and a carry into the third column.

The general rules are shown in this table:

Inputs			Results	
Operand #1	Operand #2	Carry	Sum	Carry
0	0	0	0	0
0	1	0	1	0
1	0	0	1	0
1	1	0	0	1
0	0	1	1	0
0	1	1	0	1
1	0	1	0	1
1	1	1	1	1

Signed Numbers

Until now, we have been discussing the binary representation of *unsigned numbers*. In an unsigned number, each bit carries a certain weight (as we discussed earlier), according to its position. The least-significant bit has a weight of 2^0 and each more-significant bit has a weight twice that of its predecessor. Therefore, if all bits in a byte contain 0, the byte holds the value 0, and if all bits contain 1, the byte holds the value 255.

However, many of your calculations will involve positive or negative values; that is, *signed numbers*. When a byte contains a signed number, only the seven least-significant bits represent data; the most-significant bit (Bit 7, represents the sign of the number. *The most-significant bit is 0 if the number is positive or zero and 1 if the number is negative.* Figure 0-2 shows the arrangement of signed and unsigned bytes.

Bytes holding positive numbers can represent values between 0 (binary 00000000) and +127 (binary 01111111). Bytes holding negative numbers can represent values between -1 (binary 11111111) and -128 (binary 10000000).

2s-Complement Representation

Why is -1 represented in binary as 11111111, instead of 10000000? The answer is that negative signed numbers are represented in their *2s-complement form.* Computer scientists invented the 2s-complement form to eliminate the problems associated with letting zero be represented in two different ways, all 0s ("positive zero") and all 0s with a 1 in the sign position ("negative zero").

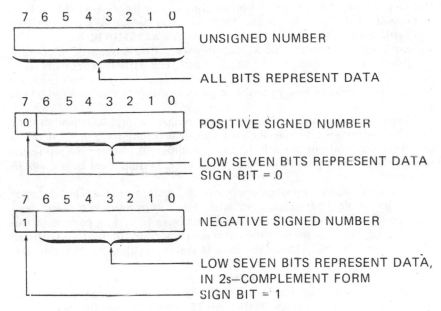

Figure 0-2. Representation of signed and unsigned numbers.

To find the binary representation of a negative number (that is, to find its 2s-complement form), simply take the positive form of the number and reverse each bit—change each 1 to a 0 and each 0 to a 1—then add 1 to the result. The following example shows the steps required to calculate the 2s-complement binary representation of -32:

```
 00100000   +32

 11011111   Reverse all bits
+       1   Add 1
 11100000   2s-complement
```

You also use the same procedure (reverse all bits and add 1) to find the positive form of a negative number.

Fortunately, most assembler programs let you enter numbers in decimal form (signed or unsigned), and make all the proper conversions for you. However, you may occasionally want to interpret a negative number that is stored in memory or in a register, so you should know how to make these conversions yourself.

0.2 The Hexadecimal Numbering System

Although the binary numbering system is an accurate way to represent numbers in memory, strings of nothing but 1s and 0s are very difficult to work with. They are very prone to errors, too, because a number like 10110101 is extremely easy to enter incorrectly as 10110110.

Years ago, programmers found that they were always required to operate on *groups* of bits, rather than individual bits. The earliest processors were four-bit devices (they processed information four bits at a time), so the logical alternative to binary numbering was a system that numbered bits in groups of four.

As you know, four bits can represent the binary values 0000 through 1111 (which is equivalent to the decimal values 0 through 15), a total of 16 possible combinations. If each digit of a numbering system is to represent one of those 16 combinations, that numbering system must be a *base 16* system.

If the word binary is used to denote a base 2 system and the word decimal is used to denote a base 10 system, what word is appropriate to describe a base 16 system? Well, whoever named the base 16 system combined the Greek word "hex" (for six) with the Latin word "decem" (for ten), and formed the word hexadecimal. Hence, the base 16 system is called the *hexadecimal numbering system*.

Of the 16 digits in the hexadecimal numbering system, the first 10 are labeled 0 through 9 (decimal values 0 through 9) and the last six are labeled A through F (decimal values 10 through 15). Table 0-1 lists the binary and decimal equivalents for each of the 16 hexadecimal digits.

Table 0-1. Hexadecimal Numbering System.

Hexadecimal Digit	Binary Value	Decimal Value
0	0000	0
1	0001	1
2	0010	2
3	0011	3
4	0100	·4
5	0101	5
6	0110	6
7	0111	7
8	1000	8
9	1001	9
A	1010	10
B	1011	11
C	1100	12
D	110T	13
E	1110	14
F	1111	15

Like binary and decimal digits, each hexadecimal digit has a "weight" that is some power of its base. Since the hexadecimal numbering system is based on 16, each hexadecimal digit has a weight 16 times greater than the digit to its immediate right. That is, the rightmost digit has a weight of 16^0, the second digit has a weight of 16^1, and so on. For example, the hexadecimal value 3AF has a decimal value of 943, because

$$(3\times16^2)+(A\times16^1)+(F\times16^0)$$

reduces to the decimal form

$$(3\times256)+(10\times16)+(15\times1)=943$$

Uses of Hexadecimal Numbers

Unlike BASIC and other high-level languages, most assembly language information is displayed in hexadecimal form. This includes addresses, instruction codes, and the contents of memory locations and registers. Therefore, to get maximum benefit from your programming you must learn to "think hexadecimal." This is difficult at first, but becomes easier as you gain more experience. To help you along, Appendix A provides tables for converting decimal numbers to hexadecimal, and vice versa.

Study Exercises (answers on page 277)

1. Convert the following decimal values to binary:
   (a) 12   (b) 17   (c) 45   (d) 72
2. Convert the following unsigned binary values to decimal:
   (a) 1000   (b) 10101   (c) 11111
3. How do you represent the three binary numbers in Exercise 2 in hexadecimal?
4. List the decimal equivalent of hexadecimal D8 if:
   (a)   the value represents an unsigned number
   (b)   the value represents a signed number

1

Introduction to Assembly Language Programming

1.1 Why Assembly Language?

Human beings can communicate with computers just like they communicate with each other: through an established language. If both participants use the same language, the communication is direct and requires no translation. However, two people speaking different languages can also communicate, if one is bilingual and can translate the other's language into his or her own.

Being an electronic instrument, a computer can "understand" only electrical signals. Thus, those signals are the basis of the computer's "native language." To communicate with the computer, you could (if you wish) learn this electrical language and conduct all your communications—that is, your *programs*—using it. This approach was, in fact, used in the early days of computers, when programmers were forced to write their programs as sequences of numeric codes, which corresponded to the signals inside the computer. These programs were said to be written in *machine language*.

Machine language potentially produces the most efficient programs, because it lets you directly control the "brain" of the computer—it's *processor*—with minimal code-to-electrical-signal translation. But you pay a price for this convenience, because machine language programming requires you to enter instructions in *numeric form*, as groups of binary or hexadecimal digits.

For example, to enter an add instruction in machine language, you might have to type in the binary pattern 10000011, or its hexadecimal equivalent, 83. Similarly, to enter a subtract instruction, you might have to type in the binary pattern 00101101 or the hexadecimal equivalent, 2D. As you might

9

expect, this approach is not only time-consuming and difficult, but it's extremely error-prone as well.

As time went by, and computers were used to solve more complex problems (which meant bigger programs), someone got the idea of replacing each numeric code with a meaningful, English-like abbreviation that programmers could easily remember. For instance, an add instruction might be represented by the abbreviation ADD rather than binary 10000011, and a subtract instruction might be represented by SUB rather than 00101101.

Of course, this also required an additional program to convert the abbreviations to the numeric codes the processor could recognize. The program that makes these abbreviation-to-number conversions is called an *assembler,* and the sum total of all abbreviations the assembler can convert is called (appropriately) the *assembly la. ·Jage.*

At the next level up from assembly language are languages that make the machine language completely "transparent" to the programmer, by replacing an entire *group* of machine level instructions with a single English-like word or phrase. These "high-level" languages (such as BASIC, Pascal and Fortran) allow you to develop programs much faster than with assembly language, but the resulting program usually takes up much more space in memory and runs slower than its assembly language equivalent. Moreover, high-level languages are unsuitable for many applications where precise control of the system is crucial.

The choice of language is up to you, but if your application program must fit into a small amount of memory or must run quickly — or if you just want to have more direct control over the resources of the Personal Computer — assembly language programming can provide the key. As a starting point, however, you must understand the features and capabilities of the Personal Computer's microprocessor, an integrated circuit (or "chip") called the 8088. Let us begin.

1.2 The 8088's Family Tree

You can consider the 8088 as being either an 8-bit microprocessor or a 16-bit microprocessor, depending on your viewpoint. By standard industry terminology, the 8088 might be characterized as an 8-bit microprocessor, because it transfers information eight bits at a time, over an *8-bit data bus.* However, the 8088's internal busses are 16 bits wide and it can operate on 8- or 16-bit numbers with equal ease, so the 8088 can also rightfully be called a 16-bit microprocessor.

To avoid getting bogged down in nomenclature, you might like to think of the 8088 as a *16-bit processor with an 8-bit data bus* (an "8/16-bit" processor). But again, the choice is up to you.

Why would a company design a 16-bit microprocessor with an 8-bit data bus? The answer to this question is wrapped up in this processor's chronology.

The Intel 8008, introduced in 1972, was the first commercial 8-bit micro-processor, and is still considered the foremost "first-generation" 8-bit micro-processor. Designed with a calculator-like architecture, the 8008 had an accumulator, six scratchpad registers, a stack pointer (a special address register for temporary storage), eight address registers, and special instructions to perform input and output. In 1973, Intel introduced a "second-generation" version of the 8008, and christened it the 8080.

The 8080 is essentially an upgraded 8008, and has more addressing and I/O capability, more instructions and executes instructions faster. The internal organization is better too, although the overall 8008 architectural philosophy is maintained in the 8080. The 8080 is historically the de facto standard in second-generation microprocessors; the device many people still think of first when someone mentions microprocessors.

By 1976, advances in technology allowed Intel to produce an enhanced version of the 8080, called the 8085. Essentially a repackaged 8080, the 8085 added such features as an on-chip oscillator, power-on reset (to initialize the microprocessor), vectored interrupts (to service the needs of peripherals), a serial I/O port (for printers and other serial peripherals), and a single, +5-volt power supply (the 8080 requires two supplies).

By the time the 8085 was introduced, Intel had lots of competition in the 8-bit microprocessor marketplace. Zilog Corporation's 8080 enhancement, the Z80, was catching on, as were non-8080 designs such as the Motorola 6800 and the MOS Technology (now Commodore) 6502. Rather than continue the struggle on the now-diluted 8-bit front, Intel made a quantum leap forward in 1978 by introducing the 8086, a 16-bit microprocessor that can process data ten times as fast as the 8080.

The 8086 is software-compatible with the 8080 at the assembly language level, which means that with some minimal translation, existing 8080 programs can be reassembled and executed on the 8086. To allow for this, the 8080 registers and instruction set appear as subsets of the 8086 registers and instructions. With this compatibility, Intel could capitalize on its experience with the 8080 to gain acceptance in more sophisticated applications.

In the same vein, realizing that many designers will still want to use the cheaper 8-bit support and peripheral chips in their 16-bit systems, Intel produced a version of the 8086 with the same 16-bit internal data paths, but with an 8-bit data bus coming out of the chip. This microprocessor, the 8088, is identical to the 8086, except the 8088 takes more time to make 16-bit transfers because it must perform them with two separate 8-bit transfers.

As an assembly language programmer you won't notice this difference unless your application is time-critical. Even then, for applications that primarily deal with 8-bit quantities rather than 16-bit quantities, the 8088 can approach to within 10 percent of the 8086's processing power!

Thus, if you wish, you can consider your IBM Personal Computer as having a 16-bit microprocessor. (This also means you can refer to the large body of literature written around the 8086. Incidentally, Intel literature usually refers to the 8086 and the 8088 as the iAPX 86 and the iAPX 88, respectively, so you may come across those designations as well.) With this prologue aside, we can now take a look at the features of the 8088.

1.3 Overview of the 8088 Microprocessor

The 8088 has *12 data and address registers,* plus a 16-bit instruction pointer (similar to the program counter in most microprocessors) and a 16-bit "flags" register. The 12 data and address registers can be divided into three groups of four registers, called *data registers, pointer and index registers,* and *segment registers.*

Addressing

Since the instruction pointer and all data and address registers are 16 bits wide, you would expect the 8088 to address no more than 64K bytes (65,536 bytes) of memory—the standard addressing range of 8-bit microprocessors. However, the 8088 employs a technique where it generates a *20-bit address* by adding a 16-bit offset to the contents of a segment register multiplied by 16. That is:

Physical Address = Offset Address + (16×Segment Register)

In reality, the 8088 doesn't actually *multiply* the segment address by 16, but instead uses the segment register as if it had four zeroes appended (see Figure 1-1). The result is the same, however, because each time a binary number is displaced one bit position to the left, it is effectively multiplied by two. Thus, displacing the segment register *four* bit positions to the left "multiplies" its contents by 16, since 2x2x2x2 = 16.

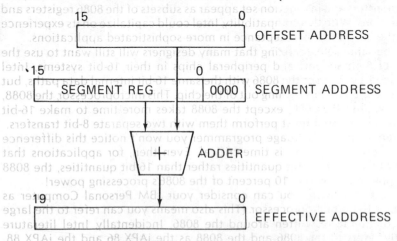

Figure 1-1. How a 20-bit address is generated.

For example, if the offset address has the value 10H—where the H suffix means hexadecimal—and the segment register contains 2000H, the 8088 calculates the physical address as follows (operands are shown in binary form):

```
  0000 0000 0001 0000     Offset address
+0010 0000 0000 0000 0000  Segment address
 0010 0000 0000 0001 0000  Physical address
```

Therefore, the memory location referenced here has the 20-bit address 20010H.

With a 20-bit address at its disposal, the 8088 can access any of *1M bytes* (1,048,576 bytes). Or *1024K bytes*, if you like. That's 16 times the addressing range of the 8080!

Segments and Offsets

Because the 8088 forms memory addresses by combining two components (a segment number and an offset), memory addressing operations in your programs are somewhat different than with other microprocessors. With most microprocessors, you can reference a memory address as a single number, but with the 8088 each memory reference requires *two* "attributes:" a segment number and an offset. However, you generally only give the offset, and let the 8088 provide the segment number. We discuss this point in more detail later in the book.

Software Features

The software features of the 8088 are impressive by any standard, but will be especially welcomed by programmers who struggled with the earlier 8-bit microprocessors. The 8088 can perform arithmetic operations on signed or unsigned binary numbers of either 8 bits or 16 bits, and on decimal numbers stored in either "packed" (two digits per byte) or "unpacked" (one digit per byte) form.

Byte and word data can reside at any address in memory, in contrast to some microprocessors (for example, the Motorola 68000) that require word data to start at even-numbered addresses. The 8088 can also operate on character strings of either bytes or words up to 64K bytes long.

The 8088 instruction set has 92 basic instruction types and provides seven different addressing modes for accessing data. The combination of the 92 instruction types, the seven addressing modes (each with a variety of operand combinations), and the various data types we just mentioned means there are *thousands* of instructions that the 8088 can execute. In fact, the combined power of these features allows the 8088 to deliver twice the performance of an 8085, if both processors are driven at the same speed.

The Personal Computer drives the 8088 at 4.77 MHz. That is, the microprocessor's clock (a small crystal, similar to the crystal in a digital watch) operates at 4,770,000 cycles per second. This means each clock cycle takes about 210 nanoseconds, where a nanosecond (abbreviated ns) is one billionth of a second, or 10^{-9} seconds.

The fastest instructions—for example, an instruction that copies the contents of one register into another—execute in two cycles, or 420 ns. The slowest instruction, a signed 16-bit by 16-bit division, can take up to 206 clock cycles, or about 43 microseconds, to execute. (A microsecond, usually abbreviated μs, is one millionth of a second, or 10^{-6} seconds.) As you can see, even this "slowest" instruction executes in the remarkable time of 0.000043 seconds!

Input/Output Space

In addition to its one-megabyte memory space, the 8088 can address 64K I/O ports (that is, 65,536 ports). The first 256 ports—ports 0 through 255—are directly addressable with input and output instructions Other instructions let you access any of the 64K I/O ports indirectly, by putting its identifying number (0 through 65535) in a data register. Like locations in memory, any port may be 8 or 16 bits wide.

Memory Allocation

Most of the 1M-byte address space is available for system and user programs, but the 8088 uses some of the highest and lowest locations for special purposes. The highest 16 bytes of memory hold one or more system reset instructions. The 8088 automatically executes these instructions when you turn on the power.

The lowest 1024 bytes of memory hold interrupt vectors—the addresses of programs the 8088 executes when it is interrupted. In the IBM Personal Computer, these locations reside in RAM. Other areas of memory hold the Personal Computer's system programs, so these locations are also unavailable to you. However, the IBM Disk Operating System is designed to put your programs at any convenient spot in memory, so you normally don't worry about how memory is allocated.

Interrupts

We are all confronted with interruptions from time to time. Some are pleasant, some are unpleasant, and some are neutral. You can ignore some interruptions, if you like; a telephone or doorbell ringing, perhaps, or a child tugging at your sleeve. (On second thought, it's pretty difficult to ignore the child!) You simply can't ignore other kinds of interruptions, such as getting a flat tire on the expressway; you must deal with them as soon as possible.

Whatever their cause, interruptions are essentially requests for our attention. In the same way, peripherals in a computer system can request the attention of the processor. The event that makes a processor stop executing its program to perform some requested activity is called an *interrupt.*

Interrupts increase the overall efficiency of a computer system, because the external devices request the attention of the processor as needed. If a system had no interrupts, the processor would have to *poll* every device in the system periodically, to see if any of them required attention, This would be like having a telephone with no bell. You would have to pick up the receiver every so often to see if anyone is on the line!

The 8088 can process two kinds of interrupts; those it can ignore and those it must service as soon as they occur. Interrupts can be generated by external devices, such as disks and other high-speed peripherals, or internally, by interrupt-generating instructions or (under certain conditions) by the 8088 itself.

Types of Interrupts

The 8088 can recognize 256 different interrupts, each with a unique *type code* that identifies it to the microprocessor. The 8088 uses this type code (a number between 0 and 255) to point to a location in an *interrupt vector table* in memory, which contains the address of the routine that handles the interrupt.

Of the 256 possible interrupt types, five are allocated to *internal interrupts.* These are:

- *Type 0, divide error,* occurs if a divide instruction produces a quotient that is too large to be contained in the result register, or if you attempt to divide by zero.
- *Type 1, single-step,* occurs when the 8088's "single-step" debugging mode is active.
- *Type 2, non-maskable interrupt,* is a type of interrupt that cannot be "locked out" under program control, as all other interrupt types can. This interrupt type generally informs the 8088 of some catastrophic event, such as imminent loss of power.
- *Type 3, interrupt instruction,* is a special one-byte instruction that is used to set up "breakpoints" (stopping points) in software debugging programs.
- *Type 4, overflow,* is triggered by another interrupt instruction (INTO) if a previous operation has produced an "overflow" condition. Overflow is discussed in Section 1.4.

Besides these five internal interrupt types, the 8088 provides 251 unassigned types that are available for additional interrupts, either internal or external. Some of the 251 available interrupts are reserved for the use of the Personal Computer's operating program (called the Basic I/O System, or *BIOS)* and others are used by its Disk Operating System (DOS) and BASIC. We'll discuss the system interrupts in Chapter 6.

Buses and Other Lines on the Chip

The 8088 microprocessor is packaged as a 40-pin integrated circuit, or "chip." Memory addresses come out of the chip on a *20-line address bus*. The first eight lines of the address bus are also used to transfer data into and out of the microprocessor; they form its *8-bit data bus*. Thus, we say the 8088's address bus and the data bus are "multiplexed." The four high order address lines are also multiplexed; they hold status information during memory and I/O operations.

The 8088 operates from a 5-volt power supply, and has one pin for power and two pins for ground. Since the processor also needs a clock (4.77 MHz in the Personal Computer), one more pin accepts the clock input. The remaining 16 pins on the chip carry *control signals,* which we discuss later.

1.4 The 8088's Internal Registers

Since this book is primarily devoted to programming the 8088 (specifically, the 8088 in the IBM Personal Computer), the most logical place to begin is by discussing the internal registers at your disposal. Figure 1-2 shows the three groups of data and address registers, the 16-bit Instruction Pointer (IP), and the 16-bit Flags register.

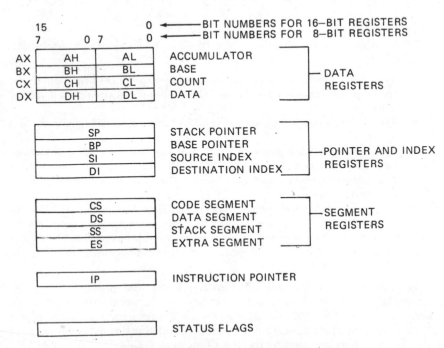

Figure 1-2. Programmable registers within the 8088.

Data Registers

Your programs can treat the data registers as either four 16-bit registers or eight 8-bit registers, depending on whether you operate on byte quantities or word quantities. The 16-bit registers are named AX, BX, CX and DX. The 8-bit registers are named AL, AH, BL, BH, CL, CH, DL and DH; here, the L and H suffixes identify the low-order and high-order bytes of the 16-bit "X" registers.

Any of these data registers can be used for general programming purposes, but certain instructions also make use of them implicitly. Specifically:

- *AX, the Accumulator,* is used in word-size multiplication, division and I/O operations, and in some string operations. The *AL register* is used in the byte-size counterparts of these same operations, and in translate and decimal arithmetic operations. The *AH register* is also used in byte-size multiplications and divisions.
- *BX, the Base register,* is used heavily to address data in memory.
- *CX, the Count register,* acts as an iteration counter for loop operations and as an element counter for repetitive string operations. The *CL register* can be used to hold the shift count for multiple-bit shift and rotate operations.
- *DX, the Data register,* is used in word-size multiplication and division operations. It can also provide the port number in I/O operations.

Former 8080 or 8085 programmers will note that AH is the only data register unique to the 8088; the other registers are relabeled 8080/8085 registers. In the 8080, AL is called A and BX, CX and DX are called HL, BC and DE.

The data registers are the only 8088 registers you may reference as either 8- or 16-bit registers. The registers in the next group are exclusively 16-bit registers.

Segment Registers

8086- and 8088-based computers keep programs and data in two separate areas of memory. These program and data areas, which can be up to 64K bytes long, are called "segments." The 8088 can work with up to four segments at any given time; it holds their starting addresses in four *segment registers.* The functions of these four registers are:

- The *code segment (CS) register* points to the segment that holds the program currently being executed. The 8088 combines the contents of CS (multiplied by 16) with the contents of the instruction pointer (IP) to derive the memory address of the next instruction to be executed.
- The *stack segment (SS) register* points to the current stack segment. A stack is a data structure in memory that functions as a temporary depository for data and addresses. The 8088 uses the stack to hold a return address while a

subroutine·is being executed, but you may also use it to preserve the contents of registers that a subroutine alters. We will talk more about stacks later.

- The data segment (DS) register points to the current data segment, which usually holds program variables.
- The extra segment (ES) register points to the current "extra" segment, which is used in string operations.

In large systems, the four segments may lie in different parts of memory. In systems that have no more than 64K bytes of memory, these segments often overlap.

Pointer and Index Registers

Just as the 8088 combines a base address in CS with an offset in IP to calculate the address of an instruction within the code segment, it accesses data in other segments by combining a base address in a segment register with an offset in another register. In accessing the stack segment, the 8088 gets the base address from SS and the offset from one of the pointer registers (SP or BP). In accessing the data segment, the 8088 gets the base address from DS and the offset from BX, or from one of the index registers (SI or DI).

Although the 8088 always assumes these register combinations, you may override these assignments. For instance, you can access a location in the extra segment by directing the 8088 to apply ES, rather than SS, to an offset in BP. We discuss segment overrides in more detail in Chapter 2.

Instruction Pointer

Most microprocessors execute a program by fetching an instruction from memory, executing that instruction, then fetching the next instruction, and so on. This approach naturally introduces some delay, because the microprocessor must wait until each new instruction has been fetched from memory before execution can begin. The 8088 eliminates much of this instruction-fetching overhead by assigning these two tasks—fetching instructions and executing instructions—to separate functional units within the chip.

One of these, the Bus Interface Unit (BIU), is solely responsible for fetching instructions from memory and passing data between the execution hardware and the "outside world." The other, the Execution Unit (EU), only executes instructions. Because these units are independent, the BIU can fetch a new instruction from memory at the same time the EU is executing a previously-fetched instruction.

Each time the BIU fetches an instruction, it adds that instruction to an instruction pipeline (or queue) within the microprocessor. Thus, when the EU finishes executing a given instruction, it can usually find the next instruction in the pipeline.

Since the BIU has no way of knowing the sequence in which the program will execute, it always fetches instructions from consecutive memory locations. Therefore, the only time the EU must wait for an instruction to be fetched is when program execution transfers to a new, non-sequential address. At that time, the EU must wait for the BIU to clear the pipeline and fetch the next instruction. Then, and only then, the EU waits in the same way most microprocessors wait for *every* instruction to be fetched. Figure 1-3 shows parallel fetching and executing in the 8088.

Because the 8088 works in this rather unique way, the people at Intel chose to differentiate their "next-execution-address" register from other manufacturers' "next-fetch-address" register by calling it an *instruction Pointer (IP)* instead of a program counter (PC). The IP always contains the offset of the next instruction to be executed by the 8088's EU. Because the IP is a special-purpose register, you cannot perform arithmetic on its contents, but the 8088 has instructions that cause the IP to change and to be transferred to and from the stack.

Flags

You will often want your program to make a "decision" based on the result of the instruction just executed. For example, you may wish to do one thing if the result of an addition is zero and something entirely different if the result is not zero. The 8088's 16-bit *Flags register* helps your program make these decisions by reporting various status conditions in six of its bits. Three additional bits let you control the 8088 from within a program.

Figure 1-4 shows how these nine "flags" are arranged in the Flags register. The flags operate as follows:

- *Bit 0, the Carry Flag (CF)*, is 1 if an add operation produces a carry or a subtract operation produces a borrow; otherwise it is 0. CF also holds the value of a bit that has been shifted or rotated out of a register or memory location, and reflects the result of a compare operation. Finally, CF also acts as a result indicator for multiplications; see the description of the OF flag, bit 11, for details.

- *Bit 2, the Parity Flag (PF)*, is 1 if the result of an operation has an even number of logic 1 bits; otherwise it is 0. PF is primarily used in data communications applications.

- *Bit 4, the Auxiliary Carry Flag (AF)*, is similar to the CF bit, except AF reflects the presence of a carry or borrow out of bit 3 of the operand. CF is useful for operating on "packed" decimal numbers.

- *Bit 6, the Zero Flag (ZF)*, is 1 if the result of an operation is zero; a non-zero result clears ZF to 0.

- *Bit 7, the Sign Flag (SF)*, is meaningful only during operations on signed numbers. It is 1 if an arithmetic, logical, shift, or rotate operation produces a negative result; otherwise it is 0. In other words, SF reflects the most-significant bit of the result, regardless of whether the result is 8 or 16 bits long.

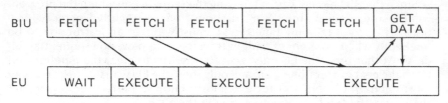

Figure 1-3. Parallel operation in the "pipelined" 8088.

- *Bit 8, the Trap Flag (TF)*, puts the 8088 into a "single-step" mode for debugging purposes.
- *Bit 9, the Interrupt Enable Flag (IF)*, allows the 8088 to recognize interrupt requests from external devices in the system. Clearing IF to 0 causes the 8088 to ignore these interrupt requests.
- *Bit 10, the Direction Flag (DF)*, causes the 8088 to automatically decrement (DF = 1) or increment (DF = 0) the index register(s) after a string instruction is executed.
  If DF is 0, the 8088 progresses forward through a string (toward higher addresses, or "right to left"). If DF is 1, it progresses backward through a string (toward lower addresses, or "left to right").
- *Bit 11, the Overflow Flag (OF)*, is primarily an error indicator during operations on signed numbers.
  OF is 1 if the addition of two like-signed numbers, or the subtraction of two opposite signed numbers, has produced a result that exceeds the two's-complement capacity of the operand; otherwise it is 0.
  OF is also 1 if the most-significant (sign) bit of the operand is changed at any time during an arithmetic shift operation; otherwise it is 0.
  The OF flag, in combination with the CF flag, also indicates the length of a multiplication result. If the upper half of the product is non-zero, CF and OF are 1; otherwise both bits 0.
  Finally, OF is 1 if the quotient produced by a divide operation overflows the result register.

The shaded bit positions in Figure 1-4 (1, 3, 5, and 12 through 15) are unused. If you ever read the status of the Flags register, these bits will be 0.

When you first turn on the power to the Personal Computer, all nine flags are 0. However, don't make the mistake of assuming how the flags are configured at any given time. The 8088 has instructions that let you set or reset flags as you choose. When in doubt, *use* these instructions.

The 8088 has conditional transfer instructions that test the state of the Carry (CF), Parity (PF), Zero (ZF), Sign (SF) and Overflow (OF) flags, and cause program execution to continue in line or at some other location in memory, depending on the result of the test.

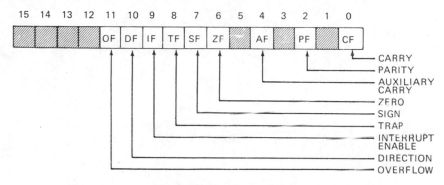

Figure 1-4. The Flags register.

Study Exercises (answers on page 277)

1. How does the instruction set of the 8088 differ from that of the 8086?
2. What physical address is generated when you combine an offset value of 2H with a segment register containing 4000H?
3. If the AX register contains 1A2BH, what does AL contain?
4. Which segment register normally accesses variables in your programs?
5. Which bit in the Flags register tells you whether a preceding subtract operation produced a negative result?

2

Using an Assembler

2.1 Introducing the Assembler

In Chapter 1 you found that assembly language lets you write programs at
the level the microprocessor understands, but doesn't force you to memo-
rize a set of numeric codes. Instead, you write your instructions as English-
like abbreviations, then run an *assembler* program to convert these abbreviations to their numeric equivalents.

By convention, the program written with abbreviations is called the
"source program" and the numeric, microprocessor-compatible form of this
program is called the "object program". Therefore, the assembler's job is to
convert source programs *you* can understand into object programs the
microprocessor can understand.

The Small Assembler and the MACRO Assembler

Several different assemblers are available for the Personal Computer.
Rather than try to describe every possible assembler that readers may use,
we will concentrate on just one typical software package: IBM's *Macro
Assembler*, which runs under the Disk Operating System (DOS). However,
the features provided in this package should be similar to those of any other
package you might own.

The Macro Assembler disk holds two separate assembler programs: the
Small Assembler (ASM), designed for systems that have at least 64K bytes of
memory, and the *MACRO Assembler (MASM)*, designed for systems that
have at least 96K bytes of memory. As its name indicates, the MACRO
Assembler lets you define "macros" — instruction sequences you reference
by a single word in a program — whereas the Small Assembler does not.

This chapter discusses both assemblers and identifies their differences,
where applicable. But rather than attempt an exhaustive description of
these two programs, we will summarize only their main features, and pro-

vide some tables for quick reference. For the full details, consult your IBM *Macro Assembler* manual.

2.2 The Steps in Developing a Program

There are essentially seven steps in developing an assembly language program:

1. Define what you want the computer to do, step by step. This often requires you to draw a *flowchart*, a diagrammed "plan" of the program.
2. Write the program instructions on a piece of paper.
3. Type the written program into the computer, using the *editor* program (more on this later).
4. Assemble the program. If the assembler spots any errors, correct them with the editor, then re-assemble the program.
5. Convert the assembler output to an executable *run module*.
6. Execute (run) the program.
7. Check the results of the program. If the results differ from what you expected, you must "debug" the program.

If your program is very short, or very simple, you should be able to perform most of these steps quickly and easily. But longer and more complex programs will require you to spend more time on each step; especially the initial step, defining the program. These steps are illustrated in an example program at the end of this chapter, to help you learn the ground rules and mechanics of developing programs. For now, we will concentrate on Steps 2 through 6.

The Editor

Step 3 refers to an *editor*, a program we haven't mentioned before in the book. An editor is a utility program you use to enter and manipulate the "text" that constitutes your *source program*. When you run the assembler (Step 4), this source program is converted to a numeric *object program*.

In the Personal Computer, the editor program is called *EDLIN* (a convoluted acronym for Line Editor), which is provided on the DOS disk. You will learn how to use EDLIN in Section 2.7.

The Assembler

EDLIN is a word processing-like program that accepts whatever you type at the keyboard, without making any judgments as to the *quality* of your work. You could type a poem, and EDLIN would accept it. You could type your shopping list, and EDLIN would accept that, too.

The computer can't directly use the information you put into EDLIN. Something must convert that information (hopefully, a program rather than a shopping list) into information the computer can understand. The "something" that makes this conversion is a program called the *assembler.*

The assembler program takes the output of EDLIN (your source program) and converts everything it can into valid instructions the 8088 can understand (Step 4). If the assembler finds anything it can't convert, it tells you with an error message. Once you have corrected all the errors the assembler has spotted, you are ready to apply the Linker.

The Linker

The IBM Disk Operating System has the ability to store a program at any convenient place in memory, which frees you from having to tell it where to put the program. To use this feature, you must convert the assembled program to a "relocatable" machine language program (Step 5), using a utility program called the Linker.

The IBM literature refers to an assembled program as an *object module* and a relocatable machine language program as a *run module.*

A Second Job For the Linker

At this point, you may wonder why the people who developed the Macro Assembler package didn't just make the assembler program generate a relocatable run module, thereby saving you the trouble of running a Linker program. Well, they *could* have done that, but that approach wouldn't have allowed you to do any "linking." Clearly, this calls for more explanation.

The IBM Disk Operating System lets you build programs one section at a time, as you might build a model airplane. With this technique, you write one section of the program, assemble it into an object module, and modify it if the assembler spots any errors. Once this first module assembles without an error, you repeat the process for the second module, then for the third module (if any), and so on. Thus, you eventually wind up with two or more object modules that, in combination, do whatever you designed the program to do.

Now you can guess what the Linker's second major job is. The Linker links assembled object modules to form one large run module.

You must run the Linker for every program you write, even if it has only one object module. For programs with one module, the Linker simply makes the module relocatable. For programs with two or more modules, the Linker combines object modules, then makes the *result* relocatable.

2.3 Source Statements

Having considered the overall approach to developing a program, we can now look at what it contains. The program you write—the *source program*— is a sequence of statements that tell the microprocessor what to do. A source statement (a line in your program) can be either an assembly language instruction or a pseudo-operation.

Assembly language instructions are symbolic representations of the 8088 microprocessor's instruction set. The *Macro Assembler* manual refers to these as "machine instructions," because they tell the "machine" (the 8088) what to do.

By contrast, *pseudo operations*—or "pseudo-ops," for short—tell the *assembler* what to do (with the instructions and data you enter).

Source statements of either kind can also include *operators,* which give the assembler information about an operand, where ambiguities exist. We discuss assembly language instructions, pseudo-ops, and operators in the sections that follow.

Constants in Source Statements

The assembler lets you enter constants in five different forms:

1. *Binary*—A sequence of 1's and 0's followed by the letter B; for example, 10111010B.

2. *Decimal*—A sequence of the digits 0 through 9, with or without the letter D; for example, 129D or 129.

3. *Hexadecimal*—A sequence of the digits 0 through 9 and the letters A through F, followed by the letter H. The first character must be one of the digits 0 through 9; for example, 0E23H.

   The 0 prefix in the preceding example tells the 8088 that E23H is a *number,* rather than a symbol or a variable name.

4. *Octal*—A sequence of the digits 0 through 7, followed by either the letter O or the letter Q; for example, 14770 or 1477Q. (The octal notation is rarely used these days, so you can probably ignore it.)

5. *Character*—A string of letters, numbers, or symbols enclosed in single or double quotes; for example, "Your input is too large."

It is also possible to specify a *negative* number. If the number is a decimal value, you simply precede it with a minus sign (e.g., –10). If the number is a binary, hexadecimal, or octal value, you must enter the number in its "two's complement" form. For example, –32D, 11100000B, 0E0H, and 340Q are alternate forms of decimal –32.

2.4 Assembly Language Instructions

Each assembly language instruction in a source program is comprised of up to four *fields*, as follows:

    . [Label] Mnemonic [Operand] [Comment]

Of these, only the mnemonic field is always required. The label and comment fields are always optional; you may include or omit them at your discretion. The operand field only applies with instructions that *require* an operand; otherwise you must omit it. (The label, operand, and comment fields are shown in brackets here to identify them as optional; *don't* type the brackets into your programs.)

You may enter these fields anywhere on a line, as long as you separate them with at least one blank space. An assembly language instruction that uses all four fields is;

    GETCOUNT: MOV CX,DI ;Initialize count

Here are the details on each of the four fields in an assembly language instruction.

The Label Field

The label field assigns a symbolic *name* to the starting location of an assembly language instruction. This lets other instructions in the program reference the labeled instruction by name, rather than by its numeric location. Any assembly language instruction can be labeled, but labels usually identify the "target" of a jump or procedure (subroutine) call instruction.

A label may be up to 31 characters long, and comprised of:

* *Alphabetic letters:* A through Z (lower-case letters are automatically converted to uppercase on input)
* *Numeric digits:* 0 through 9
* *Special characters:* ? . @ _ $

You can start a label with any character except a digit, but if you use a period (.) in the label, it must be the first character. The symbols AH, AL, AX, BH, BL, BX, BP, CH, CL, CX, CS, DH, DL, DX, DI, DS, ES, SI, and SP are register designators known implicitly by the assembler; you can't use them as labels. You can't use assembler mnemonics (listed in Chapter 3) as labels either.

Although you can't put a space in a label, you can get the same effect by using an underscore character (_). For example, you could write our previous sample instruction line as

    GET_COUNT: MOV CX,DI ;Initialize count

Clearly, this new label (GET_COUNT) is more readable than its predecessor (GETCOUNT).

Using Colons With Labels

Although most labels need a colon at the end, not all do. This statement calls for an explanation.

The 8088 has instructions that can make the processor jump from one place to another in a program. For example, the instruction

```
·JMP   GET_COUNT
```

makes the 8088 transfer control to the instruction stored at the location labeled GET_COUNT. (In the preceding example, GET_COUNT is the starting location of a MOV instruction.)

The 8088 can make this transfer in two ways:

1. If the label is in the *same* code segment as the control-transfer instruction (JMP in this case), the 8088 must only load the offset of the label into the Instruction Pointer (IP); the Code Segment (CS) register can remain as is.
2. If the label is in a *different* code segment than the transfer instruction, the 8088 must load the label's offset into IP and its segment number into CS.

The 8088 "knows" which approach to take based on whether the label has a colon suffix. If the label has a colon, the 8088 assumes it will only be referenced from within the segment. If the colon is omitted, the 8088 assumes the label will be referenced from another code segment.

Since the 8088 executes numeric machine language codes rather than symbolic instructions, how does it know whether a particular label had a colon suffix? The assembler "tells" it with a *distance attribute*.

Distance Attributes (NEAR and FAR)

When the assembler assembles a program, it examines the instruction labels and assigns one of two distance attributes to each label's location in memory. If the label has a colon suffix, the assembler assigns a NEAR attribute to that location. Otherwise, if the label has no colon suffix, the assembler assigns a FAR attribute to that location. For example, the instruction

```
GET_COUNT:   MOV   CX,DI
```

is NEAR, whereas

```
GET_COUNT    MOV   CX,DI
```

is FAR.

The 8088 automatically "knows" that NEAR locations require it to change only IP whereas FAR locations require it to change both IP and CS.

If you attempt to transfer to an un-coloned instruction label in the same segment, the assembler will produce an error message. *Remember to append a colon to all labels that you reference from within the segment*—and that will apply to most labels in your programs.

The Mnemonic Field

The mnemonic field (the leading "m" is silent in the word mnemonic) holds the two- to six-letter acronym for the microprocessor instruction. For example, MOV is the acronym for a move instruction and ADD is the acronym for an add instruction. The assembler uses an internal conversion table to translate each acronym, or *mnemonic*, in the program into its numeric equivalent.

In addition to the mnemonic, many 8088 instructions require you to specify either one or two operands. The mnemonic "tells" the assembler how many operands, and which types of operands, should be obtained from the operand field. The legal mnemonics are described in Chapter 3, so we will not list them here.

The Operand Field

The operand field "tells" the 8088 where to find the data to be operated on. For example, in this *move* instruction:

```
MOV   CX,DX
```

the operand CX , DX tells the 8088 to copy the contents of the DX register into the CX register.

The operand field is mandatory with some instructions and prohibited with others. If present, the operand field will contain either one or two operands, separated from the mnemonic by at least one blank space. If two operands are required, they must be separated by a comma (,).

For two-operand instructions, the first operand is the *destination operand* and the second operand is the *source operand*. The source operand references the value that will be added to, subtracted from, compared to, or stored into the destination operand. (In the preceding MOV example, source operand DX is stored into destination operand CX.) For this reason, the source operand is never altered by the operation, whereas the destination operand is nearly always altered. In Chapter 3 we will discuss the addressing characteristics for each instruction in the 8088's instruction set.

The Comment Field

The optional comment field is used to describe statements in the source program, thereby making the program easier to understand. When applied to a statement, you must precede a comment with a semicolon (;) and separate it from the preceding field by at least one blank space. Comments are ignored by the assembler, but are printed when you list the program.

Your comments should describe the function that is being performed, and not just restate the instruction. For example,

```
MOV  CX,0    ;Clear the count register
```

is more meaningful than

```
MOV  CX,0    ;Move 0 into CX
```

Stand-Alone Comments

In addition to describing individual lines in a program, comments can also be used by themselves, to introduce a program or a portion of a program (a procedure, for example). To include a stand-alone comment in a program, enter a semicolon (;) in column 1. Recognizing the semicolon as the beginning of a comment line, the assembler ignores that line.

The COMMENT pseudo-op, described in Section 2.5, lets you enter an entire *block* of stand-alone comments (several lines, a paragraph, or whatever) by simply enclosing it with asterisks or any other delimiter of your choice.

2.5 Pseudo Operations

Pseudo operations (or *pseudo-ops* for short) give directions to the assembler, rather than to the microprocessor. Pseudo-ops can define symbols, allocate memory for temporary storage, and perform a variety of other important "housekeeping" functions. But unlike assembly language instructions, most pseudo-ops generate no object code.

Pseudo-op statements are comprised of up to four fields:

```
[Name] Pseudo-op [Operand] [Comment]
```

As the brackets show, only the pseudo-op field is always required. A name is mandatory with some pseudo-ops, prohibited with others, and optional with the rest. The same applies to an operand. The comment field is always optional.

As with assembly language instructions, pseudo-op fields can be placed anywhere on a line, but they must be separated by at least one blank space.

The MACRO Assembler provides 59 different pseudo-ops. The Small Assembler provides a subset of these 59. In this section we discuss the most frequently used pseudo-ops (listed in Table 2-1), and postpone discussing the rest until Section 2.8. Table 2-1 divides the pseudo-ops into three groups: data, macro, and listing. Note that the macro pseudo-ops are only available with the MACRO Assembler.

Table 2-1. Frequently-used pseudo-ops.

Type	Pseudo-ops*		
Data	ASSUME	END	EXTRN
	COMMENT	ENDP	INCLUDE
	DB	ENDS	PROC
	DW	EQU	PUBLIC
	DD	= (Equal	SEGMENT
		Sign)	
Macro	*ENDM*	*IRPC*	*PURGE*
	EXITM	*LOCAL*	*REPT*
	IRP	*MACRO*	
Listing	PAGE	SUBTTL	TITLE

*Pseudo-ops printed in *italics* are not supported by the Small Assembler (ASM).

Data Pseudo-ops

The assembler's data pseudo-ops can be divided into five functional groups, as shown in Table 2-2.

Symbol Definition Pseudo-Ops

The symbol definition pseudo-ops let you assign a symbolic *name* to an *expression*. The expression may be a 16-bit constant, an index reference, another symbolic name, a segment prefix and operand, or instruction name. Once you assign the name, you may use it anywhere you would normally use the expression.

The symbol definition pseudo-ops, EQU (short for "equate") and = (equal sign) are similar, but you can redefine symbols defined with =, whereas symbols defined with EQU are permanent. Some examples of EQU are:

```
K      EQU  1024      ;A constant value
B      EQU  [BP+8]    ;An index reference
P8     EQU  DS:[BP+8] ;A segment prefix and operand
COUNT  EQU  CX        ;Another symbolic name
```

In the last example, COUNT represents an alternate name for the CX register, rather than a data value.

Some examples of the = pseudo-op are:

```
CONST=56      ;This is the same as CONST EQU 56, but
CONST=57      ; now CONST may be redefined, and
CONST=CONST+1 ; may refer to its previous definition
```

Table 2-2. Data Pseudo-ops.

Pseudo-Op	Function
Symbol Definition	
EQU	Format: name EQU expression
	Assigns value of *expression* to *name*, permanently.
=	Format: label = expression
	Same as EQU, except *label* can be redefined.
Data Definition	
DB	Format: [name] DB expression[,...]
	Defines a variable or initializes storage. DB allocates one or more bytes.
DW	Format: [name] DW expression[,...]
	Similar to DB, but allocates one or more two-byte words.
DD	Format: [name] DD expression[,...]
	Allocates one or more four-byte doublewords.
External Reference	
PUBLIC	Format: PUBLIC symbol[,...]
	Makes the defined *symbol*(s) available for use by other assembly modules that will be linked to this module
EXTRN	Format: EXTRN name:type[,...]
	Specifies symbols defined in another assembly module.
INCLUDE	Format: INCLUDE filespec
	Assembles source statements from an alternate source file into the current source file.
Segment/Procedure Specification	
SEGMENT	Format: seg-name SEGMENT [align-type]
	[combine-type]
	['class']
	seg-name ENDS
	Defines the boundaries of a named segment. Each SEGMENT definition must be terminated with an ENDS statement.

Table 2-2. Data Pseudo-ops. (continued)

Pseudo-Op	Function
ASSUME	Format: ASSUME seg-reg:seg-name[,...] or ASSUME seg-reg:NOTHING[,...] Tells the assembler which segment register a segment belongs to. *ASSUME NOTHING* cancels any previous ASSUME for the specified register.
PROC	Format: name PROC [NEAR] or name PROC FAR RET name ENDP Assigns a *name* to a sequence of assembler statements. Every PROC definition must end with an ENDP statement.

Assembly Control	
END	Format: END [expression] Marks the end of the source program.

Data Definition Pseudo-Ops

Most programs use locations in memory to hold *variables*—named data items that can be changed as needed. The assembler has three pseudo-ops that allocate space for variables.

Define Byte (DB) allocates 8-bit bytes in memory, *Define Word (DW)* allocates 2-byte words, and *Define Doubleword (DD)* allocates 4-byte doublewords. When defining a variable, you can either *initialize* it with a specified value or simply *reserve* the space (uninitialized) for later use by the program.

The data definition pseudo-ops have the general formats

```
[name]  DB  expression[,....]
[name]  DW  expression[,....]
[name]  DD  expression[,....]
```

where the operand *expression* can take any of several forms, depending on how you wish to define the variable. Further, you can set up *tables*—blocks of memory locations that are referenced under one name—by entering two or more expressions, separated by commas.

For instance, the expression may be a *constant*. (One exception; The Small Assembler does let you use a constant with the DD pseudo-op.) The following statements show the allowable maximum and minimum values for byte- and word-size variables, in decimal:

```
BU_MAX    DB    255      (maximum byte constant, unsigned)
BS_MAX    DB    127      (maximum byte constant, signed)
BS_MIN    DB    -128     (minimum byte constant, signed)

WU_MAX    DW    65535    (maximum word constant, unsigned)
WS_MAX    DW    32767    (maximum word constant, signed)
WS_MIN    DW    -32768   (minimum word constant, signed)
```

You can also let the assembler calculate the value of a constant, if you like, as in this example:

```
MINS_PER_DAY    DW    60*24
```

You may also use pseudo-ops to set up a data table in memory. To do this, simply list the table elements and separate them with a comma. The following sequence sets up two 12-element tables, one comprised of bytes and the other comprised of words:

```
B_TABLE    DB    0,0,0,0,8,-13               (byte table)
DB    -100,0,55,63,63,63
W_TABLE    DW    1025,567,-30222,0,901,-129  (word table)
DW    17,645,26534,367,78,-17
```

Here the elements are arranged as two lines of six values, but you may assign *any* number of variables with one pseudo-op, as long as you don't put more than 132 characters on a line.

Incidentally, note that the first four elements and the last three elements of B_TABLE have the same value (0 and 63, respectively). The assembler has a special operator, called DUP, that allows you to specify repeating operands without entering them individually. With DUP, B_TABLE could be set up with the shorter statement

```
B_TABLE    DB    4 DUP(0),8,-13,-100,0,55,3 DUP(63)
```

You may also define a variable without giving it an initial value, by putting a question mark (?) in the expression field. For example, these statements:

```
HIGH_TEMP     DB    ?
AVG_WEIGHT    DW    ?
```

reserve a total of three bytes in memory, but don't store anything into these locations. The first byte is allocated to the byte variable HIGH_TEMP; the next two bytes are allocated to the word variable AVG_WEIGHT.

Remember, these locations are *not initialized* in any way! Don't make the mistake of assuming they contain 0, or any other specific value.

You may also reserve space for a table in a similar manner. This statement;

```
BUFFER   DW   7,12,98 DUP(?)
```

allocates a block of 100 words (200 bytes) in memory, but initializes only the first two.

The Define Byte (DB) pseudo-op also accepts a *character string* as an expression. This lets you store error messages, table headers, and other text strings in memory. In this case, you must enclose the string in single quotes, as shown here:

```
POLITE_MSG   DB   'The number you have entered is too large'
             DB   ' to be properly processed. Please'
             DB   ' re-enter it.'
RUDE_MSG     DB   'Try again, dummy!'
```

Variables are also used to hold *memory addresses* that can be referenced by instructions in your program. Remember, every address has two components: a segment number and an offset.

If a label lies in the *same* segment as the referencing instruction, you only need to provide the label's offset. This can be done with the DW pseudo-op. For example, the statement

```
HERE_NEAR   DW   HERE
```

assigns the 16-bit offset of the label HERE to the variable HERE _ NEAR.

If a label lies in a *different segment* than the referencing instruction, the 8088 needs to know the label's segment number as well as its offset. You can provide both addresses with a *Define Doubleword (DD)* pseudo-op. For example, the statement

```
HERE_FAR   DD   HERE
```

assigns the 16-bit offset and 16-bit segment number of the label HERE to the variable HERE _ FAR.

With the IBM Small Assembler, this is the *only* application for DD. The MACRO Assembler also lets you use DD to allocate two-word (four-byte) blocks of memory, just as you can use DB and DW to allocate one- or two-byte blocks of memory.

External Reference Pseudo-Ops

These pseudo-ops allow you to reference information in an assembly module or file that is elsewhere in the system.

The PUBLIC pseudo-op makes the specified symbols(s) available to other assembly modules that will eventually be linked to the present module. A symbol can be a variable name or a label (including PROC labels), but cannot be a name defined by an EQU or = pseudo-op.

The EXTRN pseudo-op identifies symbols that are defined (and declared PUBLIC) in some other assembly module. EXTRN has the general form

```
EXTRN    name;type[,...]
```

where *name* is the symbol defined in the other assembly module and *type* can be BYTE, WORD, DWORD, NEAR, FAR, ABS, or a name defined by the EQU pseudo-op.

For example, suppose you want to access the memory location TOTAL from two different modules. The module in which TOTAL is defined may include these statements:

```
         PUBLIC  TOTAL
TOTAL  DW       0          ;Make total = 0 to start
```

and the module in which TOTAL is referenced may contain this statement:

```
EXTRN    TOTAL:WORD
```

The INCLUDE pseudo-op merges an entire *file* of source statements into the current source file at assembly time. For example, the statement

```
INCLUDE   B:OTHERFIL.ASM
```

reads the contents of the file OTHERFIL.ASM on Drive B into your source file, replacing the INCLUDE statement. INCLUDE is usually used to read *macros* into a program. We'll say more about this when we discuss macro pseudo-ops.

Segment/Procedure Specification Pseudo-Ops

The SEGMENT and ENDS pseudo-ops partition the assembly language source program into segments. A program may have up to four kinds of segments: data, code, extra and stack.

For example, a data segment may look like this:

```
DATASEG   SEGMENT          (start of data segment)
A         DB       ?
B         DB       ?
SQUARES   DB       1,4,9,16,25,36,49,64
DATASEG   ENDS             (end of data segment)
```

and a code segment may look like this:

```
PROGCODE  SEGMENT          (start of code segment)
          ..
          ..
          MOV      AX,BX
          MOV      CL,DH
```

```
        MOV         DI,CX
        ..
        ..
PROGCODE  ENDS                (end of code segment)
```

The words SEGMENT and ENDS merely mark the boundaries of a segment; they don't specify which *kind* of segment is being defined. A separate pseudo-op, ASSUME, informs the assembler which segment register a segment belongs to. DS references the data segment, CS references the code segment, SS references the stack segment, and ES references the extra segment.

The ASSUME pseudo-op has the general format

```
ASSUME  seg-reg:seg-name[,...]
```

where *seg-reg* is either DS, CS, SS or ES and *seg-name* is the segment name assigned by the SEGMENT pseudo-op.

Every assembly module that contains assembly language instructions with labels must have an ASSUME, to tell the assembler which segment register contains those labels. This ASSUME normally follows the code segment's SEGMENT statement. Thus, for the preceding two-segment program, the ASSUME would make two specifications, and the code segment would take this form:

```
PROGCODE  SEGMENT
          ASSUME    CS:PROGCODE,DS:DATASEG
          ..
          ..
          MOV       AX,BX
          MOV       CL,DH
          MOV       CX,DI
          ..
          ..
PROGCODE  ENDS
```

A *procedure* is a block of instructions that can be executed from various places in a program. Each time a procedure is *called*, the 8088 executes the instructions that make up the procedure, then returns to the place from which the call was made. Because a procedure is written only once in memory, it frees you from typing the sequence each time you need it, and thereby makes your programs shorter.

Every procedure begins with a PROC pseudo-op and ends with an ENDP pseudo-op. If it also contains a RET (Return from Procedure) instruction, the procedure can be called a *subroutine*. The RET instruction causes the 8088 to resume at the point where the procedure was called. Finally, if the procedure is to be accessible from another module, it must be preceded by a PUBLIC pseudo-op.

A procedure always has one of two *distance* attributes: NEAR or FAR, as specified by the operand field. Omitting the label makes the procedure NEAR. A NEAR procedure can only be called from within the segment in which it is defined, or from a segment that has the same ASSUME CS value. For example,

```
NEAR_NAME   PROC    NEAR
            . .
            . .
            RET
NEAR_NAME   ENDP
```

A FAR procedure can be called from any segment. For example,

```
            PUBLIC  FAR_NAME
FAR_NAME    PROC    FAR
            . .
            . .
            RET
FAR_NAME    ENDP
```

When a procedure is called, the 8088 pushes a return address onto the stack. This address will be retrieved when the RET instruction is executed. If the called procedure has a NEAR attribute, only an offset—the contents of the instruction pointer (IP)—is pushed onto the stack. If the called procedure has a FAR attribute, both a segment number—the contents of the code segment (CS) register—and an offset from IP are pushed onto the stack, in that order.

When the program is assembled, the assembler "tells" each RET instruction which kind of procedure it lies in. If a RET lies in a NEAR procedure, it automatically pulls one 16-bit word (IP contents) off the stack. If a RET lies in a FAR procedure, it pulls two 16-bit words (IP and CS contents) off the stack.

Assembly Control Pseudo-Op

The assembler provides several assembly control pseudo-ops, but only one, END, is frequently used. See section 2.8 for the others.

The END pseudo-op marks the end of the source program, and tells the assembler where to stop assembling. Therefore, *END must be included in every source program*. Its general form is

```
END  [expression]
```

where *expression*—usually a label—identifies the starting address of your source program. For example,

```
END  MY_PROG
```

The *expression* is optional if the program consists of only one source module, but mandatory if several modules must be linked to form the final run module. Using a label with END is always good documentation practice, however.

Macro Pseudo-Ops

A *macro* is a sequence of assembler statements (instructions and pseudo-ops) that may appear several times in a program, with some optional modifications each time it is used. Like procedures, macros are assigned names. Once a macro has been defined, you can use its name in your source program instead of the repeated instruction sequence.

> *Note:* If you have never programmed in assembly language, postpone reading this section until you have gained some experience. Read at least through the end of Chapter 3 before returning here.

Macros Versus Procedures

Although macros and procedures both provide you with a shorthand reference to a frequently-used instruction sequence, they are not the same. The code for a procedure occurs once in a program, and the processor transfers to the procedure as needed. In contrast, the assembler replaces each occurrence of a macro name with the instructions that name represents. (Computer people say the assembler *expands* the macro.) Therefore, when you execute the program, the processor executes the macro instructions "in-line," without transferring elsewhere in memory, as it does with a procedure. Hence, *a macro name is a user-defined assembler directive;* it directs assembly rather than program execution.

Like procedures, macros make source programs shorter and easier to change. (If you change the macro definition, the assembler incorporates the change for you every time the macro is used.) However, macros have a major disadvantage that procedures do not have: since a macro gets expanded every time it is used, it tends to make machine language programs longer by filling memory with repeated instruction sequences. Still, programmers often prefer macros for three reasons:

1. Macros are *dynamic.* You can easily modify the macro each time it is invoked, by changing its input parameters. You can only pass parameters to procedures in memory locations or registers, making procedures much more inflexible.

2. Macros make faster-executing programs, because the processor is not delayed by call and return instructions, as it is with procedures.

3. Macros can be entered into a *macro library* that programmers can draw from to create other programs.

Table 2-3 summarizes the macro pseudo-ops provided by the IBM MACRO Assembler. These pseudo-ops are not supported by the Small Assembler.

Macro-Defining Pseudo-Ops

Every macro definition has three parts:

1. *Header*—The MACRO pseudo-op, with the *name* of the macro in the label field and a *dummy-list* in the operand field. The *dummy-list* identifies the parameters that change each time the *name* appears in your source program.
2. *Body*—The sequence of assembler statements that define what the macro does.
3. *Terminator*—The ENDM pseudo-op, which marks the end of the macro definition.

A macro may be as simple as this:

```
ADD_MEM   MACRO     XX,YY,ZZ
          MOV       AX,XX
          ADD       AX,YY
          MOV       ZZ,AX
          ENDM
```

With the ADD_MEM macro defined, the statement

```
ADD_MEM   PAT,ROGER,RYAN
```

in a source program tells the assembler to replace every occurrence of the word ADD_MEM (the "macro call") with the sequence

```
MOV       AX,PAT
ADD       AX,ROGER
MOV       RYAN,AX
```

This particular macro requires you to supply three *dummy-list* parameters: two operand addresses and a destination address. However, you needn't specify all the *dummy-list* entries every time you call the macro. If you specify fewer parameters than there are entries in the *dummy-list*, the assembler ignores any macro statements that reference the unspecified entries. Similarly, if you specify more parameters than there are entries in the *dummy-list*, the assembler ignores the excess parameters.

Table 2-3. Macro Pseudo-ops.

Pseudo-Op	Function
MACRO	Format: name MACRO dummy-list
	. .
	. .
	ENDM
	Assigns a *name* to a sequence of assembler statements. Every MACRO definition must end with an ENDM pseudo-op.
LOCAL	Format: LOCAL dummy-list
	Causes the assembler to create a unique symbol for each entry in *dummy-list*, and substitute that symbol for each occurrence of the entry in the expansion.
REPT	Format: REPT expression
	. .
	. .
	ENDM
	Causes the statements between REPT and ENDM to be repeated *expression* times.
IRP	Format: IRP dummy, <argument-list>
	. .
	. .
	ENDM
	Causes the statements between IRP and ENDM to be repeated once for each argument in *<argument-list>*. Each repetition substitutes the next item in *<argument-list>* for each occurrence of *dummy* in the block.
IRPC	Format: IRPC dummy,string
	. .
	. .
	ENDM
	Causes the statements between IRPC and ENDM to be repeated once for each character in *string*. Each repetition substitutes the next character in *string* for every occurrence of *dummy* in the block.
EXITM	Format: EXITM
	Terminates a macro expansion based on the result of a preceding test.
PURGE	Format: PURGE macro-name[,...]
	Deletes the specified macro(s) from the assembler's internal tables, allowing its space to be reused.

The LOCAL Pseudo-Op

If your macro contains labeled instructions, you will want the assembler to change those labels every time it expands the macro; otherwise you'll end up with "Symbol is Multi-Defined" errors. The LOCAL pseudo-op eliminates these errors by telling the assembler which labels to change with each expansion.

For example, this macro makes the processor wait until the value COUNT has been decremented to zero:

```
WAIT    MACRO   COUNT
        LOCAL   NEXT
        MOV     CX,COUNT
NEXT:   LOOP    NEXT
        ENDM
```

Incidentally, it is no accident that LOCAL immediately follows the MACRO statement. If used, *LOCALs must be the first statements in the body of the macro.*

Repeat Pseudo-Ops

The MACRO Assembler has three pseudo-ops that cause the assembler to *repeat* sequences of assembler statements in the macro. For each of these pseudo-ops—REPT, IRP, and IRPC—the repetition count is based on an expression in the operand field. These pseudo-ops can be used within a macro definition or by themselves.

The operand for REPT is an *expression* that must evaluate to a repetition count. For example, this macro allocates LENGTH bytes in memory, and initializes these bytes with the values 1 through LENGTH, respectively:

```
ALLOCATE   MACRO   LENGTH
VALUE      =       0
           REPT    LENGTH
VALUE      =       VALUE+1
           DB      VALUE
           ENDM
```

The ALLOCATE macro could then be used to set up a 40-byte table called TABLE __ 40, with this sequence:

```
DATA       SEGMENT
TABLE_40   ALLOCATE   40
DATA       ENDS
```

The second repeating pseudo-op, IRP, lets you list the arguments that are to be substituted for a *dummy* symbol with each repetition. For example, the sequence

```
IRP     VALUE, <1,2,3,4,5,6,7,8,9,10>
DW      VALUE*VALUE*VALUE
ENDM
```

sets up a 10-word table in memory that contains the cubes of the integers 1 through 10.

The final repeating pseudo-op, IRPC, is convenient for establishing string variables in memory. IRPC takes two operands, a *dummy* symbol and a *string*, and repeats the statements in the block once for each character in the string. Each repetition substitutes the next character in the string for every occurrence of *dummy* in the block.

For example, the sequence

```
IRPC    CHAR,0123456789
DB      CHAR
ENDM
```

sets up a 10-byte text string in memory that contains the ASCII codes for the digits 0 through 9.

The EXITM Pseudo-Op

EXITM makes the macro expansion terminate early, based on the result of a preceding test. For example, suppose you have a program that calculates various lengths. One version of the program displays the lengths in feet, another displays both feet and meters. You can use EXITM to assemble the program with or without the meters display, like this:

```
DISP L  MACRO   TYPE
        ..              {INSTRUCTIONS TO DISPLAY FEET}
        ..
        IFE     TYPE
        EXITM
        ENDIF
        ..              {INSTRUCTIONS TO DISPLAY METERS}
        ..
        ENDM
```

Here, the assembler inserts the display-in-feet instructions, then tests the value of TYPE. The IFE pseudo-op, which we will discuss in Section 2.8, tells it to perform the statements between IFE and ENDIF (that is, exit) if TYPE is 0 and skip those statements if TYPE has any other value.

The PURGE Pseudo-Op

The PURGE pseudo-op deletes macro(s) from the assembler's internal tables, freeing the memory space for reuse. This just makes the *assembler* "forget" the macro after it's been referenced for the last time. PURGE does not delete any macro's source or object program that is elsewhere on disk.

You needn't PURGE a macro if you just wish to *redefine* it later in a program.

Reading Macros Into a Source Program

Before a source program can use a macro that is stored in a disk library, you must direct the assembler to read in the macro definition with an INCLUDE pseudo-op. However, if you do this with a statement like *INCLUDE MY_MACRO*, the assembler unnecessarily reads in the macro on both pass 1 and pass 2. Moreover, if the assembler reads the macro in pass 2, the macro is printed whenever you list the assembler listing file (.LST).

To avoid both problems, you should put the INCLUDE in an IF1 *conditional structure* preceding the source program. This structure causes the assembler to read in the macro during pass 1, and ignore it during pass 2. The correct form is as follows:

```
IF1
   INCLUDE MY_MACRO
ENDIF
```

We will look at all of the assembler's conditional pseudo-ops in Section 2.8.

Listing Pseudo-Ops

The six listing pseudo-ops summarized in Table 2-4 control the format and content of the assembly listing.

Format Control Pseudo-Ops

The PAGE pseudo-op has the general format

```
PAGE  [operand-1][,operand-2]
```

where *operand-1* and *operand-2* set the length and width of the pages printed out during assembly. The length can range from 10 to 255 lines; the width can range from 60 to 132 characters. The default values are 66 lines and 80 characters.

As an example, the statement

```
PAGE 25,100
```

limits each page to 25 lines vertically and 100 characters horizontally. Typically, however, you will want to print a 132-column listing on standard 66-line paper, so the statement you normally use is

```
PAGE ,132
```

Table 2-4. Listing Pseudo-Ops.

Pseudo-Op	Function
Format Control	
PAGE	Format: PAGE [operand-1][,operand-2] Sets the length and width of the page according to *operand-1* and *operand-2*, respectively.
TITLE	Format: TITLE text Specifies a title to be listed on the second line of each page.
SUBTTL	Format: SUBTTL text Specifies a subtitle to be listed on the third line of each page.
Macro Listing	
.LALL	Format: .LALL Lists the complete macro text for all expansions.
.SALL	Format: .SALL Suppresses listing of all text and object code produced by macros.
.XALL	Format: .XALL Lists only source lines that generate object code. This is the default condition.

(If you are using standard 8-1/2 inch paper, set the printer to its smallest type size, usually 16.5 characters per inch.)

On the top line of each page the assembler prints a chapter number and a page number, separated by a dash. The page number increments when a page is full or when PAGE alone (no operands), is encountered. The chapter number increments only when the form

```
PAGE  +
```

is encountered. Both conditions make the printer advance to the top of the next page.

The TITLE pseudo-op lists a title, left-justified, on the second line of each page. Typically, this title describes the assembly module, and gives its filename. The SUBTTL pseudo-op lists a *subtitle* on the third line of each page, centered. The subtitle usually identifies the contents of that particular page. For example, the beginning of a listing might have these headers:

```
TITLE   GALAXY CENSUS PROGRAM   (COUNT_ALL.ASM)
SUBTTL  Venusian Data Segment
```

A statement at the end of the first data segment might change the subtitle in this way:

```
SUBTTL  Plutonian Data Segment
```

Titles and subtitles may be up to 60 characters long.

Macro Listing Pseudo-Ops

Normally, the only macro lines the assembler includes in a listing are those that generate object code. The .LALL pseudo-op lets you list all macro text for all expansions. The .SALL pseudo op turns off .LALL.

2.6 Operators

An operator is a modifier used in the operand field of an assembly language statement or a pseudo-op statement. There are five kinds of operators:

1. Arithmetic operators
2. Logical operators
3. Relational operators
4. Value-returning operators
5. Attribute operators

Table 2-5 summarizes the individual operators in these five groups.

Arithmetic Operators

The assembler's arithmetic operators combine numeric operands and produce a numeric result. The most frequently used arithmetic operators are those that add (+), subtract (-), multiply (*), and divide (/).

A typical use of the addition operator is:

```
TABLE_PLUS_2   DW    TABLE+2
```

where the variable TABLE_PLUS_2 holds the offset address of the second byte after the location TABLE (*not* the contents of TABLE plus 2).

Similarly, the subtraction operation

```
BYTE_DIFF   DW   TABLE1-TABLE
```

gives BYTE_DIFF the distance in bytes between TABLE1 and TABLE.

A typical use of the multiplication operator is:

```
MINS_PER_DAY   EQU   60*24
```

where you let the assembler calculate a value. The constant MINS_PER_DAY gets the value decimal 1440.

Table 2-5. Legal Operators.

Operator	Function
Arithmetic	
+	Format: value-1 + value-2
	Adds value-1 and value-2.
-	Format: value-1 - value-2
	Subtracts value-2 from value-1.
*	Format: value-1 * value-2
	Multiplies value-2 by value-1.
/	Format: value-1 / value-2
	Divides value-1 by value-2, and returns the quotient.
MOD	Format: value-1 MOD value-2
	Divides value-1 by value-2, and returns the remainder.
SHL	Format: value SHL expression
	Shifts *value* left by *expression* bit positions.
SHR	Format: value SHR expression
	Shifts *value* right by *expression* bit positions.
Logical	
AND	Format: value-1 AND value-2
	Takes logical AND of value-1 and value-2.
OR	Format: value-1 OR value-2
	Takes logical inclusive-OR of value-1 and value-2.
XOR	Format: value-1 XOR value-2
	Takes logical exclusive-OR of value-1 and value-2.
NOT	Format: NOT value
	Reverses the state of each bit in *value*; that is, it takes the one's complement of *value*.
Relational	
EQ	Format: operand-1 EQ operand-2
	True if the two operands are identical.
NE	Format: operand-1 NE operand-2
	True if the two operands are not identical.
LT	Format: operand-1 LT operand-2
	True if operand-1 is less than operand-2.
GT	Format: operand-1 GT operand-2
	True if operand-1 is greater than operand-2.
LE	Format: operand-1 LE operand-2
	True if operand-1 is less than or equal to operand-2.
GE	Format: operand-1 GE operand-2
	True if operand-1 is greater than or equal to operand-2.

Table 2-5. Legal Operators (continued).

Operator	Function
Value-Returning	
SEG	Format: SEG variable
	or
	SEG label
	Returns the segment value of *variable* or *label*.
OFFSET	Format: OFFSET variable
	or
	OFFSET label
	Returns the offset value of *variable* or *label*.
TYPE	Format: TYPE variable
	or
	TYPE label
	If the operand is a variable, TYPE returns 1 (BYTE), 2 (WORD), or 4 (DOUBLEWORD). If the operand is a label, TYPE returns -1 (NEAR) or -2 (FAR).
SIZE	Format: SIZE variable
	Returns a count of the number of bytes allocated for the variable.
LENGTH	Format: LENGTH variable
	Returns a count of the number of units (bytes or words) allocated for the variable.
Attribute	
PTR	Format: type PTR expression
	Overrides the type (BYTE or WORD) or distance (NEAR or FAR) of a memory address operand. *type* is the new attribute and *expression* is the identifier whose attribute is to be overridden.
DS:	Format: seg-reg:addr-expr
ES:	or
SS:	seg-reg:label
	or
	seg-reg:variable
	Overrides the segment attribute of a label, variable, or address expression.
SHORT	Format: JMP SHORT label
	Modifies the NEAR attribute of a JMP target label to indicate it is no farther than +127 bytes or -128 bytes from the next instruction.

Table 2-5. Legal Operators (continued).

Operator	Function
THIS	Format: THIS attribute or THIS type Creates a memory address operand of either distance attribute (NEAR or FAR) or either type attribute (BYTE or WORD) at an offset equal to the current value of the location counter and a segment attribute of the enclosing segment.
HIGH	Format: HIGH value or HIGH expression Returns the high-order byte of a 16-bit numeric value or address expression.
LOW	Format: LOW value or LOW expression Returns the low-order byte of a 16-bit numeric value or address expression.

The divide operator (/) returns the quotient produced by a divide operation. For example, the statement

```
PI_QUOT  EQU  31416/10000
```

returns the value 3.

The assembler also has a MOD operator that returns the *remainder* of a divide operation. The statement

```
PI_REM  EQU  31416 MOD 10000
```

defines a constant called PI__REM that has the value 1416.

Finally, operators SHL and SHR displace a numeric operand to the left or right. About the only time you need this capability is when you set up "masks" that you'll apply to binary patterns in memory. For example, if you set up a mask with the statement

```
MASK  EQU  110010B
```

the statement

```
MASK_LEFT_2  EQU  MASK SHL 2
```

sets up a new constant with the value 11001000B. Similarly,

```
MASK_RIGHT_2  EQU  MASK SHR 2
```

sets up a new constant with the value 1100B.

Logical Operators

Like the SHL and SHR operators in the preceding section, the logical operators are primarily used to manipulate binary values instead of decimal values. However, SHL and SHR operate on an entire group of bits (by shifting the group left or right, en masse), while the logical operators manipulate individual bits within the group.

To draw an analogy, imagine a group of patients seated on a bench at a medical clinic. If the clinic operates in "shift" fashion, the nurse may order the first three patients to report to a waiting room, and have the remaining patients shift to the left. In doing this, the nurse essentially performs an *SHL 3* operation.

Conversely, if the clinic operates in "logical" fashion, the nurse may order just certain patients (perhaps only those with broken bones) to report to the waiting room. With this approach, the remaining patients stay seated where they are, and don't shift left nor right on the bench.

The logical operators AND, OR, and XOR combine two operands to produce a result; NOT requires just one operand. Let's examine each of these operators in detail.

The AND operator is primarily used to filter, mask, or strip out certain bits. To do this, AND sets the result bit to 1 for each bit position in which both operands contain a 1. For any other bit combination, AND clears the result bit to 0. (See Table 2-6.)

For example, the operation

    00110100B AND 11010111B

produces the result 00010100B. As you can see, AND operates like a house with a double-lock door. If neither lock is engaged (1 = unlocked), you can enter the house, but if either or both locks are engaged (0 = locked), you are shut outside. Here, a "1" result means you can enter and a "0" result means you cannot enter.

The OR operator sets the result bit to 1 for each position in which either or both operands contain a 1. Conversely, for bit positions where both operands contain 0, OR clears the result bit to 0. (See Table 2-6.)

Using the preceding operand combination,

    00110100B OR 11010111B

produces the result 11110111B. To make another "door" analogy, OR operates like a house with two doors. If either or both doors are unlocked (1 = unlocked), you can enter the house, but if both doors are locked (0 = locked), you are shut outside.

The XOR operator is a variation of the OR operator where 1's in both operands produce a 0, rather than a 1, in the result. (Again, see Table 2-6.) The name XOR is derived from "exclusive-OR" (because it excludes the 1-and-1 combination), to distinguish it from the "inclusive-OR" condition labeled OR.

Table 2-6. The AND, OR, and XOR Combinations.

Operand #1	Operand #2	Result AND	Result OR	Result XOR
0	0	0	0	0
0	1	0	1	1
1	0	0	1	1
1	1	1	1	0

The NOT operator simply reverses the state of each bit in the operand. That is, it changes each 1 to 0 and each 0 to 1. For example,

```
NOT 01101001B
```

produces the result 10010110B.

The 8088 also has assembly language instructions named AND, OR, XOR and NOT, which are discussed in Chapter 3. The basic difference between the logical operators and the logical instructions is that the operators do their job when the program *assembles*, whereas the instructions do their job when the program *executes*.

Relational Operators

Relational operators compare two numeric values or memory addresses in the same segment, and produce a numeric result. The result is always one of two numbers: 0 if the relationship is "false" or 0FFFFH if the relationship is "true."

For example, if CHOICE is a pre-defined constant, the statement

```
MOV AX,CHOICE LT 20
```

assembles as

```
MOV AX,0FFFFH
```

if CHOICE is less than 20, and as

```
MOV AX,0
```

if CHOICE is greater than or equal to 20.

Because the relational operators can only produce two values, 0 and 0FFFFH, they are rarely used alone. Instead, they are usually combined with other operators to form a decision-making expression. For instance, suppose AX is to be loaded with the value 5 if CHOICE is less than 20 and with 6 otherwise. A statement that performs this task is:

```
MOV AX,((CHOICE LT 20) AND 5) OR ((CHOICE GE 20) AND 6)
```

Here, if CHOICE is less than 20, the clause (CHOICE LT 20) is "true" and the clause (CHOICE GE 20) is "false," so the intermediate form of the statement is

```
MOV  AX,(0FFFFH AND 5) OR (0 AND 6)
```

which the assembler evaluates as

```
MOV  AX,5
```

Conversely, if CHOICE is greater than or equal to 20, the clause (CHOICE LT 20) is "false" and (CHOICE GE 20) is "true," so the intermediate form of the statement is

```
MOV  AX,(0 AND 5) OR (0FFFFH AND 6)
```

which the assembler evaluates as

```
MOV  AX,6
```

Value-Returning Operators

This group contains passive operators that provide information about variables and labels in your program.

The *SEG* and *OFFSET* operators return the segment and offset values of a variable or label. For example, the statements

```
MOV  AX,SEG TABLE
MOV  BX,OFFSET TABLE
```

load the segment and offset values of TABLE into AX and BX, respectively. Of course, since both segment and offset are 16-bit values, they can only be loaded into a 16-bit register.

The *TYPE* operator returns a numeric value to indicate the type attribute of a variable or the distance attribute of a label. When applied to a variable, TYPE returns 1 for a BYTE variable and 2 for a WORD variable. When applied to a label, TYPE returns –1 for a NEAR label and –2 for a FAR label.

The *LENGTH* and *SIZE* operators are only meaningful applied to variables you define with DUP. The first operator, LENGTH, returns the number of units (bytes or words) allocated for the variable. For example, the sequence

```
TABLE  DW   100 DUP(1)
       MOV  CX,LENGTH TABLE  ;Get no. of words in TABLE
```

loads 100 into CX. If you use LENGTH with any other kind of variable, it returns the value 1.

The SIZE operator returns the byte count of a variable. (That is, *SIZE* returns the product of LENGTH times TYPE.) Using the variable TABLE we just defined, the statement

```
MOV  CX,SIZE TABLE   ;Get no. of bytes in TABLE
```

loads the value 200 into CX.

Attribute Operators

Attribute operators let you specify a new attribute for an operand, and thereby override its current attribute.

The pointer (PTR) operator overrides the type (BYTE or WORD) or distance (NEAR or FAR) attribute of an operand. For instance, PTR can reference bytes in a table of words. For instance, if you define a table as

```
WORD_TABLE   DW   100 DUP(?)
```

the statement

```
FIRST_BYTE   EQU   BYTE PTR WORD_TABLE
```

assigns a name to the location of the first byte in WORD _ TABLE. After that, you can name any other byte as easily as this:

```
FIFTH_BYTE   EQU   FIRST_BYTE+4
```

As just mentioned, PTR can also change the distance attribute of a label. For example, if we have this instruction in a program:

```
START:   MOV   CX,100
```

the colon (:) suffix on the label gives START a NEAR distance attribute, which allows jump instructions in the same segment to reference the MOV instruction like this:

```
JMP   START
```

To jump to START from a different segment, you must rename START with a FAR attribute. This kind of sequence will do the job:

```
FAR_START   EQU   FAR PTR START
            JMP   FAR_START
```

The *segment override* operator (DS:, ES:, or SS:) overrides the segment attribute of a label, variable, or address expression. As mentioned in Chapter 1, when calculating a memory address, the 8088 automatically assumes SS is the segment register if the operand employs SP or BP to hold the offset. Similarly, the 8088 automatically assumes DS is the segment register if the operand employs BX, SI, or DI to hold the offset.

The segment override operator lets you specify an alternate segment register. For example, this override:

```
MOV   AX,ES:[BP]
```

directs the 8088 to use ES, rather than SS, to calculate the memory address.

The *SHORT* operator tells the assembler that a JMP target is within +127 or –128 bytes of the next instruction. With this information, the assembler encodes JMP as a two-byte instruction, rather than a three-byte instruction, which saves memory. Here is an example:

```
     JMP   SHORT THERE
     ..
     ..
THERE:
```

The *THIS* operator creates a memory address operand of a specified type (BYTE or WORD) or distance (NEAR or FAR), and gives this operand the same segment and offset attributes as the next memory address available for allocation. For example, the sequence

```
FIRST_BYTE   EQU   THIS BYTE
WORD_TABLE   DW    100 DUP(?)
```

creates FIRST_ BYTE, and gives it a BYTE type attribute with the same segment and offset attributes as WORD _ TABLE. As you see, this does the same thing as the previous statement

```
FIRST_BYTE   EQU   BYTE PTR WORD_TABLE
```

You can also use THIS to define FAR instruction locations. Returning to an earlier example,

```
START   EQU   THIS FAR
        MOV   X,100
```

gives the MOV instruction a FAR attribute, which allows JMP instructions in another segment to jump to START directly.

The *HIGH* and *LOW* operators accept a 16-bit number or address expression as an argument, and return the high- or low-order byte of the argument. For example, if you define a constant as

```
CONST   EQU   0ABCDH
```

the statement

```
MOV   AH,HIGH CONST
```

loads the value 0ABH into the AH register.

2.7 How to Edit, Assemble, and Run a Program

Since we haven't discussed the details of the 8088's assembly language instructions set (that's coming up in Chapter 3), you cannot yet write programs that add or subtract numbers, manipulate the registers, or perform the many other tasks you eventually want your Personal Computer to do. Still, you *do* have enough information to write a program that moves data around with MOV instructions, and sets up the necessary segments with pseudo-ops.

In this section we will look at a program that copies one four-byte data table in memory into another. To make it a little more interesting, the data is stored in the "destination" table in the reverse order it is stored in the "source" table.

But the details of the program are unimportant. The important point is that you will learn how to enter the program into the computer, how to assemble it, how to create listing files and a run module, and how to execute and debug the program. That is, this exercise familiarizes you with the basic steps, so you can proceed with confidence through the more complex material in the rest of the book.

The procedure described here is similar to the one in Appendix D (A Sample Session) of the IBM *Macro Assembler* manual. If you are using an IBM assembler, you should perform that procedure before using the one in this book.

You need three disks for the procedure in this section:

1. The IBM *DOS* disk (or, preferably, a back-up copy of that disk).
2. The IBM *Macro Assembler* disk (or a back-up copy).
3. A blank disk that you've initialized with the DOS FORMAT command. This will serve as your *data disk*.

We assume you have only one disk drive, although the procedure is similar (and easier) if you have two disk drives.

The Example Program for this Section

Figure 2-1 lists the instructions for our table-copying program. This program has a stack segment (STACK), a data segment (OUR_DATA), and a code segment (OUR_CODE). The stack segment will hold a return address, so the 8088 can return to DEBUG upon completing the program.

```
TITLE   Example Program (EX_PROG.ASM)
        PAGE         ,132
STACK   SEGMENT  PARA STACK 'STACK'
        DB       64 DUP('STACK   ')
STACK   ENDS
OUR_DATA SEGMENT  PARA 'DATA'
SOURCE  DB       10,20,30,40        ;This table will be
                                    ; copied into this
DEST    DB       4 DUP(?)           ; table, in reverse
                                    ; order
OUR_DATA ENDS
SUBTTL  Here is the main program.
        PAGE
OUR_CODE SEGMENT  PARA 'CODE'
OUR_PROG PROC     FAR
         ASSUME   CS:OUR_CODE,DS:OUR_DATA,SS:STACK
;
;  Set up the stack to contain the proper values so this
;  program can return to DEBUG.
```

Figure 2-1. Example program for editing and assembling.

```
            PUSH      DS              ;Put return seg. addr.
                                      ; on stack
            MOV       AX,0            ;Clear a register
            PUSH      AX              ;Put zero return addr.
                                      ; on stack
;  Initialize the data segment address.
            MOV       AX,OUR_DATA     ;Initialize DS
            MOV       DS,AX
;
;  Initialize DEST with zeroes.
            MOV       DEST,0          ;First byte
            MOV       DEST+1,0        ;Second byte
            MOV       DEST+2,0        ;Third byte
            MOV       DEST+3,0        ;Fourth byte
;
;  Copy SOURCE table into DEST table, in reverse order.
            MOV       AL,SOURCE       ;Copy first byte
            MOV       DEST+3,AL
            MOV       AL,SOURCE+1     ;Copy second byte
            MOV       DEST+2,AL
            MOV       AL,SOURCE+2     ;Copy third byte
            MOV       DEST+1,AL
            MOV       AL,SOURCE+3     ;Copy fourth byte
            MOV       DEST,AL
            RET                       ;Far return to DEBUG
OUR_PROG    ENDP
OUR_CODE    ENDS
            END       OUR_PROG
```

Figure 2-1. Example program for editing and assembling (continued).

The data segment consists of just two pseudo-op statements; one sets up the source table (SOURCE), the other reserves space for the destination table (DEST).

The code segment has four groups of assembly language instructions. The first group pushes the return address of DEBUG onto the stack. The second group initializes DS to point to the data segment. The third group stores zeroes into the four bytes of the DEST table. It does this so that each time you run the program and check the final contents of DEST, you know you're seeing the program's effect on DEST instead of the results of a previous run. The fourth group copies the table data, moving one byte at a time.

The instructions in the code segment are a single procedure enclosed by the statements

```
OUR_PROG    PROC    FAR
```

and

```
OUR_PROG    ENDP
```

Because the procedure has a FAR attribute, the final RET instruction returns the 8088 back to DEBUG, which is in a different segment of memory, after the example program has executed. A FAR attribute sets up RET to accept two addresses from the stack: an offset and a segment. *For these same reasons, most of the programs you write should be defined as procedures.*

Entering the Program

Once you've written the program, you must enter it into the computer. You do this with the Line Editor (EDLIN) program that comes on the DOS disk. EDLIN is described in Chapter 4 of the IBM *Disk Operating System* manual.

To get EDLIN running, boot the DOS disk. When you see the A > prompt, type

```
edlin b:ex_prog.asm
```

and press Enter (from now on we'll assume you know that you must press Enter after *every* line). *b:* tells EDLIN that the source program, *ex _ prog*, is on another disk. The extension *.asm* identifies it as a "source code" file.

Replace the DOS disk with your formatted data disk, then press any key. When the computer displays

```
New file
*_
```

press I to put EDLIN into the *insert* mode. The next prompt,

```
1:*_
```

tells you EDLIN is waiting for the first line of "text"—in this case, the first statement in your source program.

Now type in the source program (Figure 2-1), line by line. This figure shows the program with most words capitalized, but you may enter them in lower case if you prefer. In Figure 2-1, the fields are also neatly aligned, to make the listing more readable, but feel free to enter the fields any way you like. Just be sure you separate them by at least one space.

After you enter the entire program, take EDLIN out of the insert mode by pressing Ctrl-Break, then press the E key to save the program on the data disk. Once on disk, you can assemble this *source program* to produce an *object program*.

Assembling the Program

To start the assembly process, replace the data disk with the *Macro Assembler* disk, then type

```
asm
```

When the display shows

```
Insert diskette for drive A: and strike any key when ready
```

press Enter. The next prompt tells you that the assembler program has been read into memory, so replace the assembler disk with the data disk and press any key. Then respond to four prompts, as follows:

```
Source filename [.ASM]: ex_prog
Object filename [EX_PROG.OBJ]: (press ENTER)
Source listing [NUL.LST]: ex_prog
Cross reference [NUL.CRF]: ex_prog
```

Your responses tell the assembler to use the source file EX _ PROG.ASM to create three new files: an object file (EX _ PROG.OBJ), a listing file (EX _ PROG.LST), and a cross reference file (EX _ PROG.CRF).

The object file contains the machine language version of the source file. The listing file contains the source instructions and their numeric machine language codes—a handy, printable file for seeing how the assembler interpreted your program. The cross reference file contains cross reference information about every label and symbol in the program.

Once you've answered these prompts, the assembler converts your source program and creates the files. If you followed the preceding steps exactly, the assembler will display

```
Warning   Severe
Errors    Errors
0         0

Insert DOS disk in drive A
and strike any key when ready
```

Now, replace the data disk with the DOS disk and press a key, which will put the computer back into the Disk Operating System.

Listing the Source Program

At this point you can use the DOS *TYPE* command to display the source listing file. (If you have a printer, set it to "on line," then press Ctrl-PrtSc.) To do this, enter

```
type  b:ex_prog.lst
```

The printer will start listing as soon as you replace the DOS disk with the data disk and press a key. If the listing is directed to the screen, you can halt it at any time by pressing Ctrl-Num Lock. Press any key to resume scrolling.

Figure 2-2 shows you what the listing should look like. Note that a PAGE pseudo-op in the source program causes the listing to be produced on three pages instead of two.

The first two pages show the source program instructions and their associated object code (in hexadecimal), in this order:

- The first column gives the EDLIN line number.
- The second column shows the offset from the beginning of the segment.
- The numeric columns show the object code for that statement. For the stack and data segments, this will be the values allocated to each location. For the code segment, the values will be those of the machine language byte(s). The "R" in these columns indicates that the Linker program (to be discussed shortly) may modify memory references and produce different offsets than those listed.
- The text to the right is, of course, the source program.

The third page of the listing gives summary information about the segments and symbols in the program.

The Cross Reference Listing

For each symbol in the program, the cross reference listing identifies the line where it is defined and any other lines that reference it. Such a listing is superfluous for short programs like this, but you *should* know how to generate one.

To create the cross reference listing, insert the *assembler* disk into drive A and type

```
cref
```

When you see the prompt, replace the assembler disk with your data disk. Now, create a cross reference listing file by responding to the prompts as follows:

```
Cref filename [.CRF]:ex_prog
List filename [EX_PROG.REF]: (Press ENTER)
```

When the DOS prompt appears, display the listing file by entering

```
type ex_prog.ref
```

Figure 2-3 shows this listing. Here you see the name of each symbol in the program, along with the line number where it is defined (with a # suffix) and the line numbers of any other statements that reference the symbol. This information isn't too valuable in a small program like the one we have here, but it can be very helpful in debugging a large program.

```
The IBM Personal Computer Assembler 07-08-82            PAGE 1-1
Example Program.(EX_PROG.ASM)

                          TITLE   Example Program (EX_PROG.ASM)
 1                        PAGE    ,132
 2
 3   0000               STACK    SEGMENT PARA STACK 'STACK'
 4   0000  40 [          DB      64 DUP('STACK ')   ;This table will be copied into
 5         53 54 41 43                              ; this table- in reverse order
 6         4B 20 20 20
 7              ]
 8
 9   0200               STACK    ENDS
10   0000               OUR_DATA SEGMENT PARA 'DATA'
11   0000  0A 14 1E 28  SOURCE   DB      10,20,30,40
12   0004  04 [         DEST     DB      4 DUP(?)
13              ??
14              ]
15                      OUR_DATA ENDS
16   0008               SUBTTL  Here is the main program.
17                      PAGE
18
19   0000               OUR_CODE SEGMENT PARA 'CODE'
20   0000               OUR_PROG PROC    PAR
21                      ASSUME  CS:OUR_CODE,DS:OUR_DATA,SS:STACK
22                      ;
23                      ; Set up the stack to contain the proper values so this
24                      ; program can return to DEBUG.
```

Figure 2-2. Assembly listing for the example program in Figure 2-1.

```
25
26  0000  1E             PUSH   DS              ;Put return seg. addr. on stack
27  0001  B8 0000        MOV    AX,0            ;Clear a register
28  0004  50             PUSH   AX              ;Put zero return addr. on stack
29
30                       ; Initialize the data segment address.
31
32  0005  B8 ---- R      MOV    AX,OUR_DATA     ;Initialize DS
33  0008  8E D8          MOV    DS,AX
34
35                       ; Initialize DEST with zeroes.
36
37  000A  C6 06 0004 R 00   MOV   DEST,0        ;First byte
38  000F  C6 06 0005 R 00   MOV   DEST+1,0      ;Second byte
39  0014  C6 06 0006 R 00   MOV   DEST+2,0      ;Third byte
40  0019  C6 06 0007 E 00   MOV   DEST+3,0      ;Fourth byte
41
42                       ; Copy SOURCE table into DEST table, in reverse order.
43
44  001E  A0 0000 R      MOV    AL,SOURCE       ;Copy first byte
45  0021  A2 0007 R      MOV    DEST+3,AL
46  0024  A0 0001 E      MOV    AL,SOURCE+1     ;Copy second byte
47  0027  A2 0006 R      MOV    DEST+2,AL
48  002A  A0 0002 R      MOV    AL,SOURCE+2     ;Copy third byte
49  002D  A2 0005 E      MOV    DEST+1,AL
50  0030  A0 0003 R      MOV    AL,SOURCE+3     ;Copy fourth byte
51  0033  A2 0004 R      MOV    DEST,AL
52  0036  CE             RET                    ;Par return to DEBUG
```

Figure 2-2. Assembly listing for the example program in Figure 2-1 (continued).

```
53 0037          OUR_PROG  ENDP
54 0037          OUR_CODE  ENDS
55               END       OUR_PROG
```

The IBM Personal Computer Assembler 07-08-82   PAGE   Symbols-1
Example Program (EX_PROG.ASM)

Segments and groups:

N a m e	Size	align	combine	class
OUR_CODE	0037	PARA	NONE	'CODE'
OUR_DATA	0008	PARA	NONE	'DATA'
STACK.	0200	PARA	STACK	'STACK'

Symbols:

N a m e	Type	Value	Attr	
DEST	L BYTE	0004	OUR_DATA	Length=0004
OUR_PROG	F PROC	0000	OUR_CODE	Length=0037
SOURCE	L BYTE	0000	OUR_DATA	

```
Warning  Severe
Errors   Errors
  0        0
```

Figure 2-2. Assembly listing for the example program in Figure 2-1 (continued).

```
Symbol Cross Reference          (# is definition)  Cref-1

CODE . . . . . . . . .  19

DATA . . . . . . . . .  10
DEST . . . . . . . . .  12#  37  38  39  40  45  47  49  51

OUR_CODE . . . . . . .  19#  21  54
OUR_DATA . . . . . . .  10#  16  21  32
OUR_PROG . . . . . . .  20#  53  55

SOURCE . . . . . . . .  11#  44  46  48  50
STACK. . . . . . . . .   3#   3   9  21
```

Figure 2-3. Cross reference listing for the example program.

Creating the Run File

IBM DOS can store an object program at any convenient place in memory. To use this feature, however, you must create a *relocatable* run file.

The program that creates relocatable run files is called the *Linker*, because it can link several object files into one big run file. To run the Linker, insert the DOS disk and enter

```
link
```

When the Linker displays its Object Modules prompt, replace the DOS disk with your data disk and respond to the first two prompts as follows:

```
Object Modules: ex_prog
Run File: ex_prun
```

We intentionally gave the run file a different name (ex__prun) than all preceding files so that you can easily spot it in a directory. We could have named it ex__prog, however.

Press Enter in response to the List File and libraries prompts.* This done, you have two new files on your disk: the *run file* (EX __ PRUN.EXE) and the *list file* (EX __ PRUN.MAP). For each segment in the program, the list file shows the "start" and "stop" offsets in the segment, the length of the segment, and its class (CODE, DATA, STACK, or EXTRA).

To display the list file, press the Ctrl and PrtSc keys (if you have a printer) and enter

```
type ex_prun.map
```

The listing should look like the one shown in Figure 2-4. When the listing is completed, turn off the printer by pressing the Ctrl and PrtSc keys.

*In DOS 1.0 there are six prompts after List File. PRESS ENTER in response to all six.

```
A>type ex_prun.map
  Start  Stop   Length  Name              Class
  00000H 00036H 0037H   OUR_CODE          CODE
  00040H 00047H 0008H   OUR_DATA          DATA
  00050H 0024FH 0200H   STACK             STACK

Program entry point at 0000:0000
```

Figure 2-4. List file for the example program.

Linking Multiple Object Modules

This particular example has only one object module, ex _ prog.obj, but in later chapters of this book you will create programs that have two or more object modules. You will assemble these modules separately, then link them by giving their names in response to the Object Modules prompt. For example,

```
Object Modules:  mod1+mod2+mod3
Run File:  mod1
```

links modules mod1.obj, mod2.obj, and mod3.obj to create a run file called mod1.exe. (NOTE: DOS 1.0 uses commas to separate object module names.)

One more point: if any module contains a reference to a symbol in another module, the referencing module must contain an EXTRN pseudo-op and the referenced module must contain a PUBLIC pseudo-op. For instance, if the instructions in a module call an external procedure named EDIT, that module must include the statement EXTRN EDIT:FAR (or EXTRN:NEAR, if EDIT's code segment has the same name as the code segment that contains the call) and the module in which EDIT is defined must include the statement PUBLIC EDIT

Running the Completed Program

You now have a relocatable run file (ex _ prun.exe) ready to execute. There are two ways to execute this file:

1. With the DOS prompt on the screen, you may enter

       ex_prun

   which makes DOS load the run file and execute it. In this case, the 8088 returns to DOS.
2. You may run the program under the control of DEBUG. Here, the 8088 returns to DEBUG.

You generally only run a program under DOS when you're sure it's error-free. The example program is error-free, but in order to learn something about DEBUG — and because DEBUG will be extensively used for your program development work — you should run the example program with DEBUG.

To run DEBUG, insert the DOS disk and enter the command

```
debug
```

When you see DEBUG's hyphen prompt, replace the DOS disk with your data disk, then enter

```
n ex_prun.exe
l
```

When you see the hyphen prompt again, DEBUG is running. You may then use any of the DEBUG commands described in Chapter 6 of the IBM *DOS* manual. Figure 2-5 shows a typical session with DEBUG.

To begin, we use the Register (R) command to display the registers. Except for the flags, the contents of each 16-bit register are shown as four hexadecimal digits. The bits in the Flags register are shown as a set of eight 2-letter abbreviations. Table 2-7 tells you how to interpret these abbreviations. For example, the abbreviations produced by this Register command tell you that all Flags bits are initially in the "Clear" state; they are all set to 0.

The last line of the Register command display shows the code segment/ instruction pointer combination that specifies the address of the next instruction to be executed. In this case, the value 04AF:0000 means that CS contains 4AFH and IP contains 0. (The preceding line verifies that CS and IP do indeed hold these values.)

The last line also shows the next instruction the 8088 will execute (PUSH DS), and lists its object code (1E). Things must be working fine so far, because that *is* the first instruction in our example program.

Next we use the Trace (T) command to execute the first five instructions in the program. Each time you press T, the 8088 executes one instruction, then displays the registers and the next instruction to be executed. Thus, with the trace you get to see what the registers contain at any given time, and which paths the execution is taking. This information is invaluable in debugging a program.

Here, the first T executes the

```
PUSH  DS
```

instruction, the next T executes the

```
MOV   AX,0000
```

instruction, and so on. Notice how the registers change as each instruction executes. After the first T, the Stack Pointer (SP) has decreased from 0200H to 01FEH, reflecting the PUSH operation. Similarly, after

```
MOV   AX,04B3
```

has executed, the contents of AX have changed from 0 to 04B3H.

After these five trace commands, we use the Go (G) command to execute the rest of the program, and get the message

```
Program terminated normally
```

```
A>debug
-n ex_prun.exe
-l
-r
AX=0000  BX=0000  CX=0000  DX=0000  SP=0200  BP=0000  SI=0000  DI=0000
DS=049F  ES=049F  SS=049F  CS=04B4  IP=0000  NV UP DI PL NZ NA PO NC
04AF:0000 1E          PUSH  DS
-t

AX=0000  BX=0000  CX=0000  DX=0000  SP=01FE  BP=0000  SI=0000  DI=0000
DS=049F  ES=049F  SS=049F  CS=04B4  IP=0001  NV UP DI PL NZ NA PO NC
04AF:0001 B80000      MOV   AX,0000
-t

AX=0000  BX=0000  CX=0000  DX=0000  SP=01FE  BP=0000  SI=0000  DI=0000
DS=049F  ES=049F  SS=049F  CS=04B4  IP=0004  NV UP DI PL NZ NA PO NC
04AF:0004 50          PUSH  AX
-t

AX=0000  BX=0000  CX=0000  DX=0000  SP=01FC  BP=0000  SI=0000  DI=0000
DS=049F  ES=049F  SS=049F  CS=04B4  IP=0005  NV UP DI PL NZ NA PO NC
04AF:0005 B8B304      MOV   AX,04B3
-t

AX=04B3  BX=0000  CX=0000  DX=0000  SP=01FC  BP=0000  SI=0000  DI=0000
DS=049F  ES=049F  SS=049F  CS=04B4  IP=0008  NV UP DI PL NZ NA PO NC
04AF:0008 8ED8        MOV   DS,AX
-t
```

Figure 2-5. A DEBUG session with the example program.

```
AX=04B3  BX=0000  CX=0000  DX=0000  SP=01FC  BP=0000  SI=0000  DI=0000
DS=04B3  ES=049F  SS=04B4  CS=04B4  IP=000A  NV UP DI PL NZ NA PO NC
04AF:000A C606040000    MOV    B,[0004],00                    DS:0004=00
-g12

Program terminated normally
-r
AX=04B3  BX=0000  CX=0000  DX=0000  SP=01FC  BP=0000  SI=0000  DI=0000
DS=04B3  ES=049F  SS=04B4  CS=04B4  IP=000A  NV UP DI PL NZ NA PO NC
04AF:000A C606040000    MOV    B,[0004],0C                    DS:0004=28
-dds:0000
04B3:0000  0A 14 1E 28 28 1E 14 0A-00 00 00 00 00 00 00 00   ..((((.........
04B3:0010  53 54 41 43 4B 20 20 20-53 54 41 43 4B 20 20 20   STACK   STACK
04B3:0020  53 54 41 43 4B 20 20 20-53 54 41 43 4B 20 20 20   STACK   STACK
04B3:0030  53 54 41 43 4B 20 20 20-53 54 41 43 4B 20 20 20   STACK   STACK
04B3:0040  53 54 41 43 4B 20 20 20-53 54 41 43 4B 20 20 20   STACK   STACK
04B3:0050  53 54 41 43 4B 20 20 20-53 54 41 43 4B 20 20 20   STACK   STACK
04B3:0060  53 54 41 43 4B 20 20 20-53 54 41 43 4B 20 20 20   STACK   STACK
04B3:0070  53 54 41 43 4B 20 20 20-53 54 41 43 4B 20 20 20   STACK   STACK
-q
```

Figure 2-5. A DEBUG session with the example program (continued).

Table 2-7. The Flags Abbreviations Used by DEBUG.

Flag Name	Set	Clear
Overflow (yes/no)	OV	NV
Direction (decrement/increment)	DN	UP
Interrupt (enable/disable)	EI	DI
Sign (negative/positive)	NG	PL
Zero (yes/no)	ZR	NZ
Auxiliary Carry (yes/no)	AC	NA
Parity (even/odd)	PE	PO
Carry (yes/no)	CY	NC

We then display the final register contents.

With the program completed, we need to check whether it operated correctly—that is, whether the SOURCE table was copied to the DEST table in reverse order. To make this check, we apply the Dump (D) command to the beginning of the data segment by entering

dds:0000

This tells DEBUG to display the contents of the data segment (ds), starting at an offset of 0.

The first four values in the top line of the display reflect the final contents of SOURCE and the next four values reflect the final contents of DEST. These eight values are displayed as

0A 14 1E 28 28 1E 14 0A

in hexadecimal, and represent the decimal values

10 20 30 40 40 30 20 10

As you can see, the program did its intended task!

Besides displaying hexadecimal values for memory locations, the dump command also displays their ASCII (text) equivalents, if any. From the display here, it is apparent that the first portion of the stack segment is being shown on the remaining lines, because the ASCII representation shows repetitions of the word STACK. Our program designed the stack to be shown in this way by defining the stack segment with the pseudo-op

DB 64 DUP('STACK   ')

which makes the unused portion of the stack highly visible.

Again, DEBUG is a very powerful debugging tool that will become an integral part of your programming work. Be sure to read about this in your *DOS* manual, to learn the details of its command set.

The final section of this chapter describes some advanced pseudo-ops. If you are a beginner, you should probably proceed to Chapter 3, then return to Section 2.8 when you are more comfortable with assembly language techniques.

2.8 Advanced Pseudo-Ops

In Section 2.5 we discussed the assembler pseudo-ops that you will probably use most often. This section discusses the pseudo-ops that are used less frequently, or used by advanced programmers. Table 2-8 lists these pseudo-ops in three groups: data, conditional, and listing.

Data Pséudo-Ops

The assembler's advanced data pseudo-ops can be divided into three functional groups, as shown in Table 2-9.

Symbol Definition Pseudo-Ops

In Section 2.5 we studied the pseudo-ops DB, DW, and DD, which allocate space in memory in blocks of one, two, and four bytes, respectively. The pseudo-ops *DQ (Define Quadword)* and *DT (Define Tenbytes)* allocate memory in blocks of eight and ten bytes, respectively.

The DQ pseudo-op is primarily used for double-precision floating point applications. The DT pseudo-op allocates its ten byte blocks in "packed" decimal form; that is, with two decimal digits per byte, For example, the statement

```
ZERO_TO_NINE   DT   0123456789
```

allocates ten bytes to the name ZERO _ TO _ NINE, but initializes only the first five bytes. Hence, this statement is identical to the longer form

```
ZERO TO NINE   DB   01H,23H,45H,67H,89H,5 DUP(?)
```

Table 2-8. Advanced Pseudo-Ops.

Type	Pseudo-ops		
Data	*DQ*	LABEL	*RECORD*
	DT	NAME	*STRUC*
	EVEN	ORG	
	GROUP	.RADIX	
Conditional	ELSE	*IFNB*	IFE
	ENDIF	*IFDEF*	IFIDN
	IF	*IFNDEF*	IF1
	IFB	IFDIF	IF2
Listing	.CREF	%OUT	*.XALL*
	.LALL	*.SALL*	.XCREF
	.LFCOND	.SFCOND	*.XLIST*
	.LIST	.TFCOND	

Note: Pseudo-ops printed in *italics* are not supported by the Small Assembler (ASM).

Block Specification Pse~~l~~o-Ops

The GROUP pseudo-op collects two or more segments under one name so they all reside within a single 64K-byte block of memory. For example, suppose a program consists of two assembly modules, with two code segments (SEG1 and SEG2) in one module and a third code segment (SEG3) in the other module. These segments can all be stored in the same 64K-byte block of memory by giving them the same name (perhaps CGROUP) with GROUP statements. To do this, the first module has this kind of format:

```
CGROUP  GROUP     SEG1,SEG2
SEG1    SEGMENT
        ASSUME    CS:CGROUP
        ..
        ..
SEG1    ENDS
SEG2    SEGMENT
        ASSUME    CS:CGROUP
        ..
        ..
SEG2    ENDS
        END
```

Table 2-9. Advanced Data Pseudo-ops.

Pseudo-Op*	Function
Symbol Definition	
DQ	Format: [name] DQ expression[,...]
	Allocates storage in blocks of eight bytes.
DT	Format: [name] DT expression[,...]
	Allocates packed decimal storage in blocks of 10 bytes.
Block Specification	
GROUP	Format: name GROUP seg-name[,...]
	Collects the specified segments under one name, so they all reside within a 64K-byte physical segment.
NAME	Format: NAME module name
	Assigns a name to a module.
LABEL	Format: name LABEL type
	Defines the attributes of *name*.
RECORD	Format: name RECORD fieldname:width[=exp],[,...]
	A record is a bit pattern you define to format bytes and words for bit-packing. The record's *name* itself becomes a pseudo-op used to allocate storage.
STRUC	Format: name STRUC
	Same as RECORD, except that STRUC has a multi-byte capability.
Assembly Control	
ORG	Format: ORG expression
	Sets location counter to the value of *expression*. Assembler will store subsequent object code starting at that address.
EVEN	Format: EVEN
	Forces location counter to an even boundary.
RADIX	Format: .RADIX expression
	Allows the default radix (decimal) to be changed to any base from 2 to 16.

*Pseudo-ops printed in *italics* are not supported by the Small Assembler (ASM).

and the second module will have this kind of format:

```
CGROUP   GROUP    SEG3
SEG3     SEGMENT
         ASSUME   CS:CGROUP
         ..
         ..
SEG3     ENDS
         END
```

The NAME pseudo-op assigns a name to a module. For example,

```
NAME THIS_MODULE
```

assigns the name THIS _ MODULE to this module. If you omit the NAME pseudo-op, the assembler names the module based on the first six characters of a TITLE statement. If these characters are illegal, or if there is no TITLE statement, then the source filename becomes the module name.

The LABEL pseudo-op defines the *segment, offset,* and type attributes of *name.*

The RECORD and STRUC pseudo-ops are so complex and so rarely used that we won't even attempt to describe them here. For details, see Chapter 5 of the IBM *Macro Assembler* manual.

Assembly Control Pseudo-Ops

The ORG (for Origin) pseudo-op alters the *location counter,* the pointer that determines where the assembler stores instructions or data in memory. With the IBM PC, you normally let DOS make the placement decisions, but ORG gives you the option of making these decisions yourself. For example,

```
ORG  120D
```

tells the assembler to store the object code for subsequent instructions starting at a location 120 bytes from the start of the segment.

You may also locate the object code *relative* to the active storage location in memory, by using a dollar sign ($) to refer to the current value of the location counter. The statement

```
ORG  $+4
```

adds a value of four to the location counter, thereby causing the assembler to reserve the next four bytes in memory.

You might never use ORG in your own programs, but you'll encounter it if you ever delve into listings of system programs, such as DOS. For this reason, you should know what ORG does.

EVEN is a seldom used pseudo-op you use to develop programs to run on an *8086*-based computer. Having a 16-bit data bus, the 8086 can transfer 16 bits of data in one operation (as opposed to the 8088, which requires two 8-bit operations to transfer 16 bits of data). However, the 8086 takes longer to transfer data that starts at an odd-numbered address than to transfer data that starts at an even-numbered address. Therefore, in time-critical applications it is advantageous to store all 16-bit data values at even-numbered addresses.

The EVEN pseudo-op forces the location counter to point to an even-numbered address. If the location counter is already *at* an even address, EVEN does nothing, but if the counter is at an odd address, EVEN causes the assembler to add a one-byte NOP (no operation) instruction, which puts it at an even address. For example, if the location counter points to the address 129H, an EVEN pseudo-op makes it point to 12AH.

As you learned in Section 2.3, you can enter data in five different forms: binary, hexadecimal, decimal, octal, and ASCII. To differentiate between these forms, you must add an identifying suffix (or, for ASCII, single quotes) for every form but decimal. This is convenient if your program primarily involves decimal values, but if you are working with a lot of binary, hexadecimal or other non-decimal numbers, you may want to enter those numbers without tacking on the standard identifier (B, H, or whatever). The .RADIX pseudo-op makes this possible, by letting you change the assembler's "default" (un-suffixed) radix from decimal to any base you choose, from 2 to 16. For example, the statements

```
.RADIX 2
.RADIX 8
.RADIX 16
```

change the default radix to binary (base 2), octal (base 8), and hexadecimal (base 16), respectively. Note that the operand is always a decimal number, regardless of the current radix.

Conditional Pseudo-Ops

Conditional pseudo-ops cause the assembler to either assemble or bypass a certain portion of the source program, based on whether a specified condition is "true" or "false" at assembly time. This selective assemble/don't-assemble capability lets you place diagnostics or special conditions in test runs, or create specialized versions of a multi-use program.

With the IBM assemblers, each portion of the source program to be "conditionally assembled" must be preceded by one of six IF pseudo-ops (see Table 2-10) and terminated by an ENDIF pseudo-op. For each pseudo-op, if the expression is evaluated as "true," the enclosed code is assembled; if the expression is evaluated as "false," the assembler skips the enclosed code, and continues with the statement that follows ENDIF.

Table 2-10. Conditional Pseudo-Ops.

Pseudo-Op*	Function
IFE	Format: IFE expression True if *expression* is 0.
IF	Format: IF expression True if *expression* is not 0.
IF1	Format: IF1 True if assembler is executing pass 1.
IF2	Format: IF2 True if assembler is executing pass 2.
IFDEF	Format: IFDEF symbol True if *symbol* is defined or has been declared external by an EXTRN pseudo-op.
IFNDEF	Format: IFNDEF symbol True if *symbol* is undefined or not declared external by an EXTRN pseudo-op.
IFB	Format: IFB <argument> True if *argument* is blank. The angle brackets around <argument> are required.
IFNB	Format: IFNB <argument> True if *argument* is not blank. Used for testing when arguments are supplied. The angle brackets around <argument> are required.
IFIDN	Format: IFIDN <argument-1>, <argument-2> True if the string *argument-1* is identical to the string *argument-2*. The angle brackets around the arguments are required.
IFIDF	Format: IFIDF <argument-1>, <argument-2> True if the string *argument-1* is different from the string *argument-2*. The angle brackets around the arguments are required.

*Pseudo-ops printed in *italics* are not supported by the Small Assembler (ASM).

For example, to include diagnostic routines in a test run, you might enclose the diagnostics with the pseudo-ops IFE and ENDIF, and set up a constant called FOR_TEST_ONLY. For any assembly in which FOR_TEST_ONLY is set to 0, the diagnostics will be included in (assembled into) the program. For any assembly in which FOR_TEST_ONLY is set to a value other than 0, the diagnostics will be excluded from the program. Thus, in the sequence

```
          IFE   FOR_TEST_ONLY
DIAG1  ..            (diagnostic test instructions)
          ..
          ENDIF
```

the instructions between DIAG1 and ENDIF are assembled only if a statement such as

```
FOR_TEST_ONLY  =  0
```

appears earlier in the program. A statement such as

```
FOR_TEST_ONLY  =  1
```

makes the assembler skip the instructions between DIAG1 and ENDIF.

You may also include an ELSE pseudo-op, to generate an *alternate* set of code if the "false" condition exists, The general format is:

```
IFxx  [argument]
..
..
[ELSE]
..
..
ENDIF
```

The ten IF pseudo-ops can be grouped into five pairs, as follows:

- IFE is true if *expression* is 0; IF is true if *expression* is not 0.
- IF1 is true when the assembler is executing pass 1; IF2 is true when the assembler is executing pass 2.
- IFDEF is true if *symbol* is defined (or has been declared external) by an EXTRN pseudo-op; otherwise, IFNDEF is true.
- IFB is true if *argument* is blank; IFNB is true if *argument* is not blank.
- IFIDN is true if the string *argument-1* is identical to the string *argument-2;* IFIDF is true if these strings are different.

The conditional pseudo-ops make it possible, for example, to write a program whose I/O section varies, depending on whether the program is being run in a disk environment or a tape environment. For this application you could assign a constant called D_OR_T to act as a disk I/O or tape I/O indicator. If D_OR_T is zero, the program is assembled for a disk environment; otherwise the program is assembled for a tape environment. The structure of the program's I/O section will look like this:

```
            IFE.  D_OR_T
DISK_I/O  ..                  (disk I/O statements)
            ..
            ELSE
TAPE_I/O  ..                  (tape I/O statements)
            ..
            ENDIF
```

You can also *nest* conditional clauses, to give the assembler more than two options. For instance, suppose you have four versions of a program, to service users with four different security clearance levels—say Classified, Secret, Top Secret, and For God Only. If the clearance level is based on whether the constant LEVEL has a value of 0, 1, 2, or 3, the main program may include this kind of conditional structure:

```
IFE  LEVEL
..                 (level 0 statements)
..
ELSE
   IFE LEVEL-1
   ..              (level 1 statements)
   ..
   ELSE
      IFE  LEVEL-2
      ..           (level 2 statements)
      ..
      ELSE
      ..           (level 3 statements)
      ..
      ENDIF
   ENDIF
ENDIF
```

Listing Pseudo-ops

Listing pseudo-ops tell the assembler what information to print, and how to format that information. They are summarized in Table 2-11 as four functional groups.

Listing Control Pseudo-Ops

The .XCREF and .CREF pseudo-ops let you exclude portions of your program from the cross reference file (.CRF). Similarly, .XLIST and .LIST let you exclude portions of your program from the assembler listing file (.LST). You might apply .XLIST to print just selected procedures within a long program.

Table 2-11. Listing Pseudo-Ops.

Pseudo-Op	Function
Listing Control	
.XCREF	Format: .XCREF
	Suppresses cross reference listing between here and the next .CREF (if any).
.CREF	Format: .CREF
	Restores cross reference listing.
.XLIST	Format: .XLIST
	Suppresses assembly listing between here and the next .LIST (if any).
.LIST	Format: .LIST
	Restores assembly listing.
Display Status Message	
%OUT	Format: %OUT text
	Lists the *text* message on the display, unless the display is already the listing device.
False Conditional Block Control	
.LFCOND	Format: .LFCOND
	Lists conditional blocks that evaluate as "false."
.SFCOND	Format: .SFCOND
	Suppresses the listing of conditional blocks that evaluate as "false."
.TFCOND	Format: .TFCOND
	Reverses the setting that controls whether false conditional blocks are listed.

Display Status Message Pseudo-Op

The %OUT pseudo-op outputs a message to the display while a program is being assembled. This facility is often used to show which path—"true" or "false"—is being taken in a conditional assembly, but it can also be used to report on progress during a long assembly.

For example, in the *Conditional Pseudo-Ops* section we discussed a program whose I/O section can take two differen* forms, depending on whether the program is assembled for a disk environment or a tape environment. If we add %OUT pseudo-ops to indicate which environment is being used, the I/O section may have this kind of format:

```
           IFE   D OR T
           %OUT  ASSEMBLING FOR DISK ENVIRONMENT
DISK_I/D   ..    (disk I/O statements)
           ..
           ELSE
           %OUT  ASSEMBLING FOR TAPE ENVIRONMENT
TAPE_I/O   ..    (tape I/O statements)
           ..
           ENDIF
```

False Conditional Block Control Pseudo-Ops

From our preceding discussion of conditional assembly, you know that if an IF pseudo-op evaluates as "false," the assembler will ignore the statements between that point and the next ENDIF. That is, statements enclosed by an IF/ENDIF combination are not assembled. However, you will probably want to list those unassembled statements at one time or another, so you now can see your program in its entirety. The pseudo-ops .SFCOND, .LFCOND, and .TFCOND control the listing of "false" conditional blocks.

.LFCOND causes false conditional blocks to be listed, .SFCOND turns off the false conditional block listing, and .TFCOND reverses the listing control setting (turns it on if it is off, and turns it off if it is on).

Study Exercises (answers on page 278)

1. How many *bytes* does the following sequence allocate in memory?

```
VAR1   DB   ?
VAR2   DW   4 DUP(?),20
VAR3   DB   10 DUP(?)
```

2. What value does the assembler put into VAR1 in Exercise 1?
3. How do the following statements differ?

```
K   EQU   1024
K   =     1024
```

4. Tell what is wrong with this sequence:

```
CONST   DB        ?
        MOV       CONST,256
```

5. Which two pseudo-ops must appear in every procedure?
6. What is the difference between a NEAR procedure and a FAR procedure?
7. Which pseudo-op must appear in every source program?
8. What does the DOS Linker program do?

3

The 8088 Instruction Set

3.1 About This Chapter

In Chapter 2 you began working with the "foundation" of assembly language—the instructions that control the 8088 microprocessor. This chapter provides a detailed description of the 8088's instruction set and operand addressing modes.

Many books cover the instructions individually, discussing them one by one, in alphabetical order. Although that approach has definite merit in a technical reference manual, it tends to leave you bored and bewildered after the fifth or sixth instruction.

In this book, we group instructions by function, so similar instructions are described together. That is, we group add instructions with subtract instructions, shift instructions with rotate instructions, and so on. This approach is intended to help you *understand* the instruction set, and how individual instructions "fit together," so you don't learn them as a bunch of disjointed entities.

Later, after running a few programs, you will only need to refer to this chapter occasionally, to look up the details of specific instructions. Once you feel comfortable with the instruction set, you can resolve most questions by referring to Appendix D, where the instructions are summarized alphabetically. Appendix C is also useful. It lists the execution time for each instruction.

3.2 Addressing Modes

The 8088 provides a variety of ways to access the operands your programs are to operate on. Operands can be contained in registers, within the instruction itself, or in memory or an I/O port. Some of the manufacturers' marketing literature claims that the 8088 has 24 operand addressing modes — perhaps justifiably, if you consider all the possible operand combinations. In this book, however, we divide the addressing modes into seven groups:

1. Register addressing
2. Immediate addressing
3. Direct addressing
4. Register indirect addressing
5. Base relative addressing
6. Direct indexed addressing
7. Base indexed addressing

The microprocessor determines *which* of the seven addressing modes to use by examining the contents of a "mode field" in the instruction. The bits in the mode field are encoded by the assembler, based on how the operand(s) appear in your source program. For instance, if you write an instruction as

        MOV   AX,BX

the assembler encodes both operands (AX and BX) for the register addressing mode. However, if you put brackets around the source operand, and write the instruction as

        MOV   AX,[BX]

the assembler still encodes the destination operand (AX) for register addressing, but it encodes the source operand (BX) for the register *indirect* addressing mode.

Table 3-1 shows the assembler format, and which segment register is used to calculate the physical address, for the 8088's seven operand addressing modes. Note that all modes assume you are accessing the data segment (DS is the segment register) except those that involve BP, in which case the stack segment is assumed (SS is the segment register).

> *Important:* The 8088's string instructions, which are described in Section 3.8, assume that DI references a location in the extra segment, rather than the data segment, and uses ES as the segment register. All other instructions follow the assignments in Table 3-1.

Of the seven addressing modes, the 8088 processes register and immediate operands fastest, because its Execution Unit (EU) can fetch them from registers (for register addressing) or from the instruction queue (for immediate addressing). The five other modes take longer to process because the

Table 3-1. The 8088 addressing modes.

Addressing Mode	Operand Format	Segment Register
Register	reg	None
Immediate	data	None
Direct	disp	DS
	label	DS
Register indirect	[BX]	DS
	[BP]	SS
	[DI]	DS
	[SI]	DS
Base relative	[BX] + disp	DS
	[BP] + disp	SS
Direct indexed	[DI] + disp	DS
	[SI] + disp	DS
Base indexed	[BX][SI] + disp	DS
	[BX][DI] + disp	DS
	[BP][SI] + disp	SS
	[BP][DI] + disp	SS

Notes: 1. *disp* is optional for base indexed addressing
2. *reg* can be any 8- or 16-bit register, except IP.
3. *data* can be an 8- or 16-bit constant value.
4. *disp* can be an 8- or 16-bit signed displacement value.

Bus Interface Unit (BIU) must compute a memory address, then fetch the operand and pass it to the EU.

Each addressing mode description in this section includes an example of the mode's usage. In most cases, the 8088's move instruction is used to demonstrate the mode.

Register and Immediate Addressing

In *register addressing* the 8088 fetches an operand from (or loads it into) a register. For example, the instruction

    MOV   AX,CX

copies the 16-bit contents of the count register (CX) into the accumulator register (AX). The contents of CX are unaffected. In this example, the 8088 uses register addressing to fetch the source operand from CX and to load it into the destination register, AX.

Immediate addressing lets you specify an 8- or 16-bit constant value as a source operand. This constant is contained in the instruction (where it was put by the assembler), rather than in a register or a memory location. For example,

```
MOV  CX,500
```

loads the value 500 into the CX register and

```
MOV  CL,-30
```

loads -30 into the CL register.

Of course, the immediate operand may also be a symbol that was defined by an EQU or = pseudo-op, so this kind of form is valid:

```
K EQU  1024
 ..
 ..
MOV  CX,K
```

To avoid problems, remember that 8-bit signed numbers are limited to values between 127 (7FH) and -128 (80H), and that 16-bit signed numbers are limited to values between 32767 (7FFFH) and -32768 (8000H). For unsigned numbers, the maximum 8- and 16-bit values are 255 (0FFH) and 65535 (0FFFFH), respectively.

Immediate Values are Sign-Extended

Immediate values are always sign-extended in the destination. This means the most-significant bit of the source value is replicated to fill the 8 or 16 bits of the destination operand.

For instance, the source operand for our first example, decimal 500, can be represented by the 10-bit binary pattern 0111110100. When loading this value into a 16-bit register (CX), the 8088 extends the 10-bit pattern to 16 bits by putting a copy of the "sign" bit, 0, into the six highest bit positions of CX. Therefore, CX will end up containing the binary pattern *000000*0111110100.

In the second example, the 8088 loads the 8-bit binary pattern for -30 (11100010) into CL.

Memory Addressing Modes

As mentioned in Chapter 1, accessing memory involves a joint effort by the 8088's Execution Unit (EU) and Bus Interface Unit (BIU). When the EU needs to read or write a memory operand, it must pass an offset value to the BIU. The BIU adds this offset to the contents of a segment register (with four 0s appended) to produce a 20-bit physical address, then uses that address to access the operand.

The Effective Address

The offset that the Execution Unit calculates for a memory operand is called the operand's *effective address,* or EA. The EA represents the operand's distance in bytes from the beginning of the segment where it resides. Being a 16-bit unsigned value, the EA can reference operands that lie up to 65,535 bytes beyond the first location of the segment.

The amount of time the Execution Unit takes to calculate the EA is one of the prime factors in determining how long an instruction takes to execute. Depending on which addressing mode is used, deriving the EA may involve nothing more than fetching a displacement from within the instruction. Then again, it may require some lengthy calculation, such as adding a displacement, a base register, and an index register. Regardless of whether the execution time is critical in the application programs you write, it is worthwhile to appreciate these time factors as you read the addressing mode descriptions that follow.

Direct Addressing

With direct addressing, the EA is contained in the instruction, just as the immediate data value is contained in an immediate instruction. The 8088 adds the EA to the (shifted) contents of the Data Segment (DS) register to produce the operand's 20-bit physical address.

The direct addressing operand is normally a label instead of a displacement value. For example, the instruction

    MOV AX,TABLE

loads the contents of data memory location TABLE into the AX register. Figure 3-1 shows how this instruction works.

Incidentally, note that the 8088 stores the data in memory in the reverse order you would expect to find it; with the high-order byte *following* (rather than preceding) the low-order byte. To keep this straight, just remember that *the high (most-significant) part of the data is in the highest memory address.*

Register Indirect Addressing

With register indirect addressing, the effective address of the operand is contained in base register BX, base pointer BP, or an index register (SI or DI). Register indirect operands are enclosed in square brackets to differentiate them from register operands. For example, the instruction

    MOV AX,[BX]

loads the contents of the memory location addressed by BX into the AX register. Figure 3-2 illustrates this example.

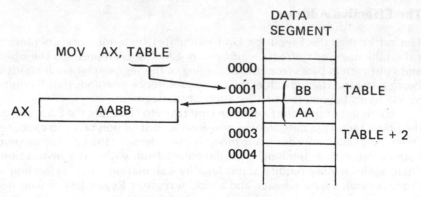

Figure 3-1. Direct addressing.

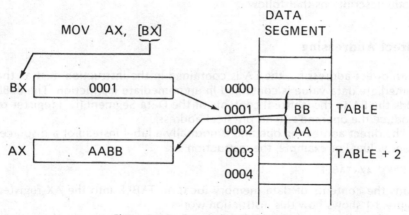

Figure 3-2. Register indirect addressing.

How do you get an offset address into BX? One way is by applying the OFFSET operator to the memory address. For instance, to load the word at location *TABLE* into AX, you could use the sequence

```
MOV   BX,OFFSET TABLE
MOV   AX,[BX]
```

Notice that these two instructions do the same job as the single instruction

```
MOV   AX,TABLE
```

except that they destroy the previous contents of BX. If you plan to access just one memory location (the contents of TABLE here), this single-instruction approach makes more sense. However, if you plan to access *several* locations, starting at that base address, having the effective address in a register is the better approach. Why? Because you can manipulate the contents of the register without fetching a new address each time. An example will make this clearer.

Recall that our "example program" in Chapter 2 includes a series of MOV instructions that copy the bytes in a source table into a destination table. Alternatively, we could have used registers to hold the table addresses and set up a *loop* to do the copying. After copying each byte, the loop could increase the source address register (perhaps BX) by one and decrease the destination address register (perhaps DI) by one. Admittedly, using a loop to move just four bytes would probably make the program longer, but a loop would be much easier to move, say, 100 bytes! We'll discuss loops later in this chapter.

Base Relative Addressing

With base relative addressing, the effective address is the sum of a displacement value plus the contents of the BX or BP register.

The BX form gives you a convenient way to access data structures located at different places in memory. To do this, you put the base address of the structure into the base register and reference elements of the structure by their displacement from the base. After that, you can access different records in the structure by simply changing the base register.

Suppose, for example, you've read some personnel records into memory from disk. Each record contains an employee's identification number, department number, division number, age, pay rate, and so on. If the division number is stored in the fifth and sixth bytes of the record, and the starting address of the record is in BX, the instruction

```
MOV   AX,[BX]+4
```

loads the employee's division number into AX. (The displacement is 4, rather than 5, because the first byte is Byte 0.) Figure 3-3 illustrates this example.

This particular example shows you how to get the division number of the employee whose record is labeled EMP_50. To get the division number of some other employee, EMP_41, you run this simple sequence:

```
MOV   BX,OFFSET EMP_41 ;Fetch base address of employee 41
MOV   AX,[BX]+4         ;and read that employee's division no.
```

Just as we used BX to access a location in the data segment, we can use BP to access stack data. The instruction

```
MOV   AX,[BP]+4
```

loads the contents of the fourth location after the BP address into AX.

The IBM assembler lets you specify the base relative operand in three different ways. The following are equivalent instructions:

```
MOV   AX,[BP]+4   ;This is the standard form, but you may
MOV   AX,4[BP]    ; put the displacement first
MOV   AX,[BP+4]   ; or within the brackets.
```

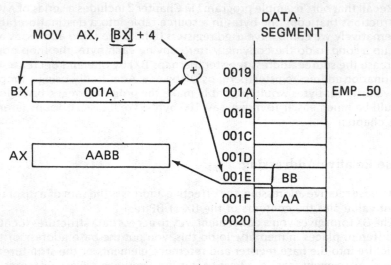

Figure 3-3. Base relative addressing.

Direct Indexed Addressing

With direct indexed addressing, the effective address is the sum of a displacement and an index register, either DI or SI. You often use this type of addressing to access elements in a table. There, the displacement points to the beginning of the table and the index register points to an element in the table

For example, if we have a byte table called B_TABLE, the instruction sequence

```
MOV  DI,2
MOV  AL,B_TABLE[DI]
```

loads the table's third element (a byte value) into the AL register.

In a word table the elements lie two bytes apart, so you *double the element number* to get its index value. With a word table called TABLE, the instruction sequence

```
MOV  DI,4
MOV  AX,TABLE[DI]
```

loads the table's third element (a word value) into the AX register. Figure 3-4 illustrates this example.

Base Indexed Addressing

With base indexed addressing, the EA is the sum of three components: a base register, an index register, and a displacement. (The displacement is optional, and may be omitted if you so choose.)

Because it offers two separate offsets, base indexed addressing is useful for accessing two-dimensional arrays. For such applications, a base register holds the starting address of the array, and the displacement and index register provide row and column offsets.

For example, suppose your Personal Computer monitors six pressure valves in a chemical processing plant. This system takes a reading of each valve once every half-hour and records these readings in memory. In one week's time these readings will form an array that has 336 blocks (48 readings per day for seven days) of six elements each, for a total of 2016 data values.

If the starting address of the array is held in BX, the block displacement (reading number times 12) is in DI and the valve number displacement is defined by the variable VALVE, you can use the instruction

```
MOV  AX,VALVE[BX][DI]
```

to load any selected pressure valve reading into AX. In Figure 3-5 this instruction extracts the value of the third reading (Reading 2) of Valve 4 from an array that has a data segment offset of 100H.

Here are some other legal formats for base indexed addressing operands:

```
MOV   AX,[BX+2+DI]   ;The operands can be put in brackets
MOV   AX,[DI+BX+2]   ; in any order
MOV   AX,[BX+2][DI]  ; and the displacement can be paired
MOV   AX,[BX][DI+2]  ; with either register.
```

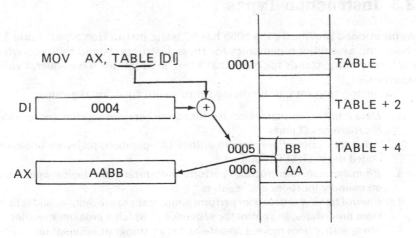

Figure 3-4. Direct indexed addressing.

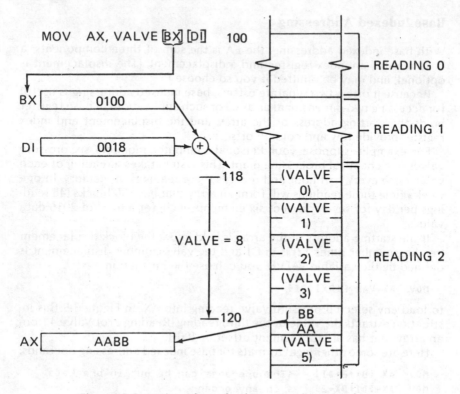

Figure 3-5. Extracting a data value from a two-dimensional array.

3.3 Instruction Types

As mentioned previously, the 8088 has 92 basic instruction types. Table 3-2 shows the assembler mnemonics for these instructions and tells you what each mnemonic stands for. Note that some instructions have several valid mnemonics.

The instruction set can be divided into seven functional groups:

1. *Data transfer instructions* move information between registers and memory locations or I/O ports.
2. *Arithmetic instructions* perform arithmetic operations on binary or binary-coded decimal (BCD) numbers.
3. *Bit manipulation instructions* perform shift, rotate, and logical operations on memory locations and registers.
4. *Control transfer instructions* perform jumps, calls to procedures, and returns from procedures, to control the sequence in which a program executes.
5. *String instructions* move, compare and scan strings of information.

Table 3-2. The 8086/8088 instruction set.

Mnemonic	Description
AAA	ASCII Adjust for Addition
AAD	ASCII Adjust for Division
AAM	ASCII Adjust for Multiplication
AAS	ASCII Adjust for Subtraction
ADC	Add with Carry
ADD	Add (without Carry)
AND	Logical AND
CALL	Call a Procedure
CBW	Convert Byte to Word
CLC	Clear Carry Flag
CLD	Clear Direction Flag
CLI	Clear Interrupt Flag
CMC	Complement Carry Flag
CMP	Compare Destination to Source
CMPS, CMPSB or CMPSW	Compare Byte or Word Strings
CWD	Convert Word to Doubleword
DAA	Decimal Adjust for Addition
DAS	Decimal Adjust for Subtraction
DEC	Decrement Destination by One
DIV	Divide, Unsigned
ESC	Escape
HLT	Halt the Processor
IDIV	Integer Divide, Signed
IMUL	Integer Multiply, Signed
IN	Input Byte or Word
INC	Increment Destination by One
INT	Interrupt
INTO	Interrupt if Overflow
IRET	Interrupt Return
JA or JNBE	Jump If Above/If Not Below nor Equal
JAE, JNB, or JNC	Jump If Above or Equal/If Not Below/If No Carry
JB, JNAE, or JC	Jump If Below/If Not Above nor Equal/If Carry
JBE or JNA	Jump If Below or Equal/If Not Above
JCXZ	Jump If CX Is Zero
JE or JZ	Jump If Equal/If Zero
JG or JNLE	Jump If Greater/If Not Less nor Equal
JGE or JNl	Jump If Greater or Equal/If Not Less
JL or JNGE	Jump If Less/If Not Greater Nor Equal

Table 3-2. The 8086/8088 instruction set (continued).

Mnemonic	Description
JLE or JNG	Jump If Less or Equal/If Not Greater
JMP	Jump Unconditionally .
JNE or JNZ	Jump If Not Equal/If Not Zero
JNO	Jump If No Overflow
JNP or JPO	Jump If No Parity/If Parity Odd
JNS	Jump If No Sign (If Positive)
JO	Jump On Overflow
JP or JPE	Jump On Parity/If Parity Even
JS	Jump On Sign
LAHF	Load AH from Flags
LDS	Load Pointer Using DS
LEA	Load Effective Address
LES	Load Pointer Using ES
LOCK	Lock the Bus
LODS, LODSB, or LODSW	Load Byte or Word String
LOOP	Loop until Count Complete
LOOPE or LOOPZ	Loop While Equal/While Zero
LOOPNE or LOOPNZ	Loop While Not Equal/While Not Zero
MOV	Move
MOVS, MOVSB, or MOVSW	Move Byte or Word String
MUL	Multiply, Unsigned
NEG	Negate (Form 2's Complement)
NOP	No Operation
NOT	Logical NOT
OR	Logical Inclusive-OR
OUT	Output Byte or Word
POP	Pop Word Off Stack to Destination
POPF	Pop Flags Off Stack
PUSH	Push Word onto Stack
PUSHF	Push Flags onto Stack
RCL	Rotate Left through Carry
RCR	Rotate Right through Carry
REP, REPE, or REPZ	Repeat String Operation/While Equal/While Zero
REPNE or REPNZ	Repeat String Operation While Not Equal/While Not Zero

Table 3-2. The 8086/8088 instruction set (continued).

Mnemonic	Description
RET	Return from Procedure
ROL	Rotate Left
ROR	Rotate Right
SAHF	Store AH into Flags
SAL or SHL	Shift Arithmetic Left/Logical Left
SAR	Shift Arithmetic Right
SBB	Subtract with Borrow
SCAS, SCASB, or SCASW	Scan Byte or Word String
SHR	Shift Logical Right
STC	Set Carry Flag
STD	Set Direction Flag
STI	Set Interrupt Enable Flag
STOS, STOSB, OR STOSW	Store Byte or Word String
SUB	Subtract (Without Borrow)
TEST	Test (Logically Compare Two Operands)
WAIT	Wait
XCHG	Exchange Two Operands
XLAT	Translate
XOR	Logical Exclusive-OR

6. *Interrupt instructions* cause the microprocessor to be interrupted, so it can service some specific condition.
7. *Processor control instructions* set and clear status flags, and change the microprocessor's execution state.

In the following sections we will describe the 8088 instruction set by groups, in the order just presented. Let us begin with the data transfer group, which includes the ubiquitous MOV instruction.

3.4 Data Transfer Instructions

Data transfer instructions move data and addresses between registers and memory locations or I/O ports. Table 3-3 summarizes these instructions and groups them into four categories; general-purpose, input/output, address transfer, and flag transfer.

Table 3-3. Data transfer instructions.

Mnemonic	Assembler Format	OF	DF	IF	TF	SF	ZF	AF	PF	CF
		Flags								
GENERAL-PURPOSE										
MOV	MOV destination,source	–	–	–	–	–	–	–	–	–
PUSH	PUSH source	–	–	–	–	–	–	–	–	–
POP	POP destination	–	–	–	–	–	–	–	–	–
XCHG	XCHG destination,source	–	–	–	–	–	–	–	–	–
XLAT	XLAT source-table	–	–	–	–	–	–	–	–	–
INPUT/OUTPUT										
IN	IN accumulator,port	–	–	–	–	–	–	–	–	–
OUT	OUT port,accumulator	–	–	–	–	–	–	–	–	–
ADDRESS TRANSFER										
LEA	LEA reg16,mem16	–	–	–	–	–	–	–	–	–
LDS	LDS reg16,mem32	–	–	–	–	–	–	–	–	–
LES	LES reg16,mem32	–	–	–	–	–	–	–	–	–
FLAG TRANSFER										
LAHF	LAHF	–	–	–	–	–	–	–	–	–
SAHF	SAHF	–	–	–	–	*	*	*	*	*
PUSHF	PUSHF	–	–	–	–	–	–	–	–	–
POPF	POPF	*	*	*	*	*	*	*	*	*

Note: * means changed and – means unchanged.

General-Purpose Instructions

Move (MOV)

The fundamental general-purpose instruction is *move (MOV)*, which can transfer byte or word data between a register and a memory location, or between two registers. It can also transfer an immediate data value into a register or memory location.

The move instruction has the general form

```
MOV  destination,source
```

Most operand combinations are legal. Here are some examples:

```
MOV  AX,TABLE      ;Move from memory into a register
MOV  TABLE,AX      ; or vice versa
MOV  ES:[BX],AX    ;A segment override may be included
MOV  DS,AX         ;Move between 16-bit registers
MOV  BL,AL         ; or 8-bit registers
MOV  CL,-30        ;Move a constant into a register
MOV  DEST,25H      ; or into memory
```

The move instruction *excludes* these combinations:

1. You cannot move data between two memory locations directly. This requires a memory-to-register transfer followed by a register-to-memory transfer.
2. You cannot load an immediate value—such as the offset address of a segment—into a segment register. You can, however, load the value into a general-purpose register, then transfer *that* register into the segment register.
3. The CS register cannot be used as the destination of a move instruction.

Push (PUSH) and Pop (POP)

Earlier we mentioned that the stack holds return addresses while a procedure is being executed. The call (CALL instruction) pushes an address onto the stack and a return (RET) instruction retrieves the address from the stack at the end of the procedure. This is one of the ways the 8088 uses the stack *automatically* without you telling it to do so.

However, the stack is also a convenient place to deposit data from your program—register and memory operands—temporarily. For instance, you might want to save the contents of the AX register while that register is being put to some other use. Two instructions that let you access the stack are *Push Word onto Stack (PUSH)* and *Pop Word Off Stack (POP)*.

PUSH deposits a word-sized register or memory operand onto the "top" of the stack. Conversely, POP retrieves a word from the top of the stack and puts it into memory or a register.

The PUSH and POP instructions have these general formats:

```
PUSH  source
POP   destination
```

where, in both cases, the operand can be a 16-bit register or a word-sized memory location. Here are some examples:

```
PUSH  SI              ;You can save a general-purpose
PUSH  DS              ; register or a segment register,
PUSH  CS              ; including CS.
PUSH  COUNTER         ;You can also save the contents of
PUSH  TABLE[BX][DI]   ; a memory location.
```

Being complementary, PUSH and POP instructions are almost always used in pairs. That is, for each PUSH in a program there must be a POP. For example, to save the contents of AX on the stack and later restore them, your program would have this form:

```
PUSH  AX    ;Save AX on top of the stack
..          (Other operations are being performed
..           with AX here.)
POP   AX    ;Retrieve AX from top of the stack
```

What do we mean by the "top" of the stack? We mean the location in the stack segment the stack pointer (SP) is pointing to. The SP always points to the word that was last pushed onto the stack. Since the stack "builds" downward in memory (at ever-decreasing addresses), the first word pushed onto the stack is stored at the highest stack address, the next word pushed is stored two bytes lower, and so on.

A PUSH instruction subtracts 2 from the stack pointer, then transfers the source operand (a word) onto the stack. Conversely, a POP instruction transfers the word addressed by SP to the destination operand, then adds 2 to the SP.

To illustrate these points, Figure 3-6 shows the stack and the stack pointer before and after a PUSH, and after a POP. After the PUSH (Fig, 3-6B), the stack pointer has moved two bytes lower in memory and those previously-unused bytes now hold the contents of AX. After the POP (Fig. 3-6C), the SP has resumed its original position. Although AX is still in memory, it is not "on the stack."

You can also save more than one word value on a stack, by performing a series of pushes. In doing so, however, remember that because each PUSH puts its data on top of the stack, *you must POP words off the stack in the reverse order you PUSHed them onto the stack.* Here is a sequence that pushes the contents of four registers onto the stack, and later restores them:

```
PUSH  AX    ;Save AX,
PUSH  ES    ; ES,
PUSH  DI    ; DI,
PUSH  SI    ; and SI
..
..
POP   SI    ;Restore SI
POP   DI    ; DI,
POP   ES    ; ES,
POP   AX    ; and AX
```

There are also special instructions that push and pop the contents of the flags register. We'll look at them in the *Flags Transfer* portion of this section.

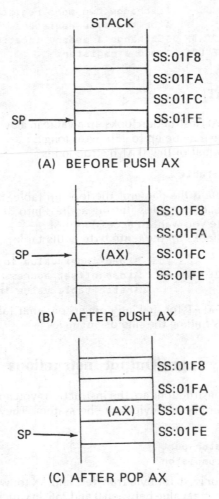

STACK

(A) BEFORE PUSH AX

(B) AFTER PUSH AX

(C) AFTER POP AX

Figure 3-6. How a PUSH and a POP affect the stack.

Exchange (XCHG)

The exchange (XCHG) instruction exchanges the byte or word source oper-
and with the destination operand. With XCHG you can exchange the contents of two registers, or exchange the contents of a register and a memory
location. Segment registers may not be used as operands with XCHG.
    Some examples are:

```
XCHG   AX,BX        ;Exchange two word registers
XCHG   AL,BH        ; or two byte registers.
XCHG   WORD_LOC,DX  ;Exchange a memory location
XCHG   DL,BYTE_LOC  ; and a register.
```

Translate (XLAT)

The translate (XLAT) instruction looks up a value in a byte table and loads it into AL. The table may be up to 256 bytes long.

The general format of the XLAT instruction is

```
XLAT   source-table
```

where *source-table* is the name of the look-up table. Before you execute XLAT, you must load the table's starting address into BX and the index into the table (the byte you want to access) into AL.

This sequence looks up the tenth byte in the table S_TAB:

```
MOV    AL,10        ;Load index value into AL
MOV    BX,OFFSET S_TAB  ;Load offset address into BX
XLAT   S_TA         ;Fetch table value into AL
```

You'll appreciate XLAT for making conversions that take a lot of time to calculate, such as finding the sine of an angle

Input/Output Instructions

The input/output instructions are the instructions you normally use to communicate with peripheral devices in the system. They have the general formats

```
IN   accumulator,port
OUT  port,accumulator
```

where *accumulator* is AL for byte transfers and AX for word transfers. Generally, *port* is a decimal value between 0 and 255, in which case it references one of the first 256 devices in the system.

The contents of the DX register may also be specified as the *port* operand, giving you access to 64K different ports. Using DX also lets you change the port number easily, perhaps to send the same data to several different ports.

Here are a few examples of the IN and OUT instructions:

```
IN   AL,200      ;Input a byte from Port 200
IN   AL,PORT_VAL ;Here the port is named by a constant
OUT  30H,AX      ;Output a word to Port 30H
OUT  DX,AX       ;Output to the port specified by DX
```

Chapter 2 of the IBM *Technical Reference* manual summarizes the ports the Personal Computer uses.

Address Transfer Instructions

Address transfer instructions transfer the *addresses* of variables rather than the *contents* of variables.

Load Effective Address (LEA)

LEA transfers the offset address of a memory operand into any 16-bit general, pointer, or index register. It has this general format:

```
LEA    reg16,mem16
```

where *mem16* is a memory operand that must have a type attribute of WORD. Unlike MOV with an OFFSET operator, the memory operand for LEA can be subscripted, which gives you a lot more addressing flexibility.
    For example, if the DI register contains 5, the instruction

```
LEA    BX,TABLE[DI]
```

loads the offset address of TABLE + 5 into BX.

Load Pointer Using DS (LDS)

The LDS instruction fetches a 32-bit doubleword from memory, and loads the high-order 16 bits into a specified word register and the low-order 16 bits into DS. The general format is

```
LDS    reg16,mem32
```

where *reg16* is any 16-bit general register and *mem32* is a memory location with a DOUBLEWORD type attribute.
    Generally, the *mem32* operand is defined with the Define Doubleword (DD) data definition pseudo-op we discussed in Section 2.5. Using the example in that section,

```
HERE_FAR    DD    HERE
```

we can get the offset address and segment number of HERE into BX and DS, respectively, with the instruction

```
LDS    BX,HERE_FAR
```

As you can see, LDS is a one-instruction replacement for a sequence of this kind:

```
MOV    BX,OFFSET HERE
MOV    AX,SEGMENT HERE
MOV    DS,AX
```

Moreover, LDS eliminates the need for a third 16-bit register (AX, here).

Load Pointer Using ES (LES)

The LES instruction is identical to the LDS instruction, except LES transfers the segment word of the pointer into ES instead of DS.

Flag Transfer Instructions

Load AH from Flags (LAHF) and Store AH into Flags (SAHF)

The LAHF instructions copies the 8080/8085 flags in the flags register into AH. It copies CF, PF, AF, ZF, and SF into the corresponding bits of AH (0, 2, 4, 6, and 7, respectively).

The SAHF instruction performs the reverse operation. It loads the five bits of AH we just mentioned into the flags register.

The LAHF instruction does not affect any flags but, of course, SAHF affects the five 8080/8085 flags. Both instructions are provided for 8080/8085 compatibility.

Push Flags onto Stack (PUSHF) and POP Flags Off Stack (POPF)

These instructions transfer the entire 16 bits of the flags register (not just the 8080/8085 flags) to and from the stack. They are essentially the same as the PUSH and POP instructions, except PUSHF and POPF require no operands—they reference the flags register implicitly.

Like PUSH and POP, PUSHF and POPF are always *paired* in a program. That is, every PUSHF must have a corresponding POPF later in the program, like this:

```
PUSHF          ;Save flags on stack
 ..       (Other, flag-altering instructions are executed here)
 ..
POPF           ;Restore flags from stack
```

Note that with PUSH, PUSHF, POP, and POPF, you now have the ability to save any registers you choose (or *all* registers, if you like) while a procedure is being executed or an interrupt is being serviced. For instance, suppose you have some valuable data in AX, DI, and SI, and need to call a procedure named CLOBBER (because it clobbers your registers) that uses these registers. Suppose also you've just performed an arithmetic operation, and need to have the flags intact after the procedure. This sequence should do the job for you:

```
PUSH   AX          ;Save the three registers
PUSH   DI
```

```
PUSH    SI
PUSHF                   ; and the flags
CALL    CLOBBER         ;Call the procedure
POPF                    ;Upon return, restore the flags
POP     SI              ; and the three registers
POP     DI
POP     AX
```

Better yet, you should put the required PUSHes and POPs *inside* the procedure, so you don't have to write those instructions every time you call it. Hence, for the preceding example, the four PUSHes should be the first four instructions in the CLOBBER procedure and the four POPs would be the last four instructions in CLOBBER. This lets you simply CALL CLOBBER each time you need it, without worrying about which registers are destroyed and which are preserved.

3.5 Arithmetic Instructions

The 8088 can perform arithmetic operations on binary numbers (either unsigned or signed) and unsigned decimal numbers (either packed or un-packed). As Table 3-4 shows, there are instructions for the four standard arithmetic functions—addition, subtraction, multiplication, and division—and two additional instructions that "sign-extend" operands, letting you operate on mixed-size data. Before discussing the instructions themselves, we should look at the formats of the various data types.

Arithmetic Data Formats

Binary Numbers

Binary numbers may be 8 or 16 bits long, and may be either unsigned or signed. In an unsigned number, all 8 or 16 bits represent data. Therefore, unsigned numbers can range from 0 to 255 (8 bits) or 65535 (16 bits). In a signed number, the high-order bit—Bit 7 or Bit 15—tells you the sign of the number; all other bits hold data. Therefore, signed numbers can range from 127 to –128 (8 bits), or from 32767 to –32768 (16 bits).

Decimal Numbers

Decimal numbers are stored as unsigned byte-size values in either "packed" or "unpacked" form. In a packed decimal number, each byte holds two *binary-coded decimal (BCD)* digits, with the cost-significant digit in the upper four bits and the least-significant digit in the lower four bits. Therefore, a packed decimal byte can hold values from 00 to 99.

Table 3-4. Arithmetic instructions.

Mnemonic	Assembler Format		OF	DF	IF	TF	SF	ZF	AF	PF	CF

ADDITION

Mnemonic	Assembler Format		OF	DF	IF	TF	SF	ZF	AF	PF	CF
ADD	ADD	destination,source	*	-	-	-	*	*	*	*	*
ADC	ADC	destination,source	*	-	-	-	*	*	*	*	*
AAA	AAA		?	-	-	-	?	?	*	?	*
DAA	DAA		?	-	-	-	*	*	*	*	*
INC	INC	destination	*	-	-	-	*	*	*	*	-

SUBTRACTION

SUB	SUB	destination,source	*	-	-	-	*	*	*	*	*
SBB	SBB	destination,source	*	-	-	-	*	*	*	*	*
AAS	AAS		?	-	-	-	?	?	*	?	*
DAS	DAS		?	-	-	-	*	*	*	*	*
DEC	DEC	destination	*	-	-	-	*	*	*	*	-
NEG	NEG	destination	*	-	-	-	*	*	*	*	*
CMP	CMP	destination,source	*	-	-	-	*	*	*	*	*

MULTIPLICATION

MUL	MUL	source	*	-	-	-	?	?	?	?	*
IMUL	IMUL	source	*	-	-	-	?	?	?	?	*
AAM	AAM		?	-	-	-	*	*	?	*	?

DIVISION

DIV	DIV	source	?	-	-	-	?	?	?	?	?
IDIV	IDIV	source	?	-	-	-	?	?	?	?	?
AAD	AAD		?	-	-	-	*	*	?	*	?

SIGN-EXTENSION

CBW	CBW		-	-	-	-	-	-	-	-	-
CWD	CWD		-	-	-	-	-	-	-	-	-

Note: *means changed, - means unchanged, and ? means undefined.

In an unpacked decimal number, each byte holds just one BCD digit, in the lower four bits. Therefore, an unpacked decimal byte can only hold values from 0 to 9. The upper four bits must be zero for multiplication and division, but may be any value for addition or subtraction.

How does the 8088 know *which* kind of data you're operating on? For instance, if you add two bytes, how does the 8088 know whether they are signed binary numbers, unsigned binary numbers, packed decimal numbers or unpacked decimal numbers? The 8088 doesn't know what kind of data you're using, nor does it care. It assumes *all* operands are binary numbers, and acts accordingly.

This approach is fine if your operands are indeed binary, but if they happen to be *decimal,* the 8088 will obviously give incorrect results. To compensate, the 8088 has a group of "adjust" instructions that make decimal operations give the proper result. We'll discuss these instructions at the appropriate places in this section.

How Numbers Are Stored in Memory

The 8088 stores numbers in the opposite way you might expect: with the least-significant byte at the lowest address. For example, if the 8088 stores the 16-bit number 1234H at a location called NUM, it stores 34H at NUM and 12H at the next byte, NUM+1. Similarly, if the 8088 stores the 32-bit *double-precision number* 12345678H starting at NUM, it is stored as 78H (NUM), 56H (NUM+1), 34H (NUM+2), and 12H (NUM+3). Be sure to remember this convoluted storage scheme when you operate on multi-byte or multi-word numbers.

Addition Instructions

Add (ADD) and Add With Carry (ADC)

Both the ADD and ADC instructions can add either 8- or 16-bit operands. The first instruction, ADD, adds a source operand to a destination operand and puts the result in the destination operand. Symbolically, this can be represented as

    destination=destination+source

The second instruction, ADC, does the same thing as ADD, except it includes the Carry Flag (CF) in the addition, like this:

    destination=destination+source+Carry

Regardless of whether you're familiar with the concept of *carry* as applied to computers, you've certainly encountered it before in adding decimal numbers with pencil and paper. For instance, in this decimal addition you have two carries:

```
  98
  13
 +79
 ----
 190
```

Adding the "ones" column produces an excess of 2, which is carried into the "tens" position, and adding this column, along with the carry, causes a 1 to be carried into the "hundreds" column. Here, carries are produced whenever a column position cannot hold the sum of all the numbers in that column.

Similarly, in a binary addition, the computer generates a carry whenever the destination operand cannot hold a sum. For instance, we know that an 8-bit register can only hold unsigned values between 0 and 255 (decimal). If we perform a binary addition of the decimal numbers 250 and 10, we get this result:

```
  1111 1010    (Binary representation of 250)
 +0000 1010    (Binary representation of 10)
1 0000 0100    (Answer=260 decimal)
```

The sum is correct, but it takes nine bit positions to represent it! If we're using 8-bit registers, the lower eight bits are returned in the destination register, and the ninth bit is returned in the *Carry Flag (CF)*.

Now you see why the 8088 has two separate add instructions. One instruction, ADD, can add single-byte or single-word numbers and the low-order terms of multi-precision numbers. The other instruction, ADC, is used to add the higher-order terms of two multi-precision numbers.

For example, the instruction

```
ADD   AX,CX
```

adds the 16-bit contents of AX and CX, and returns the result in AX. If your operands are longer than 16 bits, you can use this kind of sequence:

```
ADD   AX,CX    ;Add low-order 16 bits,
ADC   BX,DX    ; then high-order 16 bits
```

which adds the 32-bit number in CX and DX to the 32-bit number in AX and BX. Here the ADC instruction includes any carry out of (CX)+(AX) into (BX)+(DX).

These examples show how you can add register contents, but you may also add a memory operand to a general register (or vice versa), or add an immediate value to a register or to memory. The following forms are legal:

```
ADD   AX,MEM_WORD    ;Add a memory operand to a register
ADD   MEM_WORD,AX    ; or vice versa
ADD   AL,10          ;Add a constant to a register
ADD   MEM_BYTE,0FH   ; or to a memory location
```

Most combinations are legal, but you may not add memory-to-memory, nor may you use an immediate value as a destination.

The ADD and ADC instructions can affect six flags:

• The Carry Flag (CF) is 1 if the result cannot be contained in the destination operand; otherwise, CF is 0.

- The Parity Flag (PF) is 1 if the result has an even number of 1 bits; otherwise, PF is 0.
- The Auxiliary Carry Flag (AF) is 1 if the result of a decimal addition needs to be adjusted; otherwise, AF is 0.
- The Zero Flag (ZF) is 1 if the result is zero; otherwise, ZF is 0.
- The Sign Flag (SF) is 1 if the high-order bit of the result is 1; otherwise, SF is 0.
- The Overflow Flag (OF) is 1 if adding two like-signed numbers (both positive or both negative) gives a result that exceeds the 2s-complement range of the destination, which changes the sign; otherwise, OF is 0.

The status of SF and OF is only pertinent when you add signed numbers. The status of AF is only pertinent when you add decimal numbers.

The 8088 has instructions that test these flags and base an execution decision on the outcome. For instance, a negative result may cause one set of instructions to execute and a non-negative result may cause an alternate set of instructions to execute. We discuss these "decision-making" instructions later in the chapter.

Decimal Adjust for Addition (AAA and DAA)

As mentioned previously, the 8088 performs all additions as if the operands are binary. What happens if your operands are binary-coded decimal (BCD) numbers? Let's find out by looking at an example. If you add the packed BCD numbers 26 and 55, the 8088 performs this binary addition:

```
  0010 0110    (=BCD 26)
 +0101 0101    (=BCD 55)
  0111 1011    (=??)
```

Instead of the correct answer — BCD 81 — the result has a high digit of 7 and a low digit of hexadecimal B. Does this mean you can't add decimal numbers with the 8088? No, it means that you must adjust the result, to put it into BCD form.

The instructions ASCII Adjust for Addition (AAA) and Decimal Adjust for Addition (DAA) adjust the result of a decimal addition. Neither instruction takes an operand, but both assume that the result to be adjusted is in the AL register.

The AAA instruction converts the contents of AL to an unpacked decimal digit. Briefly, AAA examines the low four bits of AL. If these bits hold a valid BCD digit (a value between 0 and 9), AAA clears the high four bits of AL and the flags AF and CF. However, if the low four bits of AL hold a value greater than 9, or if AF is set to 1, AAA adjusts the result as follows:

1. Add 6 to the AL register.
2. Add 1 to the AH register.
3. Set AF and CF to 1.
4. Clear the high four bits of AL.

In Step 1, AAA adds 6 to AL because adding 6 to any hexadecimal digit between A and F produces a value between 0 and 5 (valid BCD digits) in the low four bits of the result.

The AAA instruction is used in this kind of sequence:

```
ADD   AL,BL    ;Add unpacked BCD numbers in AL and BL
AAA            ; and make the result an unpacked number
```

The result in AL is always a valid BCD digit, but now you know that if CF is 1, AH has been incremented to reflect a too-large result.

AAA updates CF and AF and leaves PF, ZF, SF, and OF undefined. AF and CF tell you whether the result is greater than 9. If CF is 1, you need an additional byte to hold the excess digit.

The DAA instruction converts the contents of AL to two *packed* decimal digits. DAA operates similar to AAA, but DAA must consider two separate digits. Here is the adjustment procedure for DAA:

1. If the low four bits of AL hold a value greater than 9, or if *AF* is 1, add 6 to AL and set AF to 1.
2. If the high four bits of AL hold a value greater than 9, or if *CF* is 1, add 60H to AL and set CF to 1.

The DAA instruction is used in this kind of sequence:

```
ADD   AL,BL    ;Add packed BCD numbers in AL and BL
DAA            ; and make the result a packed number
```

Again, the result in AL is always valid, but if CF is 1, you need an additional byte to hold an excess BCD digit.

DAA updates CF, PF, AF, ZF, and SF, and leaves OF undefined. However, only CF is pertinent, because it tells you whether the result exceeds the packed BCD limit, 99. Assume that the five other statuses are destroyed.

Increment Destination by One (INC)

The INC instruction adds 1 to a register or memory operand but, unlike ADD, affects neither the Carry Flag (CF) nor the Zero Flag (ZF). INC is often used in repetitive loop operations, to update a counter. It can also be applied to an index register or pointer when you are accessing consecutive locations in memory. You cannot increment a segment register, however.

Some examples of INC are:

```
INC  CX               ;Increment a word register
INC  AL               ; or a byte register
INC  MEM_BYTE         ;Increment a byte in memory
INC  MEM_WORD[BX]     ; or a word in memory
```

Incidentally, if you look up the execution times of INC instructions in Appendix C, you'll note that it takes the 8088 longer to increment an 8-bit (byte) register than to increment a 16-bit (word) register! Why? Only the Inte

Subtraction Instructions

How the 8088 Subtracts

Like every other general-purpose microprocessor, the 8088 has no internal unit that subtracts numbers. Does that mean you can skip this section? No! Although the 8088 has no subtraction unit, it *does* have an internal *addition* unit — an adder — and can subtract numbers by adding them. Strange as this seems, the concept is quite "elementary," as Mr. Holmes says.

To see how you can subtract by adding, consider how you subtract 7 from 10. In elementary school you learned to write this operation as

```
10-7
```

However, later (in Algebra 101, perhaps) you learned that another, yet equally valid, way to write this operation is

```
10+(-7)
```

The first form — the straight subtraction — could be performed by a processor that has a subtraction unit. Since the 8088 has no subtraction unit, it performs the subtraction in two steps. First, it negates, or *complements,* the subtrahend (the second number). This done, it adds the minuend and complemented subtrahend to produce the result. Because the 8088 works with base 2 (binary) numbers, the complement is a 2s-complement.

To obtain the 2s-complement of a binary number, you take the positive form of the number and reverse the sense of each bit (change all 1s to 0s, and all 0s to 1s), then add 1 to the result.

Applying this to our 10-7 example, the 8-bit binary representations of 10 and 7 are 00001010B and 00000111B, respectively. Take the 2s-complement of 7 as follows:

```
  1111 1000   (Reverse all bits)
+        1   (Add 1)
  1111 1001   (2s-complement of 7, or -7)
```

Now, the subtraction operation becomes

```
  0000 1010   (=10)
+ 1111 1001   (=-7)
  0000 0011   (Answer=3)
```

Eureka! We got the right answer!

Since the 8088 does the 2s-complementing automatically, there aren't many occasions when you'll want to do it yourself. However, later in this section we'll study an instruction called NEG that performs a 2s-complement, in case you ever need it.

Subtract (SUB) and Subtract with Borrow (SBB)

These instructions, SUB and SBB, are similar to their addition counterparts (ADD and ADC), but with subtraction the Carry Flag (CF) acts as a *borrow* indicator. SUB subtracts a source operand from a destination operand and returns the result to the destination. That is,

```
destination=destination-source
```

SBB does the same thing, except it also subtracts out the Carry Flag (CF), as a borrow, like this:

```
destination=destination-source-Carry
```

As with addition, the subtraction instructions perform two separate functions. One instruction, SUB, subtracts single-byte or single-word numbers, or subtracts the low-order terms of multi-precision numbers. The other, SBB, subtracts the higher order terms of two multi-precision numbers.

For example, the instruction

```
SUB   AX,CX
```

subtracts the contents of CX from the contents of AX, and returns the result in AX.

If your operands are longer than 16 bits, you can use this kind of sequence:

```
SUB   AX,CX    ;Subtract low-order 16 bits
SBB   BX,DX    ; then high-order 16 bits
```

This sequence subtracts the 32-bit number in CX and DX from the 32-bit number in AX and BX. The SBB instruction includes any borrow out of the first subtraction when it subtracts DX from BX.

Besides subtracting one register from another, you may also subtract a memory operand from a register (or vice versa), or subtract an immediate value from a register or a memory location. The following forms are all legal:

```
SUB   AX,MEM_WORD        ;Subtract memory from a register
SUB   MEM_WORD[BX],AX    ; or vice versa
SUB   AL,10              ;Subtract constant from a register
SUB   MEM_BYTE,OFH       ; or from a memory location
```

You may not subtract one memory value from another directly, nor may an immediate value be a destination.

The SUB and SBB instructions can affect six flags:

- The Carry Flag (CF) is 1 if a borrow was needed; otherwise, CF is 0.
- The Parity Flag (PF) is 1 if the result has an even number of 1 bits; otherwise, PF is 0.
- The Auxiliary Carry Flag (AF) is 1 if the result of a decimal subtraction needs to be adjusted; otherwise, AF is 0.

- The Zero Flag (ZF) is 1 if the result is zero; otherwise, ZF is 0.
- The Sign Flag (SF) is 1 if the high-order bit of the result is 1; otherwise, SF is 0.
- The Overflow Flag (OF) is 1 if you subtract a positive number from a negative number (or vice versa) and the result exceeds the 2s-complement range of the destination, which changes the sign; otherwise, OF is 0.

The status of SF or OF is only pertinent when you subtract signed numbers. The status of AF is only pertinent when you subtract decimal numbers.

Decimal Adjust for Subtraction (AAS and DAS)

As with addition, the 8088 subtracts as if the operands are binary numbers. This means that your answers may be incorrect if you are subtracting binary-coded decimal (BCD) numbers. For example, suppose you wish to subtract BCD 26 from BCD 55. The 8088 would perform a binary subtraction by taking the 2s-complement of 26, then perform this addition:

```
  0101 0101   (=BCD 55)
 +1101 1010   (=2s-complement of BCD 26)
1 0010 1111   (=??)
```

Instead of the correct answer—BCD 29—the result has a high digit of 2, a low digit of hexadecimal F, and a carry. Clearly, this result sorely needs adjusting.

The instructions ASCII Adjust for Subtraction (AAS) and Decimal Adjust for Subtraction (DAS) adjust the result after you subtract two decimal numbers. Neither instruction takes an operand, but both assume that the number to adjust is in the AL register.

The AAS instruction converts the contents of AL to a valid *unpacked* decimal digit. Briefly, AAS examines the low four bits of AL. If these bits hold a valid BCD digit (a value between 0 and 9), AAS clears the high four bits of AL and the AF and CF flags. However, if the low four bits of AL hold a value greater than 9, or if AF is set to 1, AAS performs the following adjustment procedure:

1. Subtract 6 from the AL register.
2. Subtract 1 from the AH register.
3. Set AF and CF to 1.
4. Clear the four high bits of AL.

In Step 1, AAS subtracts 6 from AL because subtracting 6 from any hexadecimal digit between A and F produces a value between 4 and 9 (valid BCD digits) in the low four bits of the result.

The AAS instruction is used in this kind of sequence:

```
SUB   AL,BL    ;Subtract BCD number in BL from AL
AAS            ; and make the result an unpacked number
```

The result in AL is always a valid BCD digit, but if CF is 1, you know AH has been decremented to reflect a too-small result.

AAS updates CF and AF and leaves PF, ZF, SF, and OF undefined. AF and CF tell you whether the result is larger than 9. If CF is 1, you need an additional byte to hold the entire result.

The DAS instruction converts the contents of AL to two *packed* decimal digits. The operation of DAS is similar to that of AAS, but two separate digits must be considered. Here is the adjustment procedure for DAS:

1. If the low four bits of AL hold a value greater than 9, or if *AF* is 1, subtract 6 from the AL register and set AF to 1.

2. If the high four bits of AL hold a value greater than 9, or if *CF* is 1, subtract 60H from the AL register and set CF to 1.

The DAS instruction is used in this kind of sequence:

```
SUB   AL,BL    ;Subtract packed BCD number in BL from AL
DAS            ; and make the result a packed number
```

Again, the result in AL is always valid, but if CF is 1, you need an additional byte to hold the complete result.

DAS updates CF, PF, AF, ZF, and SF, and leaves OF undefined. However, only CF is pertinent, because it tells you whether the result is larger than the packed BCD limit, 99. Assume that the five other statuses are destroyed.

Decrement Destination by One (DEC)

The DEC instruction subtracts 1 from a register or memory operand, but unlike SUB, affects neither the Carry Flag (CF) nor the Zero Flag (ZF). DEC is often used in repetitive loops to decrement a counter until the count becomes zero or negative. It can also be applied to an index register or pointer when you access consecutive locations in memory. You cannot decrement a segment register, however.

Some examples of DEC are:

```
DEC   CX           ;Decrement a word register
DEC   AL           ; or a byte register
DEC   MEM_BYTE     ;Decrement a byte in memory
DEC   MEM_WORD[BX] ; or a word in memory
```

Negate (NEG)

The NEG instruction subtracts the destination operand from zero, thereby forming the operand's 2s-complement.

The NEG instruction affects the flags in the same way as the SUB instruction. However, since one operand is zero, we can be more explicit about the conditions that set individual flags. Therefore, for NEG:

- The Carry Flag (CF) and the Sign Flag (SF) are 1 if the addressed operand holds a nonzero positive number; otherwise, CF and SF are 0.
- The Parity Flag (PF) is 1 if the result has an even number of 1 bits; otherwise, PF is 0.
- The Zero Flag (ZF) is 1 if the addressed operand is zero; otherwise, ZF is 0.
- The Overflow Flag (OF) is 1 if the addressed operand has the value 80H (byte) or 8000H (word); otherwise, OF is 0.

NEG is useful if you need to subtract a register or memory operand from an immediate value. For instance, you may want to subtract the contents of AL from 100. Since an immediate value can't serve as a destination, the form SUB 100,AL is illegal. As an alternative, you can negate AL and *add* 100 to the result, like this:

```
NEG   AL
ADD   AL,100
```

Compare Destination to Source (CMP)

Most programs don't execute all instructions in the order they are stored in memory. Instead, programs usually include jumps, loops, procedure calls, and other factors that cause the 8088 to transfer from one place to another in memory. We will discuss the instructions that actually produce these transfers later in this chapter, when we discuss the 8088's control transfer instructions. At this point we will discuss the CMP instruction, which is commonly used to configure the flags upon which the control transfer instructions base their transfer/no-transfer "decisions."

The CMP instruction acts very much like the SUB instruction. That is, CMP subtracts a source operand from a destination operand, and sets or clears certain flags based on the result (see Table 3-5). But unlike SUB, *CMP does not save the result of the subtraction*. That is, CMP doesn't alter the operands. CMP's sole purpose is to set up the flags for decision-making by conditional transfer instructions (see Section 3.7).

Multiplication Instructions

Multiply, Unsigned (MUL) and Integer Multiply, Signed (IMUL)

If you've endured the agony of writing a multiplication program for the 8080, 6502, or any other conventional 8-bit microprocessor, you'll be glad to hear that the 8088 has a built-in multiply capability. In fact, it has not just one, but *two*, multiply instructions.

Table 3-5. CMP instruction results.

Condition	OF	SF	ZF	CF
Unsigned Operands				
Source < Destination	D	D	0	0
Source = Destination	D	D	1	0
Source > Destination	D	D	0	1
Signed Operands				
Source < Destination	0/1	0	0	D
Source = Destination	0	0	1	D
Source > Destination	0/1	1	0	D

Note: "D" means Don't Care; "0/1" means the flag may be either 0 or 1, depending on the values of the operands.

Multiply (MUL) multiplies unsigned numbers and Integer Multiply (IMUL) multiplies signed numbers. Both can multiply a byte by a byte or a word by a word.

These instructions have the general forms

```
MUL     source
IMUL    source
```

where *source* is a byte- or word-length general register or memory location. For the second operand, MUL and IMUL use the contents of the accumulator; AL for byte operations and AX for word operations. The double-length products are returned as follows:

- A *byte* multiplication returns the 16-bit product in AH (high byte) and AL (low byte).
- A *word* multiplication returns the 32-bit product in DX (high word) and AX (low word).

Upon completion, the Carry Flag (CF) and the Overflow Flag (OF) tell you how much of the product is relevant. For MUL, if the high-order half of the result is zero, CF and OF are 0; otherwise, CF and OF are 1. For IMUL, if the high-order half of the result is a sign-extension of the low-order half, CF and OF are 0; otherwise, CF and OF are 1.

Here are some multiplication examples:

```
MUL     BX          ;Unsigned multiply of BX times AX
MUL     MEM_BYTE    ;Unsigned multiply of memory times AL
IMUL    DL          ;Signed multiply of DL times AL
IMUL    MEM_WORD    ;Signed multiply of memory times AX
```

Note that neither MUL nor IMUL lets you multiply by an immediate value directly. To do this, you must put the immediate value into a register or a memory location. For example,

```
MOV   DX,10
MUL   DX
```

multiplies AX by 10.

ASCII Adjust for Multiplication (AAM)

The AAM instruction converts the product of a preceding byte multiplication into two valid unpacked decimal operands AAM assumes the double-
length product is in AH and AL, and returns the unpacked operands in AH
and AL. For AAM to work correctly, the original multiplier and multiplicand
must have been valid unpacked operands.

To make the conversion, AAM divides the AL register by 10 (0AH) and
stores the resulting quotient and remainder in AH and AL, respectively. AAM
also updates the Parity Flag (PF), the Zero Flag (ZF), and the Sign Flag (SF) to
reflect the contents of AL. The statuses of the Carry Flag (CF), Auxiliary
Carry Flag (AF) and Overflow Flag (OF) are undefined.

To see how AAM works, assume AL contains 9 (00001001B) and BL contains 7 (00000111B). The instruction

```
MUL   BL
```

multiplies AL by BL and returns a 16-bit result in AH and AL. In this case, it
returns 0 in AH and 00111111B (that is, 63 in binary) in AL.

The subsequent instruction

```
AAM
```

divides AL by 10 (0AH), and returns a quotient of 00000110B in AH and a
remainder of 00000011B in AL. This double-length result is indeed correct—
BCD 63, in unpacked form.

The 8088 has no instruction that multiplies *packed* decimal numbers. If
you want to multiply such numbers, you must unpack them (with AAM),
multiply, then pack the result.

Division Instructions

Divide, Unsigned (DIV) and Integer Divide, Signed (IDIV)

Just as the 8088 has two separate multiplication instructions, it also has two
separate division instructions. Divide (DIV) performs an unsigned division
and Integer Divide (IDIV) performs a signed division.

These instructions have the general forms

```
DIV   source
IDIV  source
```

where *source* is a byte- or word-length divisor in a general register or a memory location. The dividend is a double-length operand in either AH and AL (8-bit operation) or DX and AX (16-bit operation). The results are as follows:

- If the source operand is a *byte*, the quotient is returned in AL and the remainder is returned in AH.
- If the source operand is a *word*, the quotient is returned in AX and the remainder is returned in DX.

Both division instructions leave the flags undefined, but if the quotient exceeds the capacity of the destination register (AL or AX), the 8088 has a dramatic way of telling you the result is invalid; it generates a *type 0 (divide by 0) interrupt*. If your program is running under DOS, the type 0 interrupt aborts the program and DOS displays the message

```
Divide Overflow
```

The following conditions cause a divide overflow:

1. The divisor is zero.
2. For an unsigned byte divide, the dividend is at least 256 times larger than the divisor.
3. For an unsigned word divide, the dividend is at least 65,536 times larger than the divisor.
4. For a signed byte divide, the quotient exceeds +127 or –128.
5. For a signed word divide, the quotient exceeds +32,767 or –32,768.

Here are some examples of division operations:

```
DIV   BX          ;Divide DX:AX by BX, unsigned
DIV   MEM_BYTE    ;Divide AH:AL by memory, unsigned
IDIV  DL          ;Divide AH:AL by DL, signed
IDIV  MEM_WORD    ;Divide DX:AX by memory, signed
```

Note that neither DIV nor IDIV lets you divide by an immediate value directly. To do this, you must put the immediate value into a register or memory location. For instance,

```
MOV   BX,10
DIV   BX
```

divides DX:AX by 10.

ASCII Adjust for Division (AAD)

The decimal adjust instructions we previously described — AAA, DAA, AAS, DAS, and AAM — all operate on the *result* of an operation. By contrast, you apply the AAD instruction *before* you execute a division operation.

AAD converts an unpacked dividend to a binary value in AL. To do this, AAD multiplies the high-order digit of the dividend (the contents of AH) by 10 and adds the result to the low-order digit in AL. Then it zeroes the contents of AH.

This sequence shows a typical use of AAD:

```
AAD        ;Adjust the unpacked dividend in AH:AL
DIV   BL   ; then perform the division
```

Sign-Extension Instructions

Two instructions let you operate on mixed-size data, by doubling the length of a signed operand. Convert Byte to Word (CBW) reproduces Bit 7 of AL throughout AH. Convert Word to Doubleword (CWD) reproduces Bit 15 of AX throughout DX. Figure 3-7 illustrates these operations.

Thus, CBW lets you add a byte to a word, subtract a word from a byte, and so forth. Similarly, CWD lets you divide a word by a word. Here are some examples:

```
CBW        ;Add a byte in AL to a word in BX
ADD   AX,BX
CBW        ;Multiply a byte in AL by a word in BX
IMUL  BX
CWD        ;Divide a word in AX by a word in BX
IDIV  BX
```

3.6 Bit Manipulation Instructions

These instructions manipulate bits within registers and memory locations. Table 3-6 divides them into three groups: logical, shift, and rotate.

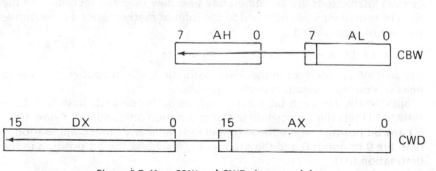

Figure 3-7. How CBW and CWD sign-extend data.

Table 3-6. Bit manipulation instructions.

Mnemonic	Assembler Format	OF	DF	IF	TF	SF	ZF	AF	PF	CF
		Flags								
LOGICAL										
AND	AND	destination,source	0	–	–	–	*	*	?	*	0
OR	OR	destination,source	0	–	–	–	*	*	?	*	0
XOR	XOR	destination,source	0	–	–	–	*	*	?	*	0
NOT	NOT	destination	–	–	–	–	–	–	–	–	–
TEST	TEST	destination,source	0	–	–	–	*	*	?	*	0
SHIFT										
SAL/SHL	SAL	destination,count	*	–	–	–	*	*	?	*	*
SAR	SAR	destination,count	*	–	–	–	*	*	?	*	*
SHR	SHR	destination,count	*	–	–	–	0	*	?	*	*
ROTATE										
ROL	ROL	destination,count	*	–	–	–	–	–	–	–	*
ROR	ROR	destination,count	*	–	–	–	–	–	–	–	*
RCL	RCL	destination,count	*	–	–	–	–	–	–	–	*
RCR	RCR	destination,count	*	–	–	–	–	–	–	–	*

Note: * means changed, – means unchanged, and ? means undefined.

Logical Instructions

Logical instructions are so named because they operate according to the rules of formal logic, as opposed to the rules of mathematics. For example, the rule of logic stated

    If A is true and B is true, then C is true

has an 8088 counterpart in the AND instruction, which applies this rule to pairs of corresponding bits in two operands.

Specifically, for each bit position where both operands have a 1 (true) state, AND sets the bit position in the destination operand to 1. Conversely, for any bit position where the two operands have any other combination— both are 0 or one is 0 and the other is 1—AND sets the bit position in the destination to 0.

Since logical operations reference certain bits within an operand, you usually use hexadecimal numbering for these operations. The 8088's logical instructions can operate on either byte or word operands, so you normally deal with either two or four hexadecimal digits.

To help you construct the correct "mask" value for a logical operation, Table 3-7 shows the hexadecimal representation of a 1 in 16 different bit positions. For example, to operate on Bit 2, the correct mask value is 4H; to operate on Bits 2 and 3, the mask value is 0CH (hex 4 + hex 8); and so on.

Logical AND (AND), Inclusive-OR (OR) and Exclusive-OR (XOR)

You already encountered AND, OR, and XOR in Section 2.6, when we discussed logical operators of the same names. However, operators do their work when the program is *assembled*, whereas instructions do theirs when the program is *executed*. But these operators and instructions have the same names because they function in the same way. Although we will describe the AND, OR, and XOR instructions here for the sake of completeness, you might wish to refer to Section 2.6 for explanations of how they operate.

The AND, OR and XOR instructions can be applied to byte or word operands, and let you combine two registers, a register with a memory location, or an immediate value with a register or a memory location.

The AND instruction primarily masks out (zeroes) certain bits in a number so that we can do some kind of processing on the remaining bits. As just mentioned, for each bit position in which both operands contain 1, the corresponding bit position in the destination is also 1. All other operand bit combinations cause the destination bit to be 0.

Table 3-8 summarizes the AND combinations. Note that *any bit ANDed with 0 will be cleared to 0, and any bit ANDed with 1 will retain its previous value.*

Some examples of AND are

```
AND    AX,BX             ;AND two registers
AND    AL,MEM_BYTE       ;AND register with memory
AND    MEM_BYTE,AL       ; or vice-versa
AND    BL,1101B          ;AND a constant with a register
AND    TABLE[BX],MASK3   ; or with memory
```

To see how AND works, suppose Port 200 is connected to the 16-bit status register of an external device in the system, and Bit 6 indicates whether that device's power is on (1) or off (0). If your program requires device power to be on before continuing, it might include the following loop:

```
CHK_PWR: IN    AX,200        ;Read device status
         AND   AX,10000000B  ;Isolate the power indicator
         JZ    CHK_PWR       ;Wait until power is on,
         ..                  ; then continue
         ..
```

The JZ (Jump If Zero) instruction, which we have not yet discussed, makes the 8088 jump back to the IN instruction at CHK __ PWR if the Zero Flag (ZF)

Table 3-7. Hexadecimal values for bit positions.

Bit Number	Hex. Value
0	0001
1	0002
2	0004
3	0008
4	0010
5	0020
6	0040
7	0080
8	0100
9	0200
10	0400
11	0800
12	1000
13	2000
14	4000
15	8000

Table 3-8. The AND, OR, and XOR bit combinations.

Source	Destination	Result		
		AND	OR	XOR
0	0	0	0	0
0	1	0	1	1
1	0	0	1	1
1	1	1	1	0

is 1, and continue to the next instruction otherwise. Here, ZF is 1 only when the power indicator—Bit 6— is 1, because the AND instruction already zeroed the other bits in AX.

The OR instruction produces a 1 result in the destination for each bit position in which either or both operands contain 1. Again, refer to Table 3-8.

OR is usually used to force specific bits to 1. For example,

```
OR   BX,0C000H
```

sets the two most-significant bits (14 and 15) of BX to 1 and leaves all other bits unchanged.

The XOR instruction is primarily used to determine which bits differ between two operands, but it can also be used to reverse the state of selected bits. XOR produces a 1 in the destination for every bit position in which the operands differ—that is, for every bit position in which one operand has 0 and the other operand has 1. If both operands contain either 0 or 1, XOR clears the destination bit to 0. Again, refer to Table 3-8.

For example,

```
XOR   BX,0C000H
```

reverses the state of the two most-significant bits of BX (14 and 15) and leaves all other bits unchanged.

Logical NOT (NOT)

The NOT instruction simply reverses the state of each bit in its register or memory operand, without affecting any flags. That is, NOT changes each 1 to 0 and each 0 to 1. In computer terminology, we say that NOT takes the *1s-complement* of its operand.

Test (TEST)

The TEST instruction logically ANDs the source and destination operands, but affects only the flags; neither operand is changed. TEST affects the flags the same as AND: it clears CF and OF to 0, updates PF, ZF, and SF, and leaves AF undefined.

If TEST is followed by a JNZ (Jump If Not Zero) instruction, the jump will be taken if there are any corresponding 1 bits in both operands.

Shift and Rotate Instructions

The 8088 has seven instructions that displace the 8- or 16-bit contents of a general register or memory location one or more positions to the left or right. Three of these instructions "shift" the operand, the other four "rotate" the operand.

For all seven instructions, the Carry Flag (CF) acts as a "9th bit" or "17th bit" extension of the operand, in that CF receives the value of the bit that has been displaced out of one end of the operand. A right shift or rotate puts the value of Bit 0 into CF. A left shift or rotate puts the value of Bit 7 (byte) or Bit 15 (word) into CF.

Shift and rotate instructions fall into two groups. *Logical* instructions displace an operand without regard to its sign. You use them to operate on unsigned numbers and non-numbers, such as masks. *Arithmetic* instructions preserve the most-significant bit of the operand, the sign bit. You use them to operate on signed numbers. Figure 3-8 shows how the various shift and rotate instructions operate.

All seven shift and rotate instructions take two operands: a *destination* and a *count*. The destination may be a general register or a memory location of either byte or word length. The count may be "1" or an unsigned value in the CL register.

Shift Instructions

Shift Arithmetic Left (SAL) and *Shift Arithmetic Right (SAR)* shift signed numbers. SAR preserves the sign of the operand by replicating the sign bit throughout the shift operation. SAL does not preserve the sign bit, but puts 1 in the Overflow Flag (OF) if the sign ever changes. Each time SAL shifts an operand, the vacated Bit 0 position receives 0.

Shift Logical Left (SHL) and *Shift Logical Right (SHR)* shift unsigned numbers. SHL does the same thing as SAL. SHR is similar to SHL, but SHR shifts operands right rather than left. Each time SHR shifts an operand, the vacated high-order bit position (Bit 7 in a byte, Bit 15 in a word) receives 0.

Besides CF and OF, the shift instructions update PF, ZF, and SF, and leave AF undefined.

To see how the shift instructions work, assume the AL register contains 0B4H and the Carry Flag is set to 1. In binary,

```
AL=10110100    CF=1
```

Here is how the four shift instructions affect AL and CF:

```
After SAL  AL,1:    AL=01101000    CF=1
After SAR  AL,1:    AL=11011010    CF=0
After SHL  AL,1:    AL=01101000    CF=1
After SHR  AL,1:    AL=01011010    CF=0
```

The shift instructions have a lot of miscellaneous uses. For instance, the following sequence uses SHL to convert two unpacked BCD numbers—a high digit in BL and a low digit in AL— into a packed BCD number in AL:

```
MOV   CL,4    ;Load shift count into CL
SHL   BL,CL   ;Shift high digit into high four bits of BL
OR    AL,BL   ;Merge AL and BL to form packed BCD number
```

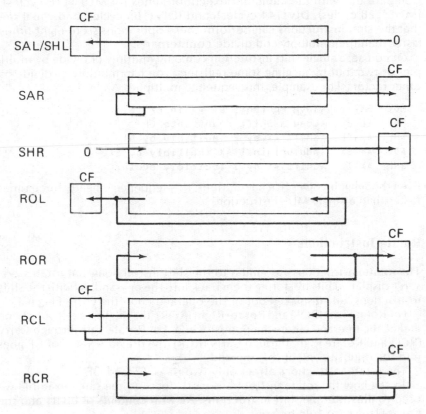

Figure 3-8. Shift and rotate operations.

The shift instructions also make fast-executing multiply and divide instructions, because *shifting an operand one bit position to the left doubles its value (multiplies it by two) and shifting an operand one bit position to the right halves its values (divides it by two.)*

The following shift instructions show you how to multiply or divide the contents of AX by four. Assume CL contains 2 in all cases.

```
SHL    AX,CL    ;Multiply an unsigned number by 4
SAL    AX,CL    ;Multiply a signed number by 4
SHR    AX,CL    ;Divide an unsigned number by 4
SAR    AX,CL    ;Divide a signed number by 4
```

You save considerable time by multiplying and dividing with shift instructions rather than with the 8088's multiply and divide instructions. Each of the preceding shift instructions takes 16 clock cycles to execute. It takes four more cycles to initialize the CL register, for a total of 20 clock cycles.

Compare this with the minimum execution times for MUL (118 cycles), IMUL(128 cycles), DIV(144 cycles), and IDIV(165 cycles) and you'll see that the shift instructions can perform these operations *six to eight times faster* than their multiply and divide counterparts!

Of course, a single shift instruction can only multiply or divide by multiples of two, but by juggling some registers, you can multiply or divide by other factors. For example, this sequence multiplies AX by 10:

```
MOV   BX,AX    ;Save contents of AX in BX
MOV   CL,2     ;Load a shift count into CL
SHL . AX,CL    ;Shift AX by 2 (multiply by 4)
ADD   AX,BX    ;Add original AX (multiply by 5)
SHL   AX,1     ;Shift AX by 1 (multiply by 10)
```

Even though it involves five instructions, this sequence is nearly three times faster than a single MUL instruction!

Rotate Instructions

The rotate instructions are similar to the shift instructions, but rotates *preserve* displaced bits by storing them back into the operand. As with the shift instructions, bits displaced out of the operand enter the Carry Flag (CF).

For Rotate Left (ROL) and Rotate Right (ROR), the bit displaced out of one end of the operand enters the opposite end. For Rotate Left through Carry (RCL) and Rotate Right through Carry (RCR), the *previous* value of CF goes into the opposite end of the operand.

The rotate instructions affect only two flags: CF and OF.

To see how the rotate instructions work, let's use the same example we used to illustrate the shift instructions: AL with contents of 0B4H and the Carry Flag set to 1. In binary,

```
AL=10110100   CF=1
```

Here is how the four rotate instructions would effect AL and CF:

```
After ROL  AL,1:  AL=01101001   CF=1
After ROR  AL,1:  AL=01011010   CF=0
After RCL  AL,1:  AL=01101001   CF=1
After RCR  AL,1:  AL=11011010   CF=0
```

3.7 Control Transfer Instructions

As mentioned in our discussion of the compare instructions, program instructions are stored consecutively in memory, but programs rarely execute in that exact order. All but the simplest programs include jumps and procedure calls that alter the sequence in which the microprocessor executes the program.

The control transfer instructions are the 8088 instructions that can trans-fer program execution from one part of memory to another. As Table 3-9 shows, these instructions can be divided into three groups: unconditional transfer instructions, conditional transfer instructions, and iteration control instructions. Note that the control transfer instructions do not affect the flags.

Unconditional Transfer Instructions

Procedures

Up to this point, the examples in this book contained instructions that perform a specific function *once*. From this you may get the idea that if you need to perform a specific operation at more than one place in your pro-gram, you must duplicate the entire sequence of instructions at each place you need it. Clearly, duplicating a sequence of instructions at many places in a program would be frustrating and time-consuming. It would also make programs much longer than they'd be if you could avoid this duplication.

As a matter of fact, you *can* eliminate this needless duplication if you define the repeat instructions as a *procedure*. A procedure—called a sub-routine in many instances—is a sequence of instructions that you write just once, but which you can execute as needed at any point in a program.

The process of transferring control from the main part of a program to a procedure is defined as *calling*. Thus, procedures are *called*. Once called, the 8088 executes the instructions in the procedure, then returns to the place where the call was made.

This description invites two questions: "How do you call a procedure?" and "How does the 8088 return to the proper place in the program?" These questions are answered in the following discussion of two procedure-related instructions, *Call a Procedure (CALL) and Return from Procedure (RET)*.

Call a Procedure (CALL) and Return from Procedure (RET)

Instructions that execute procedures must perform three functions:

1. They must include some provision for saving the contents of the Instruction Pointer (IP). Once the procedure has been executed, this address will be used to return to the proper place in the program. Therefore, this address is usually called a return address.
2. They must cause the microprocessor to begin executing the procedure.
3. They must use the stored contents of the IP to return to the program, and continue executing the program at this point.

Table 3-9. Control transfer instructions.

Mnemonic	Assembler Format		OF	DF	IF	TF	SF	ZF	AF	PF	CF
						Flags						

UNCONDITIONAL TRANSFERS

Mnemonic	Assembler Format		OF	DF	IF	TF	SF	ZF	AF	PF	CF
CALL	CALL	target	–	–	–	–	–	–	–	–	–
RET	RET	[pop-value]	–	–	–	–	–	–	–	–	–
JMP	JMP	target	–	–	–	–	–	–	–	–	–

CONDITIONAL TRANSFERS

Mnemonic	Assembler Format		OF	DF	IF	TF	SF	ZF	AF	PF	CF
JA/JNBE	JA	short-label	–	–	–	–	–	–	–	–	–
JAE/JNB	JAE	short-label	–	–	–	–	–	–	–	–	–
JB/JNAE/JC	JB	short-label	–	–	–	–	–	–	–	–	–
JBE/JNA	JBE	short-label	–	–	–	–	–	–	–	–	–
JCXZ	JCXZ	short-label	–	–	–	–	–	–	–	–	–
JE/JZ	JE	short-label	–	–	–	–	–	–	–	–	–
JG/JNLE	JG	short-label	–	–	–	–	–	–	–	–	–
JGE/JNL	JGE	short-label	–	–	–	–	–	–	–	–	–
JL/JNGE	JL	short-label	–	–	–	–	–	–	–	–	–
JLE/JNG	JLE	short-label	–	–	–	–	–	–	–	–	–
JNC	JNC	short-label	–	–	–	–	–	–	–	–	–
JNE/JNZ	JNE	short-label	–	–	–	–	–	–	–	–	–
JNO	JNO	short-label	–	–	–	–	–	–	–	–	–
JNP/JPO	JNP	short-label	–	–	–	–	–	–	–	–	–
JNS	JNS	short-label	–	–	–	–	–	–	–	–	–
JO	JO	short-label	–	–	–	–	–	–	–	–	–
JP/JPE	JP	short-label	–	–	–	–	–	–	–	–	–
JS	JS	short-label	–	–	–	–	–	–	–	–	–

ITERATION CONTROLS

Mnemonic	Assembler Format		OF	DF	IF	TF	SF	ZF	AF	PF	CF
LOOP	LOOP	short-label	–	–	–	–	–	–	–	–	–
LOOPE/ LOOPZ	LOOPE	short-label	–	–	–	–	–	–	–	–	–
LOOPNE/ LOOPNZ	LOOPNE	short-label	–	–	–	–	–	–	–	–	–

Note: – means unchanged.

These functions are performed by two instructions: *Call a Procedure (CALL)* and *Return from Procedure (RET)*.

The CALL instruction performs the return address-storing and begin-executing functions (1 and 2). The return address, which CALL pushes onto the stack, is either 16 bits long or 32 bits long, depending on whether you defined the procedure as NEAR or FAR (see Section 2.5). NEAR procedures can only be called from within the segment in which they reside. FAR procedures can be called from a different segment.

The CALL instruction has the general format

```
CALL    target
```

where *target* is the name of the procedure being called. If *target* has a NEAR attribute, CALL pushes the offset address of the next instruction onto the stack. If *target* has a FAR attribute, CALL pushes the contents of the CS register, then the offset address, onto the stack.

With the return address saved on the stack, CALL loads the offset address of the target label into IP. If the procedure is FAR, CALL also loads the segment number of the target label into the CS register.

The RET instruction makes the 8088 leave the procedure and return to the calling program. It does this by "undoing" everything CALL did. RET must always be the last instruction in the procedure to be executed. (This doesn't mean that RET must be the last instruction in the procedure—although it often is—but RET must be the last instruction the 8088 *executes*.)

When executed, RET pops a return address off the stack. If the called procedure is NEAR (it's in the same code segment), RET pops a 16-bit word off the stack and loads it into the Instruction Pointer (IP). If the called procedure is FAR (it's in a different code segment), RET pops *two* words off the stack; an offset address that is loaded into the IP, then a segment number that is loaded into CS.

To illustrate this, consider a NEAR procedure called MY_PROC. If your program needs to call MY_PROC at some point, it might execute the following sequence (offsets are also listed):

```
04F0            CALL  MY_PROC    ;Call the procedure
04F3  NEXT      MOV   AX,BX      ;Return here after the
              ..                 ; procedure
              ..
0500  MY_PROC   PROG             (start of procedure)
0500            MOV   CL,16      ;First instruction of
              ..                 ; procedure
              ..                 (additional instructions)
              ..
051E            RET              ;Return to calling program
              ..
051F  MY_PROC   ENDP             (end of procedure)
```

Upon executing the CALL instruction, the 8088 pushes the offset address of NEXT (04F3H) onto the stack, then loads the offset address of MY_PROC (0500H) into the Instruction Pointer (IP). Since the PROC pseudo-op has no distance operand, MY_PROC is, by default, a NEAR procedure. This means that MY_PROC is in the same code segment as the CALL instruction, so the 8088 leaves the Code Segment register (CS) as is.

Now that the IP has been changed, the 8088 begins executing at that new offset address. In our example, the first instruction happens to be

```
MOV  CL,6
```

When the microprocessor finally arrives at the RET instruction, it pops the return address off the stack and puts it into IP. This causes the 8088 to resume at the instruction labeled NEXT. Figure 3-9 shows the stack, the Stack Pointer (SP), and the Instruction Pointer (IP) before and after the CALL, and after RET.

Indirect Calls to Procedures

So far, we have discussed just one form of the CALL instruction, a *direct* call, in which the operand is a NEAR or FAR label in a code segment.

You may also make an *indirect* call to a procedure, through a register or a memory location. With indirect calls through memory, the 8088 fetches the procedure's IP value from the data segment, unless you use BP or specify an override. If you use BP to address memory, the 8088 fetches the IP value from the stack segment.

You may call a NEAR procedure through a register, like this:

```
CALL  BX
```

Here BX holds the procedure's offset address relative to CS. When this CALL instruction is executed, the 8088 copies the contents of BX into IP, then transfers execution to the instruction addressed by the CS:IP combination. For example, if BX holds 1ABH, the 8088 loads 1ABH into IP.

You may also call a NEAR procedure through a word-size variable, as in these examples:

```
CALL  WORD PTR [BX]
CALL  WORD PTR [BX][SI]
CALL  WORD PTR VARIABLE_NAME
CALL  WORD PTR VARIABLE_NAME[BX]
CALL  MEM_WORD
CALL  WORD PTR ES:[BX][SI]
```

The last CALL gets its procedure address from a location in the extra segment, the rest of the CALLs get their procedure address from a location in the data segment.

Similarly, you may call a FAR procedure indirectly through a doubleword-size variable, as in these examples:

```
CALL  DWORD PTR [BX]
CALL  MEM_DWORD
CALL  DWORD PTR SS:VARIABLE_NAME[SI]
```

Here, the first two CALLs get their procedure address from the data segment and the last CALL gets its address from the stack segment.

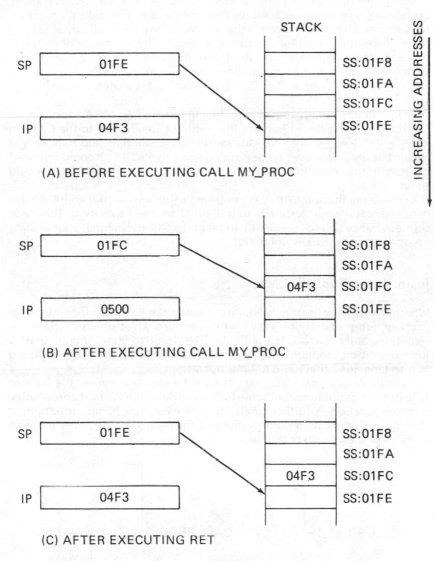

(A) BEFORE EXECUTING CALL MY_PROC

(B) AFTER EXECUTING CALL MY_PROC

(C) AFTER EXECUTING RET

Figure 3-9. How a procedure affects the stack.

How to Nest Procedures

A procedure may include one or more CALL instructions that call other procedures. For instance, a subroutine that inputs a keyboard character from a terminal may well decode that character and then call any of several other procedures, based on the decoded result. The technique of calling a procedure from within a procedure is referred to as *nesting*. Figure 3-10 shows the CALL and RET instructions for a program in which procedure PROC_1 calls procedure PROC_1 (i.e., PROC_2 is nested inside PROC_ 1).

Programmers usually describe nesting in terms of *levels*. An application like the one in Figure 3-10, where the nesting extends only to the CALL to PROC_2 (PROC_2 does not call another procedure), is said to have one level of nesting. However, there is no reason why PROC_2 could not have called a third procedure (PROC_3), with PROC_3 calling PROC_4, and so on.

Considering that each CALL instruction pushes two or four address bytes onto the stack, your nesting is only limited by the capacity of the stack segment. Since a stack segment can be up to 64K bytes long, your nesting capabilities are virtually unlimited.

Jump Unconditionally (JMP)

Whether you know it or not, you are already familiar with the basic concepts of jump operations. Have you ever read a set of instructions for something and come across a direction like "Jump to Step 5"? Well, that's a jump operation. Similarly, when the dreaded income tax form directs you to "Go to Line 36a," that's also a jump operation.

As in these everyday situations, the JMP instruction causes the 8088 to take its next instruction from some location other than the next consecutive memory location. A further similarity with everyday "jump" situations is that the JMP instruction is *unconditional*; the 8088 jumps to a new location every time it encounters JMP in a program.

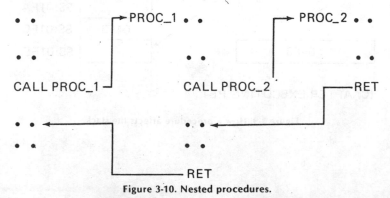

Figure 3-10. Nested procedures.

The JMP instruction has the general form

```
JMP  target
```

where *target* follows the same rules as the CALL operand. That is, *target* can be NEAR or FAR, direct or indirect. For direct jumps, the JMP instruction is three bytes long if the label is NEAR and five bytes long if the label is FAR. For instance,

```
JMP  NEAR_LABEL
```

is a three-byte instruction, and

```
JMP  FAR PTR FAR_LABEL
```

is a five-byte instruction.

If the label lies within –128 bytes or +127 bytes of the JMP instruction, you can force the assembler to make JMP a *two-byte* instruction by declaring the label SHORT. For example,

```
JMP  SHORT NEAR_LABEL
```

is a two-byte instruction. It executes in the same amount of time as

```
JMP  NEAR_LABEL
```

but takes up one less byte in memory.

You generally use JMP to skip over a group of instructions that are executed under some alternate set of conditions, or a group of instructions that are executed from some other part of the program. For example, you may see the JMP instruction used like this.

```
       . .
       . .
       MOV   AX,BX
       ADD   DX,AX
       JMP   THERE
HERE   MOV   MEM_WORD,DX
       . .
       . .
THERE  MOV   SAVE_DX,DX
```

The JMP instruction in this example jumps to a location that follows it in memory, but it could just as easily have jumped to a location that precedes it in memory.

Conditional Transfer Instructions

There are 17 different instructions that let the 8088 make an execution "decision" based on some prescribed condition, such as a register value being zero or CF being set to 1. If the condition is satisfied, the 8088 makes the jump; otherwise, it continues on to the next instruction in the program.

As you can see from Table 3-9, the assembler recognizes some of these instructions by two or three different mnemonics, which are provided for your convenience. (With these alternate mnemonics, one might well claim that the 8088 has 31 conditional transfer instructions. If that's your viewpoint, you should seriously consider a career in marketing!)

For instance, the assembler translates both JA LABEL and JNBE LABEL into the same instruction in memory. These particular instructions refer to the result of a preceding Compare (CMP) or Subtract (SUB or SBB) instruction.

The first mnemonic, JA, tells the 8088 to make the jump if the destination is "Above" (that is, greater than) the source. The second mnemonic, JNBE, tells the 8088 to make the jump If the destination is "Not Below or Equal" to the source. JA and JNBE say exactly the same thing, but in different ways. They exist strictly for your convenience, so you can write programs that are more readily understandable.

You will note from Table 3-9 that the conditional transfer instructions have the general format

```
Jx   short-label
```

where x is a one- to three-letter modifier. The operand form *short-label* tells you that the target label of the jump must be no more –128 bytes or +127 bytes away from the conditional transfer instruction. (As mentioned in Chapter 2, short labels normally have a colon suffix.) Contrast this with the Jump (JMP) instruction, which can transfer anywhere in memory.

Table 3-10 summarizes the conditional transfer instructions, and shows which conditions cause a jump to occur. Here, the mnemonics are listed individually so you don't have to search through a list of alternate mnemonics.

All conditional transfer instructions occupy two bytes in memory. (The first byte holds the operation code and the second byte holds the relative displacement.) These instructions execute in 16 clock cycles if the jump is taken, and four clock cycles if it is not taken. Because of this time differential, you should construct your programs so that, whenever possible. the expected case executes if the jump is *not taken*.

Here are a few examples of conditional transfer instructions:

1. The sequence

```
ADD   AL,BL
JC    TOOBIG
```

jumps to TOOBIG if the add operation produces a carry.

2. The sequence

```
SUB   AL,BL
JZ    ZERO
```

jumps to ZERO if the subtract operation produces a zero result in AL.

Table 3-10. The conditional transfer instructions.

Instruction	Description	Jump if...
JA	Jump If Above	CF = 0 and ZF = 0
JAE	Jump If Above or Equal	CF = 0
JB	Jump If Below	CF = 1
JBE	Jump If Below or Equal	CF = 1 or ZF = 1
JC	Jump If Carry	CF = 1
JCXZ	Jump If CX is Zero	(CX) = 0
JE	Jump If Equal	ZF = 1
*JG	Jump If Greater	ZF = 0 and SF = OF
*JGE	Jump If Greater or Equal	SF = OF
*JL	Jump If Less	SF ≠ OF
*JLE	Jump If Less or Equal	ZF = 1 or SF ≠ OF
JNA	Jump If Not Above	CF = 1 or ZF = 1
JNAE	Jump If Not Above nor Equal	CF = 1
JNB	Jump If Not Below	CF = 0
JNBE	Jump If Not Below nor Equal	CF = 0 and ZF = 0
JNC	Jump If No Carry	CF = 0
JNE	Jump If Not Equal	ZF = 0
*JNG	Jump If Not Greater	ZF = 1 or SF ≠ OF
*JNGE	Jump If Not Greater nor Equal	SF ≠ OF
*JNL	Jump If Not Less	SF = OF
*JNLE	Jump If Not Less Nor Equal	ZF = 0 and SF = OF
*JNO	Jump If No Overflow	OF = 0
JNP	Jump If No Parity (Odd)	PF = 0
*JNS	Jump If No Sign	SF = 0
JNZ	Jump If Not Zero	ZF = 0
*JO	Jump On Overflow	OF = 1
JP	Jump On Parity (Even)	PF = 1
JPE	Jump If Parity Even	PF = 1
JPO	Jump If Parity Odd	PF = 0
*JS	Jump On Sign	SF = 1
JZ	Jump If Zero	ZF = 1

*Pertinent for signed (2s-complement) arithmetic.

3. To merely *check* whether the contents of AL and BL are identical, without affecting either register, you could use a compare instruction, rather than a subtract instruction. The sequence

```
CMP   AL,BL
JE    ZERO
```

jumps to ZERO if AL and BL hold the same values. (The equivalent mnemonic JZ could have been used here, but JE is more explicit in this case.)

4. Some tests require you to choose between two different conditional transfer instructions, based on whether you are testing the result of a signed or unsigned operation. To illustrate this, suppose you want to jump to label BXMORE if the contents of BX are higher-valued than the contents of AX. The sequence

```
CMP   BX,AX
JA    BXMORE
```

applies if the operands are *unsigned*, whereas

```
CMP   BX,AX
JG    BXMORE
```

applies if the operands are *signed*.

Using Conditional Transfers With Compare (CMP)

Although you can precede conditional transfer instructions with any instruction that alters the flags, you normally precede them with a Compare (CMP) instruction. In Table 3-5 of Section 3.5 you saw how CMP affects the flags for various source and destination relationships. Now, with the wide variety of conditional transfer instructions at your disposal, it is worthwhile to look at a more practical table—one that shows which conditional transfer to use for all possible combinations of source and destination. Table 3-11 is the table you need.

To illustrate a practical application for a conditional transfer/compare combination, Example 3-1 shows a program sequence that arranges two unsigned numbers in memory in increasing order. Before this sequence is executed, the data segment offsets of the numbers are assumed to be in BX and DI, respectively. Whenever two numbers need to be exchanged, one of the numbers must be loaded into a register, because the 8088 has no memory-to-memory move instruction.

You can also combine a single compare instruction with two conditional transfer instructions, to test the "less than," "equal to", and "greater than" cases separately. Example 3-2 shows a sequence that executes one of several different groups of instructions, depending on whether the value in AL is below, equal to, or above 10.

This sequence uses a JAE instruction to determine whether AL is above or equal to 10. If it is, the 8088 jumps to the label AE10. A JA instruction then determines whether AL is above 10. If it is, the 8088 jumps to A10. Normally, the last instruction in the first two groups would be a JMP, to skip the unused options:

Table 3-11. Using conditional transfers with Compare (CMP).

To Jump If	Follow CMP with	
	For unsigned numbers	For signed numbers
Destination is greater than Source	JA	JG
Destination is equal to Source	JE	JE
Destination is not equal to Source	JNE	JNE
Destination is less than Source	JB	JL
Destination is less than or equal to Source	JBE	JLE
Destination is greater than or equal to Source	JAE	JGE

Example 3-1. Arranging Two Numbers in Increasing Order

```
; This sequence Arranges two unsigned 16-bit numbers in
; memory in order of value, with the lower-numbered value
; in the lower address. The offset of the first number is
; in BX; the offset of the second number is in DI.
        MOV     AX,[BX]     ;Load first number into AX
        CMP     AX,[DI]     ;Compare it with second number
        JBE     DONE        ;Is first no. below or equal to second
        XCHG    AX,[DI]     ; no.?  If not, swap the two numbers
        MOV     [BX],AX
DONE;   ..
```

Example 3-2. A Three-Way Decision Sequence

```
; This sequence causes one of three different groups of
; instructions to be executed, based on whether the un-
; signed number in AL is below, equal to, or above 10.
        CMP     AL,10       ;Compare AL to 10
        JAE     AE10
        ..
                            ;These instructions execute if AL<10
        ..
AE10:   JA      A10
        ..
                            ;These instructions execute if AL=10
        ..
A10:    ..                  ;These instructions execute if AL>10
```

Iteration Control Instructions

The iteration control instructions are conditional transfers, but have a very special purpose: They set up repetitive loops. In the 8088, the Count register (CX) is designed to act as the counter for loops. Each of the iteration control instructions decrement CX by 1, then make a jump/no-jump "decision" based on the result.

The basic instruction of this group is *Loop until Count Complete (LOOP)*. LOOP decrements CX by 1 and transfers control to a *short-label* target operand if CX is not zero. For example, to perform a certain set of operations 100 times, you might use this kind of sequence:

```
·       MOV  CX,100    ;Load repetition count into CX
START:  ..             (The instructions to be repeated go here)
        ..
        LOOP  START    ;If CX is not zero, jump to START
        ..             ;Otherwise continue here
```

However, LOOP by itself only terminates the loop if CX has been decremented to zero. Many applications involve loops that must also terminate if something happens *within* the loop before CX reaches zero. The instructions that provide for this are *Loop If Equal (LOOPE)* and *Loop If Not Equal (LOOPNE)*.

LOOPE, which has the alternate form *Loop If Zero (LOOPZ)*, decrements CX by 1, then jumps if CX is not zero and the Zero Flag (ZF) is 1. Thus, looping continues until CX is zero or ZF is 0, or both. Therefore, you normally use LOOPE to find the first non-zero result in a series of operations. To illustrate, Example 3-3 shows a sequence that finds the first non-zero byte in a block of memory. The offset addresses of the first and last bytes are in BX and DI, respectively.

LOOPNE, which has the alternate form *Loop If Not Zero (LOOPNZ)*, decrements CX by 1, then jumps if CX is not zero and the Zero Flag (ZF) is 0. Thus, looping continues until CX is zero or ZF is 1, or both. Therefore, you normally use LOOPNE to find the first zero result in a series of operations. If you replace LOOPE with LOOPNE in Example 3-3, the sequence will find the first *zero* byte in a block of memory rather than the first non-zero byte.

3.8 String Instructions

The string instructions let you operate on blocks of bytes or words in memory. These blocks, or *strings,* may be up to 64K bytes long, and may consist of numeric values (either binary or BCD), alphanumeric values (such as ASCII text characters) or, for that matter, any kind of information that can be stored in memory as binary patterns.

The string instructions provide five basic operations, called *primitives,* that process strings one element (byte or word) at a time. These primitives— move, compare, scan for a value, load, and store—are summarized in Table 3-12.

Table 3-12. String instructions.

Mnemonic	Assembler Format	OF	DF	IF	TF	SF	ZF	AF	PF	CF
		Flags								
REPEAT PREFIXES										
REP	REP	–	–	–	–	–	–	–	–	–
REPE/ REPZ	REPE	–	–	–	–	–	–	–	–	–
REPNE/ REPNZ	REPNE	–	–	–	–	–	–	–	–	–
MOVE										
MOVS	MOVS dest-string,source-string	–	–	–	–	–	–	–	–	–
MOVSB	MOVSB	–	–	–	–	–	–	–	–	–
MOVSW	MOVSW	–	–	–	–	–	–	–	–	–
COMPARE										
CMPS	CMPS dest-string,source-string	*	–	–	–	*	*	*	*	*
CMPSB	CMPSB	*	–	–	–	*	*	*	*	*
CMPSW	CMPSW	*	–	–	–	*	*	*	*	*
SCAN										
SCAS	SCAS dest-string	*	–	–	–	*	*	*	*	*
SCASB	SCASB	*	–	–	–	*	*	*	*	*
SCASW	SCASW	*	–	–	–	*	*	*	*	*
LOAD AND STORE										
LODS	LODS source-string	–	–	–	–	–	–	–	–	–
LODSB	LODSB	–	–	–	–	–	–	–	–	–
LODSW	LODSW	–	–	–	–	–	–	–	–	–
STOS	STOS dest-string	–	–	–	–	–	–	–	–	–
STOSB	STOSB	–	–	–	–	–	–	–	–	–
STOSW	STOSW	–	–	–	–	–	–	–	–	–

Note: – means unchanged and * means changed.

As you see, each primitive has three separate instruction forms. The first form takes one or two operands (for example, MOVS takes two operands) and the other two take no operands (for example, MOVSB and MOVSW). The no-operand forms represent the two instructions that the 8088 can actually execute. The assembler always converts the more general operand form to one of these two instructions when you assemble the program.

The 8088 assumes the destination string is in the extra segment and the source string is in the data segment. The processor addresses the destination string with DI and the source string with SI For example, MOVSB copies the data segment byte addressed by SI into the extra segment location addressed by DI.

Intel probably chose DI and SI here because they are easy-to-remember abbreviations for Destination Index (DI) and Source Index (SI). Clever, no?

Incidentally, although the 8088 assumes the destination string is in the extra segment and the source string is in the data segment, you *can* change these assignments. We'll show you how later

Example 3-3. Find a Non-Zero Location in a Memory Block

```
; This sequence finds the first non-zero byte in a speci-
; fied block of memory. The offset of the starting address
; is in BX; the offset of the ending address is in DI. The
; offset of the non-zero byte is returned in BX. If no
; non-zero bytes are found, BX will hold the same value as
; DI upon return.

              SUB   DI,BX          ;Byte count=
              INC   DI             ; (DI)-(BX)+1
              MOV   CX,DI          ;Move byte count into CX
              DEC   BX
NEXT:         INC   BX             ;Point to next location
              CMP   BYTE PTR [BX],0 ;and compare it to 0
              LOOPE NEXT           ;Go compare next byte
              JNZ   NZ_FOUND       ;Non-zero byte found?
              ..                   ; No. (BX)=(DI)
              ..
NZ_FOUND:     ..                   ; Yes. Offset of the non-
              ..                   ; zero entry is in BX.
```

Because the string instructions are designed to operate on a *series* of elements, they automatically update the pointer(s) to address the next element in the string. For example, MOVS increments or decrements its source string pointer (SI) and its destination string pointer (DI) at the end of each execution cycle.

What determines whether SI and DI increment or decrement at the end of a string instruction? It is the state of the Direction Flag (DF) bit in the 8088's Flags register. If DF is 0, SI and DI *increment* after every instruction; if DF is 1, SI and DI *decrement* after every instruction.

For example, MOVS copies an element in the source string to a location in the destination string. If DF is 0, the 8088 increments SI and D after the move, thereby addressing the following element in memory. If DF is 1, the 8088 decrements SI and DI after the move, thereby addressing the preceding element in memory.

You control the state of DF with the instructions *Set Direction Flag (STD)* and *Clear Direction Flag (CLD)*. These instructions are discussed in Section 3.10.

A single string instruction can operate on a number of consecutive elements in memory, if you precede it with a *repeat* prefix (see Table 3-12). These prefixes are not instructions, but one-byte modifiers that cause the 8088 hardware to repeat a string instruction. With this approach, the 8088 processes long strings much faster than it could with a software loop.

Repeat Prefixes

Repeat prefixes cause a string instruction to be executed the number of times specified in the CX register. For example, the sequence

```
        MOV   CX,500
   REP  MOVS  DEST,SOURCE
```

executes the MOVS instruction 500 times (we'll discuss MOVS momentarily), and decrements the CX register after each repetition. You should interpret the REP prefix to mean "repeat while not end-of-string"; that is, repeat while CX is not 0.

The remaining repeat prefixes include the Zero Flag (ZF) in the repeat/exit "decision," and therefore only apply to the compare and scan string instructions, which effect ZF. The prefix Repeat While Equal (REPE), which has the alternate name Repeat While Zero (REPZ), causes the instruction to be repeated as long as ZF is 1 and CX is not zero. If you prefix a *string compare instruction (CMPS)* with REPE, the compare operation repeats until a mismatch occurs. Specifically, the sequence

```
        MOV   CX,100
   REPE CMPS  DEST,SOURCE
```

compares the strings SOURCE and DEST, element by element, until 100 elements have been compared or until the 8088 finds an element in DEST that does not match the corresponding element in SOURCE.

The prefix *Repeat While Not Equal (REPNE)*, which has the alternate name Repeat While Not Zero (REPNZ), has the opposite effect of REPE. That is, REPNE causes the prefixed instruction to be repeated while ZF is 0 and CX is not zero. Therefore, the sequence

```
         MOV   CX,100
   REPNE CMPS  DEST,SOURCE
```

compares SOURCE to DEST, element by element, until 100 elements have been compared or until the 8088 finds an element in DEST that *matches* the corresponding element in SOURCE.

Move-String Instructions

Move String (MOVS)

The Move String (MOVS) instruction copies a byte or word from one portion of memory to another. MOVS has the general format

```
MOVS  dest-string,source-string
```

where *source-string* is a string in the data segment and *dest-string* is a string in the extra segment. As with CMPS, the 8088 uses SI to address the data segment and DI to address the extra segment. So *MOVS copies one byte or word from the data segment to the extra segment.*

You may override the segment assignment for SI, but not for DI. For instance, you might override SI to copy a string from one part of the extra segment to another.

Although MOVS moves only one element, you can move a string of up to 64K bytes (32K words) by applying the REP prefix. Example 3-4 shows a sequence that copies a 100-byte string called SOURCE in the data segment into the extra segment, where it is called DEST. As demonstrated here, every multi-element MOVS operation involves five steps:

1. Clear DF (with CLD) or set DF (with STD), depending on whether you want the move to progress toward higher addresses in memory or lower addresses in memory, respectively.
2. Load the offset of the source string into SI.
3. Load the offset of the destination string into DI.
4. Load the element count (number of bytes or words to be moved) into CX.
5. Execute the MOVS instruction, with a REP prefix.

Example 3-4. A Multi-Byte Move Operation

```
;  This sequence copies 100 bytes from a string called
;  SOURCE in the data segment to a string called DEST in
;  the extra segment.
;
        CLD                       ;Set DF=0, to move forward
        LEA    SI,SOURCE          ;Load offset of SOURCE into SI
        LEA    DI,ES:DEST         ; and offset of DEST into DI
        MOV    CX,100             ;Load element count into CX
REP     MOVS   DEST,SOURCE        ;Move the bytes
```

Of course, in addition to these five instructions your program must include an *extra segment* that holds space for the destination string and a *data segment* that holds the source string. Generally, you define the destination string with a pseudo-op such as

```
DEST    DB    100 DUP(?)
```

How does the assembler know whether you are moving bytes or words? It determines this based on the *type* of the source and destination labels in the operand field.

If these labels have the type attribute BYTE (that is, if they were set up with DB pseudo-ops), the assembler encodes MOVS as a MOVSB instruction. Conversely, if the operand labels have the type attribute WORD (that is, if they were set up with DW pseudo-ops), the assembler encodes MOVS as a MOVSW instruction. Therefore, if you define SOURCE and DEST with DW pseudo-ops, the sequence in Example 3-4 copies 100 words instead of 100 bytes.

Move Byte String (MOVSB) and Move Word String (MOVSW)

Because it has operands, the MOVS instruction has two advantages:

1. It can explicitly identify the strings involved in the operation, which makes for better program documentation.
2. It lets you reassign the source string to a segment other than the data segment. For instance, *MOVS [DI],ES:[SI]* copies a string element from one area of the extra segment to another.

However, the operands are also a possible limitation in that they tie MOVS to two specific strings. If you intend to include a move operation in a general-purpose procedure, you are better off using one of the non-specific forms, either MOVSB or MOVSW. These instructions implicitly reference SI and DI for the starting source address and destination address, and perform the move. As with MOVS, DF determines the direction.

For example, if you have a general-purpose procedure of this kind:

```
GEN_MOVE    PROC
            ..
            ..
REP         MOVSB
            ..
            ..
GEN_MOVE    ENDP
```

you could use it to move 500 bytes from SOURCE to DEST with this calling sequence:

```
CLD
LEA     SI,SOURCE
LEA     DI,ES:DEST
MOV     CX,500
CALL    GEN_MOVE
```

Elsewhere in the program, you could move 1000 bytes from SOURCE to another destination string, say DEST1, with this calling sequence:

```
CLD
LEA    SI,SOURCE
LEA    DI,ES:DEST1
MOV    CX,1000
CALL   GEN_MOVE
```

Moving Strings in the Data Segment

As you learned earlier, SI normally addresses the data segment, but you can change this assignment by using the MOVS form of the instruction with a *segment* override applied to source operator. For example,

```
MOVS DEST,ES:SOURCE
```

copies an element from the SOURCE string in the extra segment to the DEST string in the extra segment.

Since you can't override DI, it appears the destination must always be a string in the extra segment. Does this mean you can never copy a string into the data segment? No, you *can* copy a string into the data segment, but to do this you must use some trickery.

To copy a string into the data segment, you need only to make the extra segment register (ES) have the same value as the data segment register (DS). Once this has been done, and you execute MOVS, the 8088 will "think" it is copying a string from the data segment to the extra segment, as usual. But *you* know the 8088 is in fact copying a string from one place in the data segment to another!

Example 3-5 shows how this "trick" can be used to copy 100 bytes from the string SOURCE__ D to the string DEST __ D, where both strings are in the data segment. Note that except for the first two instructions, this sequence is identical to the sequence in Example 3-4.

Incidentally, you can also apply this technique to the other string instructions we discuss in this section.

Example 3-5. A Data Segment Move Operation

```
;  This sequence copies 100 bytes from a string called
;  SOURCE_D to a string called DEST_D, where both strings
;  are in the data segment.
      MOV    ES,DS          ;Make ES point to data
      MOV    ES,SI          ; segment
      CLD                   ;Set DF=0, to move forward
      LEA    SI,SOURCE_D    ;Load offset of SOURCE_D into
                            ; SI
```
(continued on next page)

```
     LEA    DI,DEST_D         ; and offset of DEST_D into
                              ; DI
     MOV    CX,100            ;Load element count into CX
REP  MOVS   DEST_D,SOURCE_D   ;Move the bytes
```

Compare-String Instructions

Compare Strings (CMPS)

Like the Compare (CMP) instruction we discussed in Section 3.5, the *Compare Strings (CMPS)* instruction compares a source operand to a destination operand, and returns the results in the flags. CMPS, like CMP, affects neither operand.
The general form of CMPS is:

```
CMPS   dest-string,source-string
```

where *source-string* is a string in the data segment addressed by SI and *dest-string* is a string in the extra segment addressed by DI. Therefore, CMPS compares an element (byte or word) in the data segment with an element in the extra segment.
Like the CMP instruction, CMPS compares the two operands by subtracting them. However, CMP subtracts the source operand from the destination operand, but *CMPS subtracts the destination operand from the source operand!* This means the conditional transfer instructions that follow a CMPS instruction must be different than those that follow a CMP instruction. Table 3-13 is the table you need with CMPS.
To compare more than one element, you must apply a repeat prefix to the CMPS instruction. Here, REP would be meaningless, because it would only return the flags result of comparing the two final elements. With CMPS, you must use either REPE (REPZ) or REPNE (REPNZ).
REPE causes the strings to be compared until (CX) is zero or an element mismatch occurs. Thus,

```
     CLD
     MOV    CX,100
REPE CMPS   DEST,SOURCE
```

compares up to 100 elements of SOURCE and DEST in an attempt to find two elements that are unalike.
REPNE causes the strings to be compared until (CX) is zero or an element match occurs. Thus,

```
      CLD
      MOV    CX,100
REPNE CMPS   DEST,SOURCE
```

Table 3-13. Using conditional transfers with CMPS.

To Jump If	Follow CMPS with:	
	For unsigned numbers	For signed numbers
Source is greater than Destination	JA	JG
Source is equal to Destination	JE	JE
Source is not equal to Destination	JNE	JNE
Source is less than Destination	JB	JL
Source is less than or equal to Destination	JBE	JLE
Source is greater than or equal to Destination	JAE	JGE

compares up to 100 elements of SOURCE and DEST in an attempt to find two elements that are alike.

As with MOVS, the Direction Flag (DF) determines whether the operation proceeds forward (DF = 0) or backward (DF = 1) in memory, and SI and DI are updated after each operation.

Checking Results

Since repeated compare operations can terminate on either of two conditions—contents of CX are zero or ZF changed to 0 (REPE) or 1 (REPNE)—you will usually want to determine which of these caused the termination. The easiest way to find out what stopped the compare is to follow CMPS with a conditional transfer instruction that tests ZF—either JE (JZ) or JNE (JNZ).

For example, the following sequence causes the 8088 to jump to NOT_ FOUND if DEST and SOURCE have no common elements in the first 100 elements:

```
            CLD
            MOV   CX,100
REPNE       CMPS  DEST,SOURCE   ;Search for a match
            JNE   NOT_FOUND     ;Matching elements found?
            ..                  ; Yes. Continue here.
            ..
NOT_FOUND:  ..                  ; No. Continue here.
```

Compare Byte Strings (CMPSB) and Compare Word Strings (CMPSW)

Like MOVSB and MOVSW, the CMPSB and CMPSW instructions have no operands, and are thereby convenient for use in a general-purpose procedure.

Scan-String Instructions

The scan-string instructions let you search a string in the extra segment for a specified value. The offset of the string's first element is in DI.

If you are scanning a byte string, the search value must be in AL. If you are scanning a word string, the search value must be in AX. The scan operation is nothing more than a compare-with-accumulator operation, affecting the flags in the same way as the string-compare instructions.

Scan String (SCAS)

The basic instruction in this group, *Scan String (SCAS)*, has the general form

```
SCAS  dest-string
```

where the operand *dest-string* identifies a string in the extra segment whose offset is in DI. This operand tells the 8088 whether the search value is a byte in AL or a word in AX.

As with CMPS, to operate on more than one string element, you should apply the repeat prefix REPE (REPZ) or REPNE (REPNZ). For example, this sequence

```
      CLD
      LEA   DI,ES:B_STRING
      MOV   AL,10
      MOV   CX,100
REPE  SCAS  B_STRING
```

scans up to 100 elements of the byte string B_STRING, attempting to find the first element that does not contain 10. If such an element is found, the offset of the *next* element is returned in DI and ZF is 0. A subsequent JCXZ instruction will tell you whether the element was found (jump not taken) or not found (jump taken).

Scan Byte String (SCASB) and Scan Word String (SCASW)

These instructions have no operand, which means you can scan many different strings with just one SCASB or SCASW instruction by just changing the contents of DI.

Load-String and Store-String Instructions

Once you have located a desired string element with a compare-string or scan-string instruction, you normally want to perform some operation on that element. You may want to read the element into a register for subsequent processing (perhaps determine its exact value) or change the element in memory. The load-string and store-string instructions provide these operations.

Load String (LODS)

The *Load String (LODS)* instruction transfers a *source-string* operand, addressed by SI, from the data segment to accumulator AL (byte operation) or AX (word operation), then adjusts SI to point to the next element. If DF is 0, SI is incremented; if DF is 1, SI is decremented. You don't normally repeat LODS.

For example, the following sequence compares the 500-byte strings DEST and SOURCE to find the first non-matching elements. If a mismatch is detected, the SOURCE string element is loaded into AL.

```
        CLD
        LEA     DI,ES:DEST      ;Get offset of DEST
        LEA     SI,SOURCE       ; and SOURCE
        MOV     CX,500          ;Element count
REPE    CMPSB                   ;Search for a mismatch
        JCXZ    MATCH           ;Mismatch found?
        DEC     SI              ; Yes. Adjust SI,
        LODS    SOURCE          ;   read element into AL,
        ..                      ;   and process it
        ..
MATCH:  ..                      ; No mismatch. Continue
        ..                      ; here.
```

Because this is a byte operation, the element pointer (SI) is either incremented by 1 (if DF = 0) or decremented by 1 (if DF = 1) by the LODS instruction.

As usual, LODS has the optional shorter forms *Load Byte String (LODSB)* and *Load Word String (LODSW)*.

Store String (STOS)

The *Store String (STOS)* instruction transfers an operand from accumulator AL (byte operation) or AX (word operation) to the *destination-string* operand in the extra segment, addressed by DI, then adjusts DI to point to the next element. If DF is 0, DI is incremented; if DF is 1, DI is decremented.

As a repeated operation, STOS is convenient for filling a string with a given value. For instance, the following sequence scans the 200-word string W_STRING for the first non-zero element. If such an element is found, this word and the next five words are filled with zeroes.

```
        CLD
        LEA    DI,ES:W_STRING    ;Address string
        MOV    AX,0              ;Search value is 0
        MOV    CX,200    ·       ;Search count is 200 words
REPNE   SCASW                    ;Search the string
        JCXZ   ALL0             ;Non-zero word found?
        SUB    DI,2             ;  Yes. Adjust DI,
        MOV    CX,6             ;    then fill six words
REP     STOS   W_STRING         ;    with 0
ALL0:   ..                      ;  No. Continue here
        ..
```

3.9 Interrupt Instructions

An interrupt is similar to a procedure call because both make the 8088 save return information on the stack, then jump to an instruction sequence elsewhere in memory. A procedure call makes the 8088 jump to an instruction sequence called a procedure; an interrupt makes the 8088 jump to an instruction sequence called an *interrupt service routine.*

However, while procedure calls can be NEAR or FAR, and direct or indirect, an interrupt always makes an indirect jump to its service routine. It does this by taking the address of the routine from a 32-bit *interrupt vector* in memory. Moreover, procedure calls only save an address on the stack, but interrupts also save the flags on the stack (as a PUSHF instruction does).

Interrupts can be initiated by external devices in the system or by special interrupt instructions within a program. The 8088 has three different interrupt instructions—two "calls" and one "return"—as summarized in Table 3-14.

Interrupt (INT)

The INT instruction has the general form

```
INT  interrupt-type
```

where *interrupt-type* is the identification number of one of 256 different vectors in memory.

Table 3-14. Interrupt instructions.

Mnemonic	Assembler Format		Flags								
			OF	DF	IF	TF	SF	ZF	AF	PF	CF
INT	INT interrupt-type		–	–	0	0	–	–	–	–	–
INTO	INTO		–	–	0	0	–	–	–	–	–
IRET	IRET		*	*	*	*	*	*	*	*	*

Note: – means unchanged and * means changed.

When INT is executed, the 8088 does the following:

1. Push the Flags register onto the stack.
2. Clear the Trap Flag (TF) and the Interrupt Enable/Disable Flag (IF), to disable single-stepping and "lock out" other maskable interrupts.
3. Push the CS register onto the stack.
4. Calculate the address of the interrupt vector, by multiplying *interrupt-type* by 4.
5. Load the second word of the interrupt vector into CS.
6. Push the IP onto the stack.
7. Load the first word of the interrupt vector into IP.

In summary, After INT has executed, the flags, CS and IP are on the stack, TF and IF are 0, and the CS:IP combination points to the starting address of the interrupt service routine. Now the 8088 begins executing the interrupt service routine.

The 256 interrupt vectors are located in the lowest locations in memory. Since each is four bytes (one doubleword) long, they occupy a total of 1K bytes—absolute addresses 0 through 3FFH. For example, the instruction

```
INT   1AH
```

causes the 8088 to calculate the vector address 68H (4x1AH), and to fetch the 16-bit IP and CS values of the interrupt service routine from locations 68H and 6AH, respectively.

Figure 3-11 shows the stack, the Stack Pointer (SP), the Code Segment (CS) register, and the Instruction Pointer (IP) before and after this instruction is executed. In this example, the interrupt vector is assumed to hold the address F000:FE6E, so that is where the 8088 begins executing.

Of the 256 interrupt types, Intel has decreed that the first five (Types 0 through 4) must be allocated to internal interrupts in every 8086 or 8088 system. In the IBM Personal Computer, most of next 27 interrupt types (5H through 1FH) perform dedicated functions for the computer's *Basic I/O System (BIOS)*. Further, the IBM *Disk Operating System (DOS)* reserves interrupt types 20H through 3FH for its use. We will discuss interrupts in greater detail in Chapter 6.

Interrupt If Overflow (INTO)

The *Interrupt If Overflow (INTO)* instruction is a *conditional* INT instruction. INTO only activates an interrupt if the Overflow Flag (OF) is 1. In that case, INTO transfers control to an interrupt service routine with an indirect call through interrupt vector 4. In other words, INTO activates a Type 4 interrupt

Interrupt Return (IRET)

The *Interrupt Return (IRET)* instruction is to interrupts what RET is to procedure calls. It "undoes" the work of the original operation, and lets the 8088 make an orderly return to the main program. For this reason, IRET must be the last instruction the 8088 executes in an interrupt service routine.

When executed, IRET pops three 16-bit values off the stack, and loads them into the Instruction Pointer (IP), the Code Segment (CS) register, and the Flags register, respectively. Other program registers may be destroyed unless the interrupt service routine includes provisions to save them.

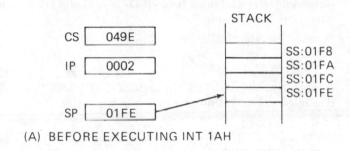

(A) BEFORE EXECUTING INT 1AH

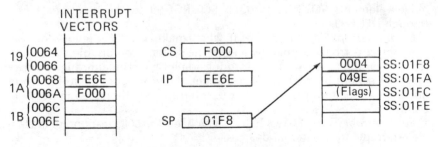

(B) AFTER EXECUTING INT 1AH

Figure 3-11. How an interrupt affects the stack.

3.10 Processor Control Instructions

These instructions let you regulate the operation of the 8088 microprocessor from within a program. As Table 3-15 shows, there are three kinds of processor control instructions: flag operations, external synchronization, and the "do-nothing" instruction, no operation.

Flag Operations

The 8088 has seven instructions that let you change the Carry Flag (CF), Direction Flag (DF), and Interrupt Enable Flag (IF).

The *Set Carry Flag (STC)* and *Clear Carry Flag (CLC)* instructions force CF to a 1 or 0 state, respectively. These are useful to pre-condition CF before an RCL or RCR rotate-with-carry operation. *Complement Carry Flag (CMC)* makes CF a 0 if it is a 1, and vice versa.

The *Set Direction Flag (STD)* and *Clear Direction Flag (CLD)* instructions force DF to a 1 or 0 state, respectively. You use STD and CLD to select the direction for a string operation. If DF is 0, the index registers SI and DI increment after each operation. If DI is 1, SI and DI decrement after each operation. For example,

```
MOV   CX,100
CLD
MOVS  DEST,SOURCE
```

moves elements SOURCE through SOURCE + 99 to the locations DEST through DEST + 99. Conversely,

```
MOV   CX,100
STD
MOVS  DEST,SOURCE
```

moves elements SOURCE through SOURCE-99 to the locations DEST through DEST-99.

Clear Interrupt Flag (CLI) zeroes IF, which makes the 8088 "ignore" maskable interrupts from external devices in the system. You disable such interrupts when the processor is performing some time-critical or high-priority task that cannot be interrupted. However, the processor will still perform *non-maskable* interrupts while IF is 0. Interrupts are discussed in detail in Chapter 6.

Set Interrupt Flag (STI) sets IF to 1, which lets the 8088 respond to maskable interrupts from external devices.

External Synchronization Instructions

These instructions are primarily used to synchronize the 8088 microprocessor with external events.

The *Halt (HLT)* instruction puts the 8088 into a halt state. In this state, the processor sits idle and executes no instructions. The 8088 only leaves the halt state if you reset it or it receives an external interrupt, either nonmaskable or (if IF is 1) maskable. You use HLT to make the processor wait for an interrupt before proceeding.

The *Wait (WAIT)* instruction also puts the 8088 into an idle state, but instead of just sitting there it checks an input line called TEST at five-clock intervals. If TEST is active, the 8088 resumes execution at the instruction that follows WAIT. The 8088 will also service interrupts while WAITing, but upon return from the interrupt it goes idle again.

After reading how HLT and WAIT put the 8088 in a idle state, you might think that *Escape (ESC)* sends the processor on vacation! Not true. ESC simply makes the 8088 fetch the contents of a specified operand and put that operand on its data bus. In this way ESC provides a mechanism by which other processors in the system may receive their instructions from the 8088 instruction stream, and make use of the 8088 addressing modes.

The general form for ESC is:

```
ESC  ext-opcode,source
```

where *ext-opcode* is a 6-bit immediate number and *source* is a register or a memory variable. If *source* is a register, the processor does nothing. If *source* is a memory variable, the 8088 reads the operand from memory and discards it. However, an external processor may "capture" the memory operand when the 8088 reads it from memory.

Lock the Bus (LOCK) is a one byte prefix that may precede any instruction. LOCK makes the 8088 activate its bus LOCK signal for as long as the LOCKed instruction takes to execute. While the LOCK signal is active, no other processor in the system can use the bus. Obviously, you only use LOCK in systems that include several microprocessors.

No Operation Instruction

The final instruction, *No Operation (NOP)*, is the simplest of all, because it does exactly what its name implies—it performs no operation whatsoever. It affects no flags, no registers and no memory locations. It does nothing other than advance the Instruction Pointer (IP).

That being the case, what good is NOP? Surprisingly, NOP has a variety of uses. For example, you can use its op-code (90H) to "patch" object code when you want to delete one or more instructions without re-assembling.

Table 3-15. Processor control instructions.

Mnemonic	Assembler Format	OF	DF	IF	TF	SF	ZF	AF	PF	CF
					Flags					
FLAG OPERATIONS										
STC	STC	–	–	–	–	–	–	–	–	1
CLC	CLC	–	–	–	–	–	–	–	–	0
CMC	CMC	–	–	–	–	–	–	–	–	*
STD	STD	–	1	–	–	–	–	–	–	–
CLD	CLD	–	0	–	–	–	–	–	–	–
STI	STI	–	–	1	–	–	–	–	–	–
CLI	CLI	–	–	0	–	–	–	–	–	–
EXTERNAL SYNCHRONIZATION										
HLT	HLT	–	–	–	–	–	–	–	–	–
WAIT	WAIT	–	–	–	–	–	–	–	–	–
ESC	ESC ext-opcode,source	–	–	–	–	–	–	–	–	–
LOCK	LOCK	–	–	–	–	–	–	–	–	–
NO OPERATION										
NOP	NOP	–	–	–	–	–	–	–	–	–

Note: – means unchanged and * means changed.

NOP is also convenient when you are testing sequences of instructions in your computer. That is, you can make NOP the last instruction in a test program — a convenient spot at which to stop a trace. You will probably find other uses for this innocuous, but handy, instruction.

Study Exercises (answers on page 278)

1. Write an instruction that stores the contents of the AX register into a word location called SAVE _ AX in the extra segment.

2. . What does this sequence do?

```
MOV    AX,0
MOV·   BX,AX
MOV    BP,AX
MOV    [BX],AX
MOV    [BP],AX
```

3. Which of the following instructions or sequences are invalid? (Assume variables are defined in the data segment and instructions are defined in the code segment.)

```
(a)  K       EQU   1024ˉ
             . .
             . .
             MOV   K,AX
(b)  TEMP    DB    ?
             . .
             . .
             MOV   AL,TEMP
(c)  TEMP    DB    ?
             . .
             . .
             MOV   TEMP,AX
(d)  TEMP    DB    ?
     T3      DB    10
             . .
             . .
             MOV   TEMP,T3
(e)  MOV     [BX][BP],AX
```

4. List two instructions that clear the AX register to zero.

5. How do these two instructions differ?

```
MOV  BX,OFFSET TABLE+4
LEA  BX,TABLE+4
```

6. Write a loop that subtracts a three-word variable called V2 from another three-word variable called V1.

7. What does this instruction do?

```
MUL  10
```

8. If AX contains 1234H and BX contains 4321H, list the contents of AX after each of these instructions is executed:

```
(a)  AND   AX,BX
(b)  OR    AX,BX
(c)  XOR   AX,BX
(d)  NOT   AX
(e)  TEST  AX,BX
```

9. Write a sequence to *normalize* AX. That is, shift AX left until the·most-significant "1" bit is in Bit 15. If AX is initially zero or Bit 15 already contains a 1, exit immediately.

10. What does this sequence do?

```
START:  MOV   CX,3
        SUB   AX,10
        LOOP  START
```

4

High-Precision Mathematics

If you have done any assembly language programming on one of the conventional microprocessors, you are probably impressed with the arithmetic potential of the 8088. For starters, the very fact that the 8088 has built-in multiply and divide instructions means the hours (or days) of time you normally spend developing multiplication and division programs are available for more stimulating activities, such as playing racquetball.

In this chapter we build on the potential offered by the multiply and divide instructions to develop some programs that tackle tougher math problems. We will begin with programs that multiply 32-bit signed and unsigned numbers. From there, we will discuss how to handle overflow situations in divide operations, and conclude with a program that calculates the square root of a 32-bit number.

4.1 Multiplication

In Chapter 3 we studied the 8088's two multiplication instructions, *Multiply, Unsigned (MUL)*, and *Integer Multiply, Signed (IMUL)*. These instructions multiply byte-length (8-bit) and word-length (16-bit) operands to produce double-length (16- or 32-bit) products.

Is it difficult to multiply numbers larger than 16 bits? No, it's not difficult at all, as you shall see. Anyone who has written a multiplication program for an earlier 8-bit microprocessor will tell you that just *having* a multiply instruction of any kind makes up for whatever inconvenience you go through to extend its capabilities.

151

Unsigned 32-Bit x 32-Bit Multiply

Although the MUL instruction can only handle 8- or 16-bit operands, you can use MUL to multiply multi-precision unsigned numbers. For instance, you can use MUL to multiply two 32-bit numbers. To do this, you let MUL generate a series of 32-bit *cross products*, then sum them to form the final 64-bit product. This method is the one you learned in elementary school to multiply decimal numbers by hand, with pencil and paper.

As you probably recall (in these days of pocket calculators, it may be a little hazy), you write the multiplicand with the multiplier below it, and perform a series of multiplications—one for each digit in the multiplier. Each individual multiplication produces a partial product, which you enter directly below the multiplier digit. Thus, each partial product is offset one digit position to the left of the preceding partial product.

For example, 124 times 103 looks like this:

```
   124   Multiplicand
 x 103   Multiplier
   372   Partial Product #1
   000   Partial Product #2
   124   Partial Product #3
 12772   Final Product
```

You offset the partial products from each other to account for the *decimal weights* of the multiplier digits. In this example, the 3 is a "ones" digit, the 0 is a "tens" digit and the 1 is a "hundreds" digit. Therefore, you could write the example as:

$$103 \times 124 = (3 \times 124) + (0 \times 124) + (100 \times 124)$$

or

$$103 \times 124 = (3 \times 1 \times 124) + (0 \times 10 \times 124) + (1 \times 100 \times 124)$$

In this section we will develop a short procedure that multiplies two 32-bit unsigned numbers and yields a 64-bit unsigned product. If you had no multiply instruction you would have to perform 32 separate multiplications, one for each bit in the multiplier.

But fortunately the 8088 has an instruction that multiplies 16-bit unsigned numbers directly. This instruction, MUL, lets us regard a 32-bit multiplier and a 32-bit multiplicand as two 2-digit numbers, where each digit is 16 bits long. Thus, we can generate the 64-bit product with just *four* multiplications.

Figure 4-1 shows a symbolic representation of the multiplier (digits A and B) and the multiplicand (digits C and D), and illustrates how the four partial products are derived and how they must be aligned in order to calculate the 64-bit final product. The circled numbers in Figure 4-1 identify the four 16-bit additions you must make to calculate the final product. (For instance, Addition 1 adds the high 16 bits of Product #1 to the low 16 bits of Product #2.)

Using Figure 4-1 as a guide, we can develop the procedure that multiplies two 32-bit numbers. Example 4-1 shows such a procedure, labeled MULU32, where the multiplier and multiplicand are entered in register pairs CX:BX and DX:AX, respectively. The 64-bit unsigned product is returned in these same four registers: DX (high 16 bits), CX (mid-upper 16 bits), BX (mid-lower 16 bits) and AX (low 16 bits). Example 4-1 also shows some scratch variable locations that you must set up in the data segment.

Example 4-1. A 32-Bit x 32-Bit Unsigned Multiply Procedure

```
;     This procedure multiplies two 32-bit unsigned numbers
;     and generates a 64-bit product.  Enter with the
;     multiplier in CX (high word) and BX (low word) and
;     the multiplicand in DX (high word) and AX (low word).
;     The product is returned in DX, CX, BX and AX (high
;     to low order).
;
;     Set up these variabies in the data segment:
;
HI_MCND   DW
LO_MCND   DW    ?
HI_PP1    DW    ?
LO_PP1    DW    ?
HI_PP2    DW    ?
LO_PP2    DW    ?
HI_PP3    DW    ?
LO_PP3    DW    ?
HI_PP4    DW    ?
LO_PP4    DW    ?
;
;     The main procedure follows.
;
MULU32    PROC
          MOV    HI_MCND,DX    ;Save multiplicand in memory
          MOV    LO_MCND,AX
          MUL    BX            ;Form partial product #1
          MOV    HI_PP1,DX     ; and save it in memory
          MOV    LO_PP1,AX
          MOV    AX,HI_MCND    ;Form partial product #2
          MUL    BX
          MOV    HI_PP2,DX     ; and save it in memory
          MOV    LO_PP2,AX
          MOV    AX,LO_MCND    ;Form partial product #3
          MUL    CX
          MOV    HI_PP3,DX     ; and save it in memory
          MOV    LO_PP3,AX
          MOV    AX,HI_MCND    ;Form partial product #4
```

```
          MUL   CX
          MOV   HI_PP4,DX    ; and save it in memory
          MOV   LO_PP4,AX
;
; Add the partial products to form the 64-bit final
;   product.
;
          MOV   AX,LO_PP1    ;Low 16 bits
          MOV   BX,HI_PP1    ;Form mid-lower 16 bits
          ADD   BX,LO_PP2    ; with sum #1
          ADC   BX,LO_PP3    ; and sum #2
          MOV   CX,HI_PP2    ;Form mid-upper 16 bits
          ADC   CX,HI_PP3    ; with sum #3
          ADC   CX,LO_PP4    ; and sum #4
          MOV   DX,HI_PP4    ;Form high 16 bits
          ADC   DX,0         ; including any propagated
                             ;  carry

          RET
MULU32    ENDP
```

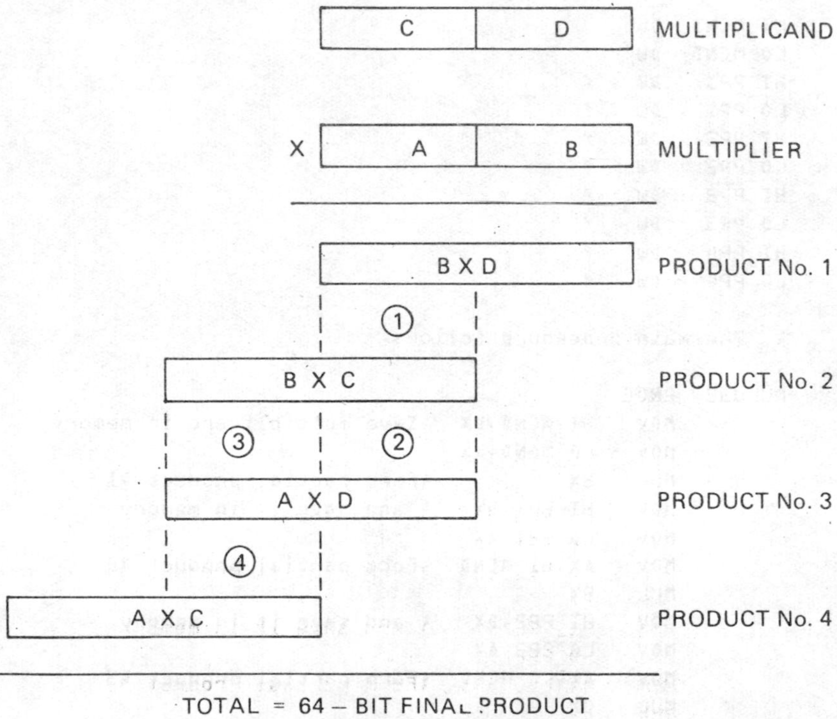

Figure 4-1. Generating a 64-bit product with four 16-bit by 16-bit multiplications.

The MULU32 procedure is fairly straightforward if you refer to Figure 4-1 as you look at the instructions and their accompanying comments. The MULU32 procedure begins by saving the multiplicand in memory, then generating the four 32-bit partial products. Once the partial products have been saved in memory, the only remaining step is to add them. Note that all additions except the first are made with ADC instructions, to propagate any carry from one add operation to another. The Carry Flag remains intact between additions because MOV does not affect CF.

Depending on the operand values, the MULU32 procedure may take up to 907 cycles, or 190.47 μs, to execute.

Because a 32-bit operand can represent unsigned values as large as 4.294×10^9, the MULU32 procedure is satisfactory for most applications. (And for those that involve larger numbers, you'll probably use floating-point math!) However, it is certainly possible to develop a procedure that multiplies 64-bit (or longer) numbers with the cross-products approach used in Example 4-1.

Signed 32-Bit x 32-Bit Multiply

Although the procedure in Example 4-1 is described as a procedure to multiply two unsigned numbers, it can also multiply two signed numbers, as long as both numbers are positive. That is, Example 4-1 provides a 32-bit x 32-bit "non-negative" multiply procedure. This procedure cannot properly multiply negative numbers because such numbers are represented in 2s-complement form.

What happens if we simply replace each MUL instruction in Example 4-1 with an IMUL (Integer Multiply, Signed) instruction? That won't do the job either because IMUL assumes that the most significant bit of each operand is a sign indicator, which is not the case when we generate cross products.

How, then, can you multiply 32-bit signed numbers? Perhaps the simplest way is to negate the negative operand(s), perform a normal unsigned multiplication, then adjust the product, if required. If just one of the operands is negative, you must 2s-complement the product. If both operands are negative, the (positive) product is correct as it stands,

We employ this simple approach in Example 4-2. There, a byte variable called NEG__IND holds a "negative indicator." This indicator is initially set to zero, and stays that way if both operands are positive. If one of the operands is negative, we take the 1s-complement of NEG__IND, which makes it all 1s. If both operands are negative, we 1s-complement NEG__IND twice, which returns it to the all-zeroes state.

Each time NEG__IND is 1s-complemented, one of the operands is negated (2s-complemented). Because the 8088's NEG instruction only operates on byte or word operands, we must 2s-complement our 32-bit operands in "brute-force" fashion. To do this, we 1s complement the operand, then add 1.

Example 4-2. A 32-Bit x 32-Bit Signed Multiply Procedure

```
;    This procedure multiplies two 32-bit signed numbers and
;    generates a 64-bit product. Enter with the multiplier in
;    CX (high word) and BX (low word) and the multiplicand in
;    DX (high word) and AX (low word). The product is re-
;    turned in DX, CX, BX and AX (high to low order).
;    This procedure calls MULU32 (Example 4-1).
;
;    Set up this variable, and those listed in Example 4-1,
;    in the data segment.
;
NEG_IND  DB    ?
;
;    The main procedure follows.
;
EXTRN     MULU32:FAR        ;MULU32 is an external procedure
MULS32    PROC
          MOV    NEG_IND,0   ;Negative indicator=0
          CMP    DX,0        ;Multiplicand negative?
          JNS    CHKCX       ; No. Go check multiplier.
          NOT    AX          ; Yes. 2s-complement multiplicand
          NOT    DX
          ADD    AX,1
          ADC    DX,0
          NOT    NEG_IND     ;    and 1s-complement indicator
CHKCX:    CMP    CX,0        ;Multiplier negative?
          JNS    GOMUL       ; No. Go multiply.
          NOT    BX          ; Yes. 2s-complement multiplier
          NOT    CX
          ADD    BX,1
          ADC    CX,0
          NOT    NEG_IND     ;    and 1s-complement indicator
GOMUL:    CALL   MULU32      ;Perform unsigned multiplication
          CMP    NEG_IND,0   ;Does product have correct sign?
          JZ     DONE        ; Yes. Exit.
          NOT    AX          ; No. 2s-complement product
          NOT    BX
          NOT    CX
          NOT    DX
          ADD    AX,1
          ADC    BX,0
          ADC    CX,0
          ADC    DX,0
DONE:     RET
MULS32    ENDP
```

This procedure calls MULU32 to perform the 32-bit by 32-bit multiplication. Since MULU32 is in another assembly module, we must declare it EXTRN at the start of the example. (Remember, the MULU32 module must have a PUBLIC MULU32 statement.) After the 8088 returns from MULU32, the state of NEG_ IND determines whether the product is correct (NEG_ IND zero) or needs to be negated (NEG_ IND nonzero).

The execution time of the MULS32 procedure depends on whether the operands are both positive, both negative, or of opposite sign. Here is a summary of these execution times, in both clock cycles and microseconds:

Operands	Maximum Time (Cycles)	Maximum Time (μs)
Both positive	1034	217.14
Opposite signs	1074	225.54
Both negative	1082	227.22

4.2 Division

There are many applications for division, but one of the most common is in taking the average of a set of numbers—perhaps the results of a series of laboratory tests. Example 4-3 shows a typical averaging program.

This procedure, AVERAGE, averages a specified number of unsigned word values pointed to by BX, with the word count contained in CX. The integer portion of the average is returned in AX and the remainder is returned in DX. For example, you could use this sequence to average a 100-word table called TABLE:

```
LEA   BX,TABLE   ;Fetch offset of TABLE
MOV   CX,100     ; and its word count
CALL  AVERAGE    ;Calculate the average
```

While describing the DIV and IDIV instructions (Section 3.5), we mentioned that a divide operation automatically aborts if the divisor is zero or if an *overflow* condition exists. An overflow occurs when the dividend is so much larger than the divisor that the result register can't hold the quotient. An unsigned division overflows if the dividend is more than 65,535 times greater than the divisor.

Both divide-by-zero and overflow cause the 8088 to automatically activate a Type 0 (Divide by Zero) interrupt. This interrupt saves the register contents, displays the message

```
. Divide Overflow
```

then terminates the program.

Example 4-3. A Word-Averaging Procedure

```
;    This procedure takes the average of a specified number
;    of unsigned word values in the data segment. The offset
;    of the first word is contained in BX and the word count
;    is contained in CX.
;    Upon return, the integer portion of the average is in AX
;    and the fractional remainder is in DX.
;
AVERAGE   PROC
          SUB    AX,AX      ;Clear dividend to start
          SUB    DX,DX
          PUSH   CX         ;Save word count on stack
ADD_W:    ADD    AX,[BX]    ;Add next word to total
          ADC    DX,0
          ADD    BX,2       ; and update the index
          LOOP   ADD_W      ;All words now totaled?
          POP    CX         ; Yes. Retrieve word count
          DIV    CX         ; | and take the average
          RET
AVERAGE   ENDP
```

Naturally, the divide operation in Example 4-3 aborts if CX holds zero upon entry. Can it abort on an overflow as well? No, overflow cannot occur here because the ratio of the dividend (word total) to the divisor (word count) can never exceed 65,536! However, some divide operations (e.g., dividing 200,000 by 2) may generate an overflow. For this reason, it is worthwhile to look at a procedure that returns a valid quotient regardless of whether or not overflow occurs.

How to Deal with Overflow

In some applications an overflow indicates an error condition. In other applications overflow is acceptable, but means that the program must be able to accommodate a quotient longer than 16 bits. Since the division aborts when the 8088 encounters an overflow condition, how can you obtain a longer quotient? Perhaps the easiest way to get this quotient is to split the 32-bit dividend into two 16-bit numbers, then perform two 16-bit by 16-bit divide operations (which can't produce an overflow).

If the divisor is a 16-bit number called X and the dividend is a 32-bit number represented by $Y_1 Y_0$, you can represent the divide operation as

$$X \sqrt{Y_1 Y_0}$$

or, more properly, as

$$X \sqrt{(Y_1 \times 2^{16}) + Y_0}$$

This division generates two 16-bit quotient digits (Q_1 and Q_0) and two 16-bit remainder digits (R_1 and R_0), as follows:

$$x \sqrt[Q_1 \times 2^{16}]{Y_1 \times 2^{16}} \text{ and } R_1 \times 2^{16}$$

$$x \sqrt[Q_0]{(R_1 \times 2^{16}) + Y_0} \text{ and } R_0$$

As you see, the combination of these two operations produce a 32-bit quotient, Q_1Q_0, and a 16-bit remainder, R_0. (The interim remainder R_1, if there is one, disappears during the second divide operation.) If no overflow occurs, Q_1 is zero, and the result is returned as $0Q_0$ and R_0.

With this approach we can develop a divide procedure that *always* returns a valid quotient and remainder, regardless of overflow. Example 4-4 gives a procedure called DIVUO that does the job. This procedure divides a 32-bit dividend in DX (high word) and AX (low word) by a 16-bit divisor in BX, and produces a 32 bit quotient in DX.AX and a 16-bit remainder in DX.

Example 4-4. A Division Procedure That Accounts for Overflow

```
;       This divide procedure determines the correct quotient
;       and remainder, regardless of overflow. Enter with the
;       16-bit divisor in BX and the 32-bit dividend in DX
;       (high word) and AX (low word).
;       The 32-bit quotient is returned in BX:AX and the 16-bit
;       remainder is returned in DX.
;
DIVUO           PROC
                CMP     BX,0                    ;Divisor=0?
                JNZ     DVROK
                INT     0                       ; Yes. Abort the divide
DVROK:          PUSH    ES                      ;Save current ES
                                                ; register,
                PUSH    DI                      ; DI register
                PUSH    CX                      ; and CX register
                MOV     DI,0                    ;Fetch current INT 0
                MOV     ES,DI                   ; vector
                PUSH    ES:[DI]                 ; and save it on the
                PUSH    ES:[DI+2]               ; stack
                LEA     CX,OVR_INT              ;Make INT 0 vector
                MOV     ES:[DI],CX              ; point to OVR_INT
                MOV     CX,SEG OVR_INT
                MOV     ES:[DI+2],CX
                DIV     BX                      ;Perform the division
                SUB     BX,BX                   ;If no overflow, make
                                                ; BX zero
```

```
RESTORE:    POP   ES:[DI+2]         ;Restore INT 0 vector
            POP   ES:[DI]
            POP   CX                ;Restore original CX,
            POP   DI                ; DI
            POP   ES                ; and ES
            RET
;
; This interrupt service routine is executed if the divide
; operation produces overflow.
;
OVR_INT:    POP   CX                ;Modify return address
            LEA   CX,RESTORE        ; offset to skip
            PUSH  CX                ; SUB BX,BX
            PUSH  AX                ;Save current AX
                                    ; register
            MOV   AX,DX             ;Set up first dividend,
            SUB   DX,DX             ; 0-Y1
            DIV   BX                ;Q1 is in AX, R1 is in
                                    ; DX
            POP   CX                ;Fetch original AX into
                                    ; CX
            PUSH  AX                ;Save Q1 on the stack
            MOV   AX,CX             ;Set up second divi-
                                    ; dend, R1-Y0
            DIV   BX                ;Q0 is in AX, R0 is in
                                    ; DX
            POP   BX                ;Final quotient is in
                                    ; BX:AX
            IRET
DIVU0       ENDP
```

The DIVUO procedure is comprised of four steps:

1. Check whether the divisor in BX is zero. If so, call the Type 0 interrupt to abort the operation.
2. Change the Type 0 interrupt vector in absolute locations 0 (offset) and 2 (segment) so that it points to a new interrupt service routine—the one labeled OVR_INT in Example 4-4.
3. Perform the division. In the absence of overflow, the 8088 continues to the next consecutive instruction (SUB BX,BX). If overflow occurs, the 8088 activates the Type 0 interrupt service routine, which is now OVR_INT.
4. Restore the original Type 0 interrupt vector from values placed on the stack.

With or without overflow, the DIVUO procedure returns a 32-bit quotient (BX:AX) and a 16-bit remainder (DX). If no overflow occurs, BX is zero.

4.3 Square Root

In this final section we will develop a program to calculate the integer square root of a 32-bit unsigned number, using the classical method of successive approximations (also known as Newton's method). This method says that *if A is an approximation for the square root of a number N, then*

$$A1 = (N/A \pm A)/2$$

is a better approximation.

To illustrate, assume that the number whose root is to be determined has the value N. The first approximation is derived using the formula $(N/200) + 2$. To derive the second approximation, divide N by the first approximation, then average the two results. To form the third approximation, divide N by the second approximation and average, and so on. For example, to find the square root of 10,000:

```
N=1000; first approximation is (10,000/200)+2, or 52
   10,000/52=192,  (192+52)/2=122
   10,000/122=81,  (122+81)/2=101
   10,000/101=99,  (101+99)/2=100
   10,000/100=100
```

So the square root of 10,000 is 100. We know that 100 *is* the square root, rather than just another intermediate approximation, because 100 multiplied by itself produces the original number exactly.

This particular number, 10,000, happens to have an integer square root, but not many numbers do. The square root of 9999, for instance, is not an integer.

This means if we try to computerize the successive approximation method and use

root x root = number

as the "all done" criteria, the processor will loop through the approximation instructions indefinitely, because the square of the *integer* approximation will never be 9999. Surely there must be a better way to stop the processor once it has found the closest, or "best," square root for a number.

You can use several different methods to end the approximation procedure. The one that best suits your needs depends on how accurate your answer must be, and how much execution time you're willing to invest to derive that answer.

For instance, you can let the 8088 execute the loop 10 times, and assume that answer is accurate enough. Although it satisfies many applications, this method is rather arbitrary in nature. For a more precise solution, you can let the 8088 repeat the loop until it finds two successive approximations that are identical, or until they only differ by one. We take the latter approach in our software example.

Example 4-5 gives a procedure (SQRT32) that calculates the integer square root of a 32-bit number by successive approximations. In this procedure, the source number is contained in DX (high word) and AX (low word), and the 16-bit square root is returned in BX.

Example 4-5. Square Root of a 32-Bit Number

```
;   This procedure calculates the square root of a 32-bit
;   integer in DX (high word) and AX (low word), and
;   returns that square root as a 16 bit integer in BX.
;   The original number in DX:AX is not affected.
;
SQRT32      PROC
            PUSH    BP          ;Save contents of BP
            PUSH    DX          ; and source number DX:AX
            PUSH    AX
            MOV     BP,SP       ;BP points to AX on the stack
            MOV     BX,200      ;As a first approximation,
            DIV     BX          ; divide source number by 200,
            ADD     AX,2        ; then add 2
NXT_APP:    MOV     BX,AX       ;Save this approximation in BX
            MOV     AX,[BP]     ;Read source number again
            MOV     DX,[BP+2]
            DIV     BX          ;Divide it by last approximation
            ADD     AX,BX       ;Average the last two results
            SHR     AX,1
            CMP     AX,BX       ;Last two approximations
                                ; identical?
            JE      DONE
            SUB     BX,AX       ; No. Check for difference of 1
            CMP     BX,1
            JE      DONE
            CMP     BX,-1
            JNE     NXT APP
DONE:       MOV     BX,AX       ;Put result in BX
            POP     AX          ;Restore source number
            POP     DX
            POP     BP          ; and scratch register BP
            RET
SQRT32      ENDP
```

To begin, the procedure saves BP (which it uses as a stack pointer), DX, and AX on the stack, then copies the Stack Pointer (SP) into BP, so that BP points to AX on the stack. The first approximation is then derived using the formula (N/200) + 2. The instruction at NXT_APP is the beginning of a loop that extends to the label DONE.

With each pass through this loop, the 8088 calculates a new approximation by dividing the 32-bit source number (read from the stack) by the preceding approximation, then averaging these two results. It averages results with a right-shift operation, which effectively divides AX by 2. Using SHR instead of DIV here saves quite a bit of execution time—2 cycles for SHR versus a minimum of 80 cycles for DIV!

The procedure checks each new approximation against the last approximation, looking for approximations that are identical or differ by only 1 (+1 or -1). When any of these three conditions occur, the processor transfers to DONE; otherwise it goes back to NXT_APP to calculate a new approximation. At DONE, the 8088 puts the final square root value in BX, then pops the source number (AX and DX) and the original value of BP off the stack.

Study Exercise (answer on page 280)

1. An interesting observation made a few years ago gives us a simple way to calculate square roots. The observation is this: *The square root of an integer is equal to the number of successively higher odd numbers that can be subtracted from it.*

    Figure 4-2 shows how you can extract the square root of 25 using this method. (Skeptics will want to try a few additional cases of their own.) In this example, a total of five odd numbers—1, 3, 5, 7, and 9—can be subtracted from 25, so the square root is 5.

    Develop a procedure that employs this algorithm to take the square root of the 32-bit unsigned number in DX (high word) and AX (low word), and returns the 16-bit square root in BX. As with Example 4-5, AX and DX should be returned intact.

```
  25
-  1     Partial square root = 1
  24
-  3     Partial square root = 2
  21
-  5     Partial square root = 3
  16
-  7     Partial square root = 4
   9
-  9     Square root        = 5
   0
```

Figure 4-2. Obtaining a square root with odd-number subtractions.

5

Operating on Data Structures

There are almost as many ways to organize information in memory as there are kinds of information to be organized. These organizational techniques vary with the application, and have such names as lists, arrays, strings, and look-up tables. All of these are different kinds of *data structures*.

The subject of data structures can (and does) fill many volumes, so we can't hope to give it an exhaustive treatment in a book like this. Instead, we will concentrate on just three basic structures: *lists, look-up tables* and *text files*.

Lists hold units of data (one or more bytes or words), called *elements* arranged sequentially in memory. The sequence can be *consecutive*, where elements occupy adjacent memory locations, or *linked*, where each element includes an address "pointer" to the next element in the list. Moreover, the elements may be randomly arranged or in ascending or descending order.

Look-up tables are data structures which hold information (either data or addresses) that has a defined relationship to a known value. A telephone directory is a look-up table; knowing a name, you can look up an associated telephone number.

Text files consist of non-numeric information such as letters, reports, telephone lists, and other similar files.

5.1 Unordered Lists

In our ordered society, where telephone book listings are arranged alphabetically and house numbers increase or decrease as you go up or down a street, unordered *anythings* somehow seem bothersome. Still, not everything can be neatly ordered, so unordered lists remain a fact of life in many applications, particularly those that involve random data or data that change with time. For example, computerized weather stations probably store hourly temperature readings in unordered lists and most manufacturers probably log monthly shipping statistics in unordered lists.

Most lists are comprised of an element count byte (or word) and one or more data elements. When you work with a list, you generally want to either add elements, delete elements, or search for an element of a certain value. These operations are fairly easy to do.

1. To add an element, you simply store it at the end of the list and add 1 to the element count.
2. To delete an element, you just move the remainder of the list (all elements following the one to be deleted) upward in memory, then subtract 1 from the element count.
3. To search for an element value, you compare each element to the search value, starting with the first element in the list.

Adding an Element to an Unordered List

Procedure ADD _ TO _ UL, shown in Example 5-1, is a sample of the kind of program you would use to create an unordered list or to add an element to an existing unordered list. In this case, the list contains word values (either signed or unsigned).

ADD _ TO _ UL starts by reading the element count into CX, then scanning the data elements for the value in AX. If this value is already in the list (the final value of ZF is 0) the 8088 pops the starting address back into DI and returns. Otherwise, it adds the value to the end of this list and increases the element count by one.

How long does this procedure take to execute? That depends on the number of elements in the list and whether the search value is already in the list. The primary determinant is how many times the Scan String (SCASW) instruction is repeated. This instruction executes in $(9+19N)$ cycles, where N is the number of repetitions. Let's examine the timing for both cases— value is not in the list and value is in the list—for a list that has N data elements.

If the search value is in the list, the SCASW instruction executes N times. The remaining instructions in the procedure execute only once, and take 135 cycles. Therefore,

$$\text{Execution Time} = 9 + 19N + 135$$
$$= 19N + 144 \text{ cycles}$$

Thus, adding an element to a 100-element list takes 2044 cycles, or 429.24 μs.

If the search value is in the list, it should take the 8088 an average of N/2 comparisons to locate it, because 50 percent of the time a search value will lie in the lower half of the list and 50 percent of the time it will lie in the upper half of the list. This means the scan should theoretically take

$(9 + 9.5N)$ cycles. The remaining instructions in the procedure take an additional 78 cycles, Therefore, on the average,

Execution Time $= 9 + 9.5N + 78$
$= 9.5N + 87$ cycles

Thus, finding an element in an unordered 100-element list takes an average of 1037 cycles, or 217.77 μs.

Example 5-1. Adding an Element to an Unordered List

```
;  This procedure adds the value in AX to an unordered list
;  in the extra segment, if that value is not already in the
;  list. The starting address of the list is in DI. The
;  length of the list, in words, is in the list's first
;  location. DI and AX are returned unaltered.
;
ADD_TO_UL  PROC
           CLD                     ;Make DF=0, to scan forward
           PUSH   DI               ;Save starting address
           PUSH CX
           MOV    CX,ES:[DI]       ;Fetch word count
           ADD    DI,2             ;Make DI point to 1st data
                                   ; element
REPNE      SCASW                   ;Value already in the list?
           POP CX
           JNE    ADD_IT
           POP    DI               ; Yes. Restore starting
           RET                     ; address and exit.
ADD_IT:    STOSW                   ; No. Add it to end of list,
           POP    DI               ; then update element count.
           INC    WORD PTR ES:[DI]
           RET
ADD_TO_UL  ENDP
```

Deleting an Element from an Unordered List

To delete an element from an unordered list, you must find the element to be deleted, then move all subsequent elements up one position. Doing this, you write over the deletion "victim." With this element removed, there is one less element in the list, so you decrease the element count (the first location in the list) by one.

To illustrate, Figure 5-1A shows a list of bytes in memory. This list has six data elements, so the first location (LIST) holds the value 6. Figure 5-1B shows what the list looks like after the fourth element (the value 14) has been deleted. After the deletion, the list has only five data elements and the values 97 and 8 have moved up in memory, eradicating the deleted value.

The DEL_UL procedure in Example 5-2 performs just such an operation, using AX to specify the value to be deleted. As in Example 5-1, DI points to the start of the list.

The instructions that precede REPNE load the element count into CX and the address of the first data element into DI, then scan the list for the search value. These instructions are identical to those at the beginning of Example 5-1. If the search value is in the list (ZF = 1), the 8088 jumps to DELETE.

At DELETE, the processor takes one of two paths. If the element to be deleted is at the end of the list (CX contains zero), the 8088 jumps to DEC_CNT, where it simply decreases the list's element count. If the element to be deleted lies within the list, the loop at NEXT_EL moves all remaining elements up one position, overwriting the deletion victim. The element count is then decreased by one to reflect the deletion.

Finding Maximum and Minimum Values in an Unordered List

In working with a list of unordered data, you often want to find the largest and smallest values in the list. One way to find these values is to initially declare the first element as both the maximum and the minimum value, then compare each of the remaining elements in the list to those values. If your program finds an element whose value is less than the minimum, you make that value the new *minimum*. Similarly, if your program finds an element whose value is greater than the maximum, you make that value the new *maximum*.

The procedure MINMAX in Example 5-3 applies this method to an unordered list of unsigned word values. When you call this procedure, the starting address of the list must be in DI. MINMAX returns the maximum value in AX and the minimum value in BX.

This procedure comes in three parts. The first part calculates the number of comparisons to make (element count -1) and sets up the first data element as both the maximum and minimum norm. The second and third parts loop through the list searching for a new minimum and a new maximum, respectively. New minimums are loaded into BX; new maximums are loaded into AX.

This particular procedure processes lists of *unsigned* word values, but you easily modify it to search for the maximum and minimum in a list of *signed* words. In Example 5-3, simply replace JAE NOMIN with JGE NOMIN and replace JBE NOMAX with JLE NOMAX. For the reason behind this, see Table 3-11 in Section 3.7.

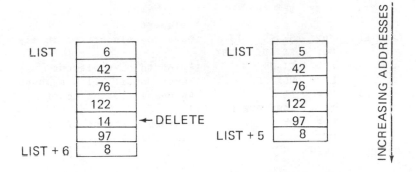

(A) BEFORE DELETION   (B) AFTER DELETION

Figure 5-1. How a deletion affects a list.

Example 5-2. Deleting an Element From an Unordered List

```
;   This procedure deletes the value in AX from an unordered
;   list in the extra segment, if that value is in the list.
;   The starting address of the list is in DI. The length of
;   the list, in words, is in the list's first location.
;   DI and AX are returned unaltered. CX is altered.
DEL_UL     PROC
           CLD                       ;Make DF=0, to scan forward
           PUSH   BX                 ;Save scratch register BX
           PUSH   DI                 ; and starting address
           MOV    CX,ES:[DI]         ;Fetch element count
           ADD    DI,2
REPNE      SCASW                     ;Value in the list?
           JE     DELETE             ; If so, go delete it.
           POP    DI                 ; Otherwise, restore registers
           POP    BX
           RET                       ; and exit.
;   The following instructions delete an element from the
;   list, as follows:
;       (1)    If the element lies at the end of the list,
;              delete it by decreasing the element count by 1.
;       (2)    Otherwise, delete the element by moving all
;              subsequent elements up by one position.
```

```
DELETE:    JCXZ  DEC_CNT          ;If (CX)=0, delete last
                                  ; element
NEXT_EL:   MOV   BX,ES:[DI]       ;Move one element up in list
           MOV   ES:[DI-2],BX
           ADD   DI,2             ;Point to next element
           LOOP  NEXT_EL          ;Repeat until all are moved
DEC_CNT:   POP   DI               ;Decrease element count by 1
           DEC   WORD PTR ES:[DI]
           POP   BX               ;Restore contents of BX
           RET                    ; and exit
DEL_UL     ENDP
```

Example 5-3. Maximum and Minimum Values in an Unordered List

```
; This procedure finds the maximum and minimum word values
; in an unordered list in the extra segment, and returns
; those values in AX and BX, respectively.
; The starting address of the list is in DI. The length of
; the list, in words, is in the list's first location.
; DI is returned unaltered.
;
MINMAX     PROC
           PUSH  DI               ;Save starting address
           PUSH  CX
           MOV   CX,ES:[DI]       ;Fetch word count
           DEC   CX               ;Get ready for count-1
                                  ; comparisons
           PUSH  CX               ;Save this count value
           MOV   BX,ES:[DI+2]     ;To start, make 1st element
           MOV   AX,BX            ; minimum and maximum
; These instructions find the minimum value in the list.
           ADD   DI,4             ;Point to 2nd element in the
           PUSH  DI               ; list and save this pointer
CHKMIN:    CMP   ES:[DI],BX       ;Compare next element to
                                  ; minimum
           JAE   NOMIN            ;New minimum found?
           MOV   BX,ES:[DI]       ; Yes.  Put it in BX
NOMIN:     ADD   DI,2             ;Point to next element
           LOOP  CHKMIN           ;Check entire list
; These instructions find the maximum value in the list.
           POP   DI               ;Point to 2nd element in the
                                  ; list
```

```
         POP   CX              ;Reload comparison counter
CHKMAX:  CMP   ES:[DI],AX      ;Compare next element to
                               ; maximum
         JBE   NOMAX           ;New maximum found?
         MOV   AX,ES:[DI]      ; Yes.  Put it in AX
NOMAX:   ADD   DI,2            ;Point to next element
         LOOP  CHKMAX          ;Check entire list
         POP DI
         POP CX
         RET
MINMAX   ENDP
```

5.2 Sorting Unordered Data

If your application involves plotting information versus time or text processing, you can probably accept the information in unordered form. However, in many applications it is more advantageous to have the information
arranged in increasing or decreasing order, because it is easier to analyze
that way.

How can you rearrange a list of unordered data? There is a considerable
amount of literature on this subject, but we'll concentrate on one common
sorting technique called the *bubble sort*. If you want to know about other
sorting techniques, D. E. Knuth's classic *The Art of Computer Programming.
Volume 3: Sorting and Searching* (Addison-Wesley) is an excellent starting
point.

Bubble Sort

The bubble sort technique is so named because it causes list elements to
"rise" upward in memory (to higher-numbered addresses), just as soap bubbles rise into the air. A bubble sort accesses elements in a list sequentially,
starting with the first element, and compare each element with the next
one in the list.

If the bubble sort program finds an element that is greater than its higher-
addressed neighbor, it exchanges these elements. The program then compares the next two elements, exchanges them if required, and so on. By the
time the 8088 gets to the last element in the list, the highest-valued element
will have "bubbled-up" to that final list position.

In sorting with this algorithm, the processor usually makes several passes
through the list, as you can see from the simple example in Figure 5-2. Here,
the first pass "bubbles" 50 to the end of the list and the next two passes
bubble 40 and 30 to the next highest positions. Therefore, this particular list
gets sorted in three passes.

Seeing pass-by-pass "snapshots" of the list, as in Figure 5 2, makes it easy for *you* to know when a list is entirely sorted, but how can a *computer* know when a list is sorted? Unless you give it a specific pass count, or tell it when to stop in some other way, the computer will go merrily along. executing pass after pass, ad infinitum. Since the number of sorting passes 'epends on the initial arrangement of the list, we have no way to provide an exact pass count in a program. As an alternative, we will set up a special indicator, called an *exchange flag,* that the computer can use to find out when to stop sorting.

The exchange flag is set to 1 before each sorting pass. Any sorting pass that includes an element exchange operation changes the exchange flag to 0. Therefore, after each pass the value of the exchange flags tells the computer whether to continue sorting. A value of 0 tells the computer to make another pass through the list. A value of 1 indicates the list is sorted, and tells the computer to stop sorting. Figure 5-3 shows a flowchart of the bubble sort algorithm.

As you can see, even if a list is already in order at the outset, it takes the processor one pass to deduce this fact. If one pass is the minimum, what *maximum* number of passes may you anticipate? Since the five-number list in Figure 5-2 was already partially sorted, we only made three sorting passes to put it in ascending order. One more pass is needed to detect that this list is indeed sorted, making four passes altogether.

If that same list had been initially arranged in descending order (the worst case), the processor would have made five passes through the list—four passes to sort the data and one additional pass to determine no further sorting was needed. From this observation we can state that *an N-element list takes from one to N passes to sort, with (N + 1)/2 passes being the average.*

A Bubble Sort Program

With the preceding background in bubble sort theory and a flowchart showing what needs to be done, we are prepared to write a program that sorts a list in memory. Example 5-4 shows a procedure (B _ SORT) that sorts a list of word values, although you can easily modify it to sort a list of bytes.

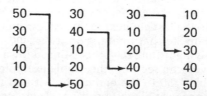

Figure 5-2. A bubble sort "bubbles" the largest numbers to the end.

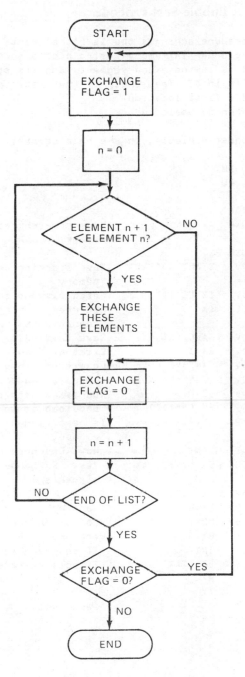

Figure 5-3. The bubble sort algorithm.

Example 5-4. A Bubble Sort Procedure

```
;  This procedure arranges the 16-bit elements of a list in
;  ascending order in memory, using bubble sort.
;  The list is in the extra segment, and its starting
;  address is in DI. The length of the list, in words, is in
;  the list's first location.
;  DI is returned unaltered.
;
;  Set up these variables in the data segment.
;
SAVE_CNT    DW  ?
START_ADDR  DW  ?
;
B_SORT  PROC
        PUSH AX                     ;Save scratch registers on
                                    ; stack
        PUSH BX
        MOV   START_ADDR,DI         ;Save starting address in
                                    ; memory
        MOV   CX,ES:[DI]            ;Fetch element count
        DEC   CX                    ;Get ready for count-1
                                    ; comparisons
        MOV   SAVE_CNT,CX           ;Save this value in memory
INIT:   MOV   BX,1                  ;Exchange flag (BX)=1
        MOV   CX,SAVE_CNT           ;Load count into CX
        MOV   DI,START_ADDR         ; and start address into DI
NEXT:   ADD   DI,2                  ;Address a data element
        MOV   AX,ES:[DI]            ; and load it into AX
        CMP   ES:[DI+2],AX          ;Is next element < this
                                    ; element?
        JAE   CONT                  ; No.  Go check next pair
        XCHG  ES:[DI+2],AX          ; Yes.  Exchange these
                                    ; elements
        MOV   ES:[DI],AX
        SUB   BX,BX                 ;  and make exchange flag 0
CONT:   LOOP  NEXT                  ;Process entire list
        CMP   BX,0                  ;Were any exchanges made?
        JE    INIT                  ; If so, make another pass
        MOV   DI,START_ADDR         ; If not, restore registers
        POP   BX
        POP   AX
        RET                         ; and exit.
B_SORT  ENDP
```

As usual, the list lies in the extra segment, and is addressed by DI. Furthermore, B_SORT uses BX to hold the exchange flag (which always holds a value of either 1 or 0) and AX to hold the element value that is being compared to the next element in the list.

The B_SORT procedure also uses two word variables in the data segment: *SAVE CNT* holds the comparison count (element count -1) and *START ADDR* holds the starting address of the list. B_SORT uses these variables to reinitialize CX and DI at the beginning of each new sort operation.

Despite the fact that it has a lot of instructions, the B_SORT procedure is quite simple. After calculating the values for SAVE_CNT and START_ADDR, the procedure initializes the exchange flag (BX — 1), the comparison counter (CX) and the element pointer (DI). At the label NEXT, the 8088 loads an element into AX, then compares it with the next element in memory.

If the second element is less than the first, the 8088 loads the second element into AX and stores the two elements back into memory, in reverse order. Because an exchange took place, the processor clears BX to zero. The LOOP instruction at CONT transfers control back to NEXT until the entire list has been processed.

When all elements have been compared, and exchanged as needed, a CMP instruction checks whether the exchange flag (BX) is zero. If it is, at least one exchange took place during the preceding sorting pass, so the 8088 jumps back to INIT to begin a new pass. Otherwise, if BX is still 1 after a sorting pass, the list is finally sorted, so the 8088 restores DI from START_ADDR and BX and AX from the stack, then returns.

Streamlining the Bubble Sort Program

The bubble sort procedure in Example 5-4 has one subtle, but noteworthy, deficiency: it sorts some elements needlessly. To be specific, during each sorting pass B_SORT compares every pair of elements in the list. However, each pass makes an element "bubble" higher in the list. The first pass bubbles the highest-valued element to the end of the list, the second pass bubbles the next highest-valued element to *its* proper position, and so on. Therefore, the elements at the end of the list are in their final (sorted) positions, so you may exclude them from subsequent sorting passes!

To exclude these sorted elements, *each pass through the list should involve one less comparison than the preceding pass.* We can make this happen by modifying our procedure so that the value in SAVE_CNT gets decremented before each new pass. Fortunately, this change is very easy to make.

To do this, you need to change the sixth, seventh and eighth instructions in the procedure to bring the decrement-count operation under the label INIT. You also need to add one more instruction after the decrement, to make the processor exit if SAVE_CNT is 0. Here is a summary of the changes:

	Old				Revised	
	DEX	CX			MOV	SAVE_CNT,CX
	MOV·	SAVE_CNT,CX		INIT:	MOV	BX,1
INIT:	MOV	BX,1			DEG	SAVE_CNT
					JZ	SORTED

Here, SORTED refers to the MOV instruction that restores the contents of DI from START_ADDR. The bubble sort procedure that has these changes (BUBBLE) is shown in Example 5-5.

For any given list, the BUBBLE procedure makes the same number of sorting passes as the B_SORT procedure in Example 5-4. But BUBBLE makes about half as many *comparisons* as B_SORT, so BUBBLE executes much faster than B_SORT.

For instance, in sorting 100 elements arranged in decreasing order, B_SORT makes 100 passes, with 99 comparisons in each pass—a total of 9,900 comparisons. By contrast, BUBBLE makes 100 passes, with 99 comparisons in the first pass and one comparison in the last pass, for an average of 50 comparisons—a total of 5,500 comparisons.

To compare BUBBLE to B_SORT, I sorted two lists of 16-bit elements using both procedures. Both lists were initially arranged in decreasing order. The first list, which had 500 elements, was sorted in 7.5 seconds by B_SORT and in 4.5 seconds by BUBBLE. The second list, which had 1000 elements, was sorted in 28.0 seconds by B_SORT and in 16.5 seconds by BUBBLE. Based on these tests, we can assume that *BUBBLE sorts a list about 40 percent faster than B_SORT.*

Incidentally, you will note that the sorting time rises dramatically as you take on longer lists. The bubble sort procedures presented here can sort lists up to 32K words long, but you'd better be prepared to wait if your lists are that extensive. In fact, a "worst-case" list of even 2000 words takes BUBBLE about 66 seconds to sort.

5.3 Ordered Lists

Now that you know how to sort a list, let us discuss how to search the list for a known value, and then see how to add and delete elements.

Searching an Ordered List

In Section 5.1 we learned that to locate a given value in an unordered list, you must search the list sequentially, element by element. This takes an average of N/2 comparisons for an N-element list. If a list is *ordered*, however, you can use any of several search techniques to find a value. For all but the shortest lists, most of these techniques are faster and more efficient than searching sequentially.

Example 5-5 A Better Bubble Sort Procedure

```
;  This procedure arranges the 16-bit elements of a list in
;  ascending order in memory, using bubble sort.
;  The list is in the extra segment, and its starting
;  address is in DI. The length of the list, in words, is in
;  the list's first location.
;  DI is returned unaltered.·
;
;  Set up these variables in the data segment.
;
SAVE_CNT      DW    ?
START_ADDR    DW    ?
;
BUBBLE    PROC
          PUSH  AX                    ;Save scratch registers on
                                      ; stack
          PUSH  BX
          MOV   START_ADDR,DI   ;Save starting address in
                                      ; memory
          MOV   CX,ES:[DI]            ;Fetch element count
          MOV   SAVE_CNT,CX          ;Save this value in memory
INIT:     MOV   BX,1                  ;Exchange flag (BX)=1
          DEC   SAVE_CNT             ;Get ready for count-1
                                      ; comparisons
          JZ    SORTED                ;Exit if SAVE_CNT is 0
          MOV   CX,SAVE_CNT          ;Load the compare count into CX
          MOV   DI,START_ADDR   ; and the start address into DI
NEXT:     ADD   DI,2                  ;Address a data element
          MOV   AX,ES:[DI]           ; and load it into AX
          CMP   ES:[DI+2],AX         ;Is next element < this
                                      ; element?
          JAE   CONT                  ; No.  Go check next pair
          XCHG  ES:[DI+2],AX         ; Yes.  Exchange these elements
          MOV   ES:[DI],AX
          SUB   BX,BX                 ; and make exchange flag 0
CONT:     LOOP  NEXT                  ;Process entire list
          CMP   BX,0                  ;Were any exchanges made?
          JE    INIT                  ; If so, make another pass
SORTED:   MOV   DI,START_ADDR   ; If not, restore registers
          POP   BX
          POP   AX
          RET                         ; and exit.
BUBBLE    ENDP
```

The Binary Search

One of the most widely-known search techniques for ordered lists is the *binary search.* Its name reflects the fact that it divides the list into a series of progressively shorter halves ("bi" is Latin for "two"), and eventually closes in on one element location in the list. A binary search starts in the middle of the list and determines whether the search value lies above or below that point. It then takes *that* half of the list and divides *it* into halves, and so on.

The flowchart in Figure 5-4 shows the steps you take to make a binary search on an ordered list. The result of the search is an address. If the search value is in the list, the address is that of the matching element. If the value is not in the list, the address is that of the last location to be compared. Of course, the program that performs this search must also return some kind of indicator that tells you whether the address reflects a successful search or an unsuccessful search.

Example 5-6 shows a procedure (B_SEARCH) you can use to search an ordered list of unsigned words. The fact that this procedure operates on words instead of bytes requires us to make a few changes to our basic algorithm. For one thing, because words lie two bytes apart in memory, we must include instructions that ensure the index is always a multiple of two; that is, an *even* value. For the same reason, we terminate a search, and declare it unsuccessful, when the index has decreased to 2 (instead of 0).

In this procedure, the search value is in AX and the starting address of the list is in DI. B_SEARCH returns the result address in SI, and CF tells whether the value was found (CF = 0) or not found (CF = 1).

The B_SEARCH procedure begins with a step that is not included in the basic binary search algorithm (see Figure 5-4): it compares the search value with the first and last elements in the list. If the search value is less than the first element or greater than the last element, or if the search value matches one of those elements, the procedure terminates without further ado. If these initial checks fail, however, the 8088 proceeds to the search operation, starting at SEARCH.

Once DI is saved in memory, the 8088 copies the index (word count) from the first location of the list into SI, and forces it to an even value, if appropriate. This index is added to DI to form the address of the middle element in the list, the starting point for the binary search. The 8088 then compares the search value to this middle element, and jumps to ALL_DONE if the values match. In the absence of a match, the 8088 determines whether to continue its search in the upper half of the list (the instructions that start at HIGHER) or the lower half of the list.

These paths are similar in that both .

1. Check whether the index is equal to 2. If it is, the 8088 sets CF to 1 (to indicate a nonmatch), then transfers to ALL_DONE to exit.
2. Divide the index by 2 by shifting it right one position.
3. Force the shifted index to an even value.

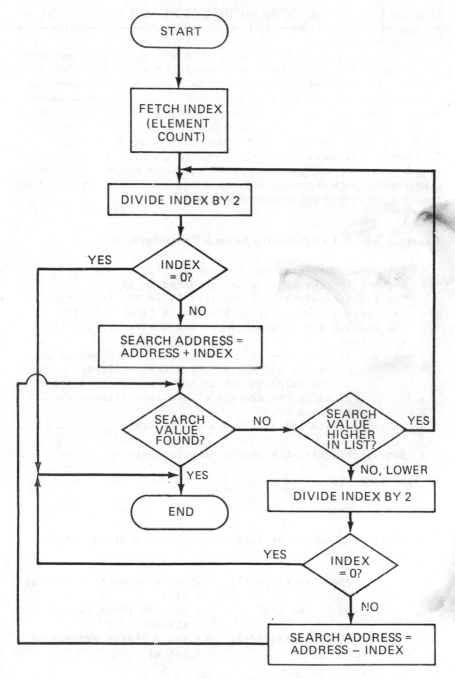

Figure 5-4. Binary search algorithm.

However, to search lower in the list, the 8088 subtracts the index (SI) from the current address (DI), whereas to search higher in the list, it adds the index to the current address.

This process repeats until the index has diminished to 2 or the search value is found. Either way, the procedure ends at ALL_DONE, where DI is moved to SI and the original contents of D1 are retrieved from memory.

How much more efficient is a binary search than a straight sequential, element-by-element scan — the kind we used in Examples 5-1 and 5-2? In his article "An Introduction to Algorithm Design" (Computer, February 1979, pp. 66-78), Jon L. Bentley stated that while a sequential search of an N-element list requires an average of N/2 comparisons, a binary search requires an average of $\log_2 N$ comparisons. Therefore, sequentially scanning a 100 element list will average 50 comparisons, but a binary search will do the same job with about seven comparisons!

Example 5-6. A 16-Bit Binary Search Procedure

```
;   This procedure searches an ordered list in the extra
;   segment for the word value contained in AX.
;   The starting address of the list is in DI. The length of
;   the list, in words, is in the list's first location.
;   The results are returned in SI and the Carry Flag (CF),
;   as follows:
;        1.  If the value is in the list, CF is 0 and SI
;            holds the address of the matching element.
;        2.  If the value is not in the list, CF is 1 and
;            SI holds the address of the last element to
;            be compared.
;   In either case, AX and DI are unaffected.
;
;   Set up this variable in the data segment.
;
START_ADDR  DW   ?
;
B_SEARCH    PROC
;
;   First find out if AX lies beyond the boundaries of the
;   list.
;
            CMP   AX,ES:[DI+2]    ;Search value < or = first
                                  ; el.?
            JA    CHK_LAST        ; No. Go check last
                                  ; element
            LEA   SI,ES:[DI+2]    ; Yes.  Fetch address of
                                  ; 1st el.
```

```
            JE      EXIT_1ST            ;If value=1st element, exit
            STC                         ;If value < 1st element,
                                        ; set CF
EXIT_1ST:   RET
CHK_LAST:   MOV     SI,ES:[DI]          ;Point to last element
            SHL     SI,1
            ADD     SI,DI
            CMP     AX,ES:[SI]          ;Search value > or=last
                                        ; el?
            JB      SEARCH              ; No.  Go search list
            JE      EXIT_LAST           ; Yes.  Exit if value=
                                        ; element
            STC                         ;If value > last element,
                                        ; set CF
EXIT_LAST: RET
;
;  Search for the value within the list.
;
SEARCH:     MOV     START_ADDR,DI       ;Save starting address in
                                        ; memory
            MOV     SI,ES:[DI]          ;Fetch index
EVEN_IDX:   TEST    SI,1                ;Force index to an even
                                        ; value
            JZ      ADD_IDX
            INC     SI
ADD_IDX:    ADD     DI,SI               ;Calculate next search
                                        ; address
COMPARE:    CMP     AX,ES:[DI]          ;Search value found?
            JE      ALL_DONE            ; If so, exit
            JA      HIGHER              ; Otherwise, find correct
                                        ; half
;
;  Search lower in the list.
;
            CMP     SI,2                ;Index=2?
            JNE     IDX_OK
NO_MATCH:   STC                         ; If so, set CF
            JE      ALL_DONE            ;  and exit
IDX_OK:     SHR     SI,1               ; If not, divide index by 2
            TEST    SI,1                ;Force index to an even
                                        ; value
            JZ      SUB_IDX
            INC     SI
SUB_IDX:    SUB     DI,SI               ;Calculate next address
            JMP     SHORT COMPARE       ;Go check this element
```

```
; Search higher in the list.
;
HIGHER:    CMP    SI,2              ;Index=2?
           JE     NO_MATCH          ; If so, go set CF and exit
           SHR    SI,1              ; If not, divide index by 2
           JMP    SHORT EVEN_IDX    ;  and go check next
                                    ;  element
;
; These are the exit instructions.
;
ALL_DONE:  MOV    SI,DI             ;Move compare address into
                                    ; SI
           MOV    DI,START_ADDR     ;Restore starting address
           RET                      ; and exit
B_SEARCH:  ENDP
```

Of course, you normally search a list for a value in order to *do* something to the matching element. Typically, you either want to add the value to the list or delete it from the list. Let's see how to perform those operations.

Adding an Element to an Ordered List

You add an element to an ordered list with four basic steps:

1. Find out where the value should be added.
2. Clear a location for the entry by moving all higher-valued elements down one position.
3. Insert the entry at the newly-vacated element position.
4. Add 1 to the list's element count, to reflect the insertion.

The B_SEARCH procedure we just developed gives us a good clue as to where the entry should be added, in that it returns the address of the element where the search stopped. To complete Step 1, we need to determine whether the entry must be inserted immediately *before* or immediately *after* that final search element. You make that determination by comparing the entry value to the final search element.

Example 5-7 shows a procedure (ADD_TO_OL) that performs the four steps we just listed. This procedure begins by calling B_SEARCH, to find out whether the entry value is already in the list. As you know, B_SEARCH returns an address in SI and a found/not-found indicator in the Carry Flag (CF).

Upon return from B_SEARCH, the ADD_TO_OL procedure interrogates CF, and exits if CF is 0 (since that means the entry is already in the list). If CF is 1, however, the procedure saves the last-searched address in BX and calculates the address of the last element (in CX). Subtracting the contents of SI from this address gives the number of bytes that must be moved higher in memory to make room for the insertion. Right-shifting this result (that is, dividing it by 2) tells you how many *words* must be moved. If the entry value is less than the last-compared element, that element must also be moved, so the move count (CX) is increased by 1.

At CHECK _ CNT, the 8088 checks whether the move count is zero. If it is, the entry is simply tacked on to the end of the list. Otherwise, this value must be inserted in the list, which requires moving all subsequent elements down one word position. The instructions starting at MOVE _ ELS move elements down, one by one, starting with the last word in the list. When all required elements have been moved, the 8088 inserts the entry (AX) in the newly-vacated slot, then increases the element count by 1.

Example 5-7. Adding an Element to an Ordered List

```
;  This procedure adds the value in AX to an ordered list in
;  the extra segment, if the value is not already in the
;  list.
;  The starting address of the list is in DI. The length of
;  the list, in words, is in the list's first location.
;  Neither AX nor DI is affected.
;  The B_ ARCH procedure (Example 5-6) is used to conduct
;  the search.
;
ADD_TO_OL   PROC
            PUSH  SI            ;Save SI and BX
            PUSH  BX
            CALL  B_SEARCH      ;Is the value in the list?
            JNC   GOODBYE       ; If so, exit
            MOV   BX,SI         ; If not, copy compare addr. to
                               ; BX
            MOV   CX,ES:[DI]    ;Find address of last element
            SHL   CX,1
            ADD   CX,DI         ; and put it in CX
            PUSH  CX            ;Save end address on the stack
            SUB   CX,SI         ;Calculate no. of words to be
                               ; moved
            SHR   CX,1
            CMP   AX,ES:[SI]    ;Should compare el. be moved,
                               ; too?
            JA    EXCLUDE
            INC   CX            ; Yes. Increase move count by 1
            JNZ   CHECK_CNT
EXCLUDE:    ADD   BX,2          ; No. Adjust insert pointer
CHECK_CNT:  CMP   CX,0          ;Move count=0?
            JNE   MOVE_ELS
```

```
                   POP   SI            ; If so, store value at end of
                                       ; list,
                   MOV   ES:[SI+2],AX
                   JMP   SHORT INC_CNT ; then go increase element
                                       ; count
     MOVE_ELS:     POP   SI            ;Start move at end of list
                   PUSH  BX            ;Save insert address on stack
     MOVE_ONE:     MOV   BX,ES:[SI]    ;Move one element down in list
                   MOV   ES:[SI+2],BX
                   SUB   SI,2          ;Point to next element
                   LOOP  MOVE_ONE      ;Repeat until all are moved
                   POP   BX            ;Retrieve insert address
                   MOV   ES:[BX],AX    ;Insert AX in the list
     INC_CNT,      INC   WORD PTR ES:[DI] ;Add 1 to element count
     GOODBYE:      POP   BX            ;Restore registers
                   POP   SI
                   RET                 ; and exit
     ADD_TO_OL     ENDP
```

Deleting an Element from an Ordered List

It's much easier to delete an element from an ordered list than it is to add one, because all the 8088 has to do is find the proper element, move all subsequent elements up one location, and decrement the element count.

Example 5-8 shows a typical delete procedure (DEL__OL), which uses B__SEARCH (see Example 5-6) to locate the intended deletion "victim." As usual, the starting address of the list is in DI and the value to be deleted is in AX.

If B__SEARCH locates the entry value in the list, the DEL__OL procedure uses its address, and the address of the end of the list, to calculate the number of words that must be moved up in memory. The four-instruction loop at MOVEM performs the move operation. When the 8088 has moved all words, it decreases the list's element count to reflect the deletion.

5.4 Look-Up Tables

Many applications use tables to hold a set of values that are required during processing. In some applications, these tables hold results of calculations that take a long time to derive mathematically, such as finding the sine of an angle. In other applications, tables hold parameters that have some defined relationship to a program input, but which cannot be calculated. For instance, you can't give the computer someone's name and expect it to calculate their telephone number.

Example 5-8. Deleting an Element From an Ordered List

```
;  This procedure deletes the value in AX from an ordered
;  list in the extra segment, if the value is in
;  the list.
;  The starting address of the list is in DI. The length of
;  the list, in words, is in the list's first location.
;  Neither AX nor DI is affected.
;  The B_SEARCH procedure (Example 5-6) is used to conduct
;  the search.
;
DEL_OL   PROC
         PUSH CX                ; Save registers
         PUSH SI
         PUSH BX
         CALL B_SEARCH          ;Is the value in the list?
         JC   ADIOS             ;If not, exit
         MOV  CX,ES:[DI]        ; If so, find address of last
                                ;   element
         SHL  CX,1
         ADD  CX,DI             ;   and put it in CX
         CMP  CX,SI             ;Is the last element to be
                                ; deleted?
         JE   CNT_M1            ; Yes.  Go decrement element
                                ; count
         SUB  CX,SI             ; No.  Calculate move count
         SHR  CX,1
MOVEM:   MOV  BX,ES:[SI+2]      ;Move one element up in list
         MOV  ES:[SI],BX
         ADD  SI,2             ;Point to next element
         LOOP MOVEM            ;Repeat until all are moved
CNT_M1:  DEC  WORD PTR ES:[DI]  ;Decrease element count by 1
ADIOS:   POP  BX               ;Restore registers
         POP  SI
         POP  CX
         RET                    ; and exit
DEL_OL   ENDP
```

Applications like these call for a *look-up table*. As the name implies, a look-up table obtains an item of information (an *argument*) based on a known value (a *function*).

Look-up tables can replace complicated or time-consuming conversion operations, such as extracting the square root or cube root of a number, or deriving a trigonometric function (sine, cosine, and so forth) of an angle. Look-up tables are especially efficient when a function covers only a small range of arguments. By using a look-up table, the microcomputer doesn't need to perform complex calculations each time a function is required.

Look-up tables reduce the execution time in all but the simplest relationships. (For instance, you wouldn't use a look-up table to store arguments that are always twice the value of a function?) But since look-up tables usually take up large amounts of memory storage space, they are most efficient in applications where you are willing to sacrifice memory space for execution speed.

Because look-up applications are so common, the 8088 instruction set has a special instruction, *Translate (XLAT)*, for this purpose. XLAT looks up a value in a byte table, using the contents of BX as a base address and the contents of AL as an index into the table, and returns the addressed byte value in AL. This section includes examples of look-up operations on both byte tables and word tables.

Look-Up Tables Can Replace Equations

You can save processing time and program development time by providing the results of complex equations in a look-up table. As typical examples, we will examine how look-up tables can provide the sine or cosine of an angle.

Sine of an Angle

As you probably recall from high school trigonometry, the sine of all angles between 0° and 360° can be graphed as shown in Figure 5-5A. Mathematically, you can approximate this curve with the formula

$$sine(X) = X - \frac{X^3}{3!} + \frac{X^5}{5!} - \frac{X^7}{7!} + \frac{X^9}{9!} \dots$$

It is possible to write a program to make this calculation, but such a program would probably require a couple of milliseconds to execute. If your application requires very precise sines, you may be forced to write such a program, but most applications are best served by an angle-to-sine look-up table instead.

If an application needs the sine of any angle between 0° and 360°, where the angle is an integer in degrees, how many sine values must the table contain? 360 sine values? No, we can get by with a table of only *91 sine values;* one value for each angle between 0° and 90°.

To understand how this can be so, look at Figure 5-5A again. If we call the leftmost quarter of the graph (angles from 0° to 90°) Quadrant I, we see that:

1. Sines in Quadrant II (91° to 180°) are the "mirror image" of those in Quadrant I.
2. Sines in Quadrant III (181° to 270°) are the "negative inverse" of those in Quadrant I.

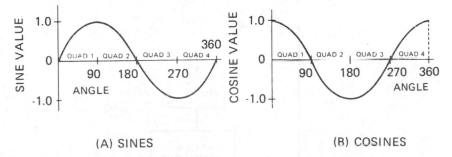

(A) SINES   (B) COSINES

Figure 5-5. The sines and cosines of angles between 0 and 360 degrees.

3. Sines in Quadrant IV (271° to 360°) are the "negative inverse, mirror image" of those in Quadrant I.

That is, the sines in Quadrants II, III, and IV bear some simple relationship to the sines in Quadrant I!

Therefore, if the values in Quadrant I are stored in a look-up table, your program can find the sine of an angle in any quadrant by making these conversions:

If the angle X is between	Take
0° and 90°	Sine(X)
91° and 180°	Sine(180 - X)
181° and 270°	-Sine(X - 180)
271° and 360°	-Sine(360 - X)

These relationships let us construct a flowchart for an angle-to-sine conversion program. This flowchart, shown in Figure 5-6, derives the sine as a sign-and-magnitude value. That is, the high-order bit of the result gives the sign of the sine (0 = positive, 1 = negative) and the remaining low-order bits give the magnitude of the sine—its absolute value.

Example 5-9 gives an angle-to-sine look-up procedure called *FIND_SINE*. This procedure accepts angles from 0° to 360° in AX and returns a 16-bit sign-and-magnitude sine value in BX. In the look-up table (SINES), the sines are stored as integers. You must divide them by 10,000 if you wish to use them as operands.

At the beginning of this procedure, the 8088 checks whether the angle is less than 181°. If it is, the processor jumps to SIN _ POS; otherwise it sets the most-significant bit of a sign register (CX) to 1—because sines above 180° are negative—and subtracts 180 from the angle.

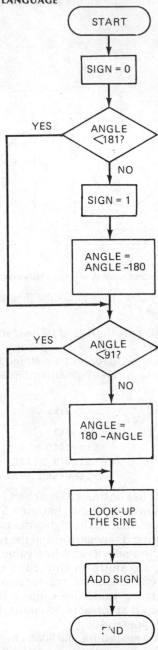

Figure 5-6. Flowchart for angle-to-sine conversion program.

Example 5-9. Look-Up the Sine of an Angle

```
;   This procedure returns the sine of the angle (0 to 360
;   degrees) contained in AX.
;   The sine, a sign-and-magnitude value, is returned in BX.
;   The contents of AX are unaffected.
;
;   Store this sine look-up table in the data segment.
;
SINES   DW    0,175,349,523,698,872        ;0-5
        DW    1045,1219,1392,1569,1736     ;6-10
        DW    1908,2079,2250,2419,2588     ;11-15
        DW    2756,2924,3090,3256,3420     ;16-20
        DW    3584,3746,3907,4067,4226     ;21-25
        DW    4384,4540,4695,4848,5000     ;26-30
        DW    5150,5299,5446,5592,5736     ;31-35
        DW    5878,6018,6157,6293,6428     ;36-40
        DW    6561,6691,6820,6947,7071     ;41-45
        DW    7193,7313,7431,7547,7660     ;46-50
        DW    7771,7880,7986,8090,8191     ;51-55
        DW    8290,8387,8480,8572,8660     ;56-60
        DW    8746,8829,8910,8988,9063     ;61-65
        DW    9135,9205,9272,9336,9397     ;66-70
        DW    9455,9511,9563,9613,9659     ;71-75
        DW    9703,9744,9781,9816,9848     ;76-80
        DW    9877,9903,9926,9945,9962     ;81-85
        DW    9976,9986,9994,9998,10000    ;86-90
;
;   This is the look-up procedure.
;
FIND_SINE   PROC
            PUSH   AX            ;Save AX
            PUSH   CX            ; and CX
            SUB    CX,CX         ;Initialize sign to 0
            CMP    AX,181        ;Angle < 181 degrees?
            JB     SIN_POS       ; Yes.  Continue with sign=0
            MOV    CX,8000H      ; No.  Set sign=1
            SUB    AX,180        ;  and subtract 180 from
                                 ;  angle
SIN_POS:    CMP    AX,91         ;Angle < 91 degrees?
            JB     GET_SIN       ; Yes. Go look up sine
            NEG    AX            ; No.  Subtract angle from
                                 ;  180
            ADD    AX,180
```

```
GET_SIN:    MOV    BX,AX            ;Make angle a word index
            SHL    BX,1
            MOV    BX,SINES[BX]     ; and look up the sine value
            OR     BX,CX            ;Combine sine with sign bit
            POP    CX
            POP    AX
            RET
FIND_SINE   ENDP
```

With tne correct sign now in Bit 15 of CX, the CMP instruction at SIN_ POS compares the input angle to 91°. If the angle is greater than or equal to 91°, its value must be subtracted from 180. You would expect to perform this subtraction with the instruction SUB 180,AX, but the 8088 does not offer this form of SUB.

That being the case, we make the subtraction by negating AX, then adding 180 to the result. The four instructions at GET_ SIN load the angle into BX, double it to form a word index, look up the sine in SINES, and OR it with the sign in CX.

The amount of time FIND _ SINE takes to return a sine value depends on which quadrant the look-up angle lies in. The execution times (excluding the time required to execute the CALL and RET instructions) are as follows:

- For angles between 0° and 90°, FIND _ SINE executes in 125 cycles, or 26.25 μs.
- For angles between 91° and 180°, FIND _ SINE executes in 120 cycles, or 25.20 μs.
- For angles between 181° and 270°, FIND _ SINE executes in 121 cycles, or 25.41 μs.
- For angles between 271° and 360°, FIND _ SINE executes in 116 cycles, or 24.36 μs.

Cosine of an Angle

As Figure 5-5B shows, the cosine curve is nothing more than the sine curve displaced one quadrant to the left. Therefore, the cosine of any given angle is equal to the sine of an angle that is 90° greater. That is,

cosine(X) = sine(X + 90)

Knowing this, we can use the SINES table in Example 5-9 to look up the cosine of an angle as well as its sine. Example 5-10 shows a procedure that does this. As with FIND _ SINE, you must divide the result of FIND _ COS by 10,000.

Incidentally, note that the sine and cosine curves are symmetric about the vertical axis, so negative angles have the same sines and cosines as their positive counterparts. For example, –25° has the same sine and cosine as + 25°. This means you can also use FIND _ SINE and FIND _ COS for angles between –1° and –360° by supplying the angle's *absolute value* in AX.

Example 5-10. Look-Up the Cosine of an Angle

```
; This procedure returns the cosine of the angle (0 to 360
; degrees) contained in AX.
; The cosine, a sign-and-magnitude value, is returned in
; BX.
; The contents of AX are unaffected.
; This procedure calls FIND_SINE (Example 5-9).
;
FIND_COS  PROC
          PUSH  AX                ;Save AX
          ADD   AX,90             ;Add 90 for use by FIND_SINE
          CMP   AX,360            ;Is the result greater than 360?
          JNA   GET_COS
          SUB   AX,360            ; If so, subtract 360
GET_COS:  CALL  FIND_SINE         ;Look-up the cosine
          POP   AX
          RET
FIND_COS  ENDP
```

Look-Up Tables Can Perform Code Conversions

Look-up tables can also hold coded data such as display codes, printer codes, and messages. Example 5-11 shows a procedure that performs multiple look-ups. It converts a hexadecimal digit in AL to its ASCII, BCD, and EBCDIC equivalents. The converted values are returned in CH, CL, and AH, respectively.

Example 5-11. Convert Hex to ASCII, BCD and EBCDIC

```
; This procedure converts a hexadecimal digit in AL to its
; ASCII, BCD and EBCDIC equivalents. The converted values
; are returned in CH, CL and AH, respectively.
; The contents of AL are unaffected.
;
; These look-up tables must be stored in the data segment.
;
ASCII  DB  '0123456789ABCDEF'
BCD    DB  0,1,2,3,4,5,6,7,8,9,10H,11H,12H,13H,14H,15H
EBCDIC DB  0F0H,0F1H,0F2H,0F3H,0F4H,0F5H,0F6H,0F7H
       DB  0F8H,0F9H,0C1H,0C2H,0C3H,0C4H,0C5H,0C6H
;
; Here is the conversion procedure.
;
```

```
CONV_HEX    PROC
            PUSH   BX           ;Save BX and DX
            PUSH   DX
            MOV    DL,AL         ;Save the input value in DL
            LEA    BX,ASCII      ;Look-up the ASCII value
            XLAT   ASCII
            MOV    CH,AL         ; and load it into CH
            MOV    AL,DL
            LEA    BX,BCD        ;Look-up the BCD value
            XLAT   BCD
            MOV    CL,AL         ; and load it into CL
            MOV    AL,DL
            LEA    BX,EBCDIC     ;Look-up the EBCDIC value
            XLAT   EBCDIC
            MOV    AH,AL         ; and load it into AH
            MOV    AL,DL         ;Restore registers
            POP    DX
            POP    BX
            RET
CONV_HEX    ENDP
```

When you transmit data between the computer and a printer, a display, or some other peripheral in the system, it takes a form called *ASCII* (for American Standard Code for Information Interchange). *EBCDIC* (Extended Binary-Coded Decimal Interchange Code) is a transmission protocol for data processing and communications systems.

Jump Tables

Some look-up tables contain *addresses* rather than data values. For instance, an error routine may use a look-up table to find the starting address of one particular message in a set of possible messages. Similarly, an interrupt service routine may use a look-up table to call one of several interrupt handler programs, depending on which type of service a particular device requested. Another routine may use a look-up table to call one of several control programs, based on which control key an operator pressed. In all of these applications (and there are many more), the look-up table that holds the addresses is called a *jump table*.

Example 5-12 illustrates a jump table that serves five different users in a multi-terminal computer system. This procedure, *SEL_USR*, interprets the contents of AL as a user identification code, and employs this code to call one of five user service procedures.

SEL_USR checks whether the entered code is valid then jumps to an error-printing routine if the code is greater than four. With a valid code, SEL_USR converts the code to an index then uses that index to perform an indirect jump to the appropriate user service procedure (USER0 through

USER4). The user's RET instruction returns control to the program that is
called SEL_USR.

Example 5-12. A Multi-user Selection Procedure

```
;  This procedure calls one of five user service procedures,
;  based on a user identification code in AL. The contents
;  of DI are affected; AL is unaffected.
;
;  This address table must be stored in the data segment.
;
U-ADDR    DD    USER0,USER1,USER2,USER3,USER4
;
;  Here is the selection procedure.
;
SEL_USR   PROC  FAR
          CMP   AL,4                    ;Invalid ID code?
          JA    U_ERROR
          MOV   DI,AL                   ; No. Move ID code into
          SHL   DI,1                    ;  DI and convert it to
          SHL   DI,1                    ;  an index
          JMP   FAR PTR U_ADDR[DI]      ;Jump to user procedure
U_ERROR:  ..                           (Print an error message)
          ..
          RET
SEL_USR   ENDP
```

5.5 Text Files

In the preceding sections we've been working with data structures that
contain numeric information. However, word processing and many other
applications involve manipulating nonnumeric information—primarily text
files.

Text files are lists whose elements are strings of ASCII characters. For
instance, a text file that holds personnel information for a corporation will
contain one element, or *record,* for each employee. In turn, each record has
several subrecords, or *fields,* that list the employee's name, identification
number, shift, pay rate, and so on. The 8088's string instructions are particularly convenient for manipulating text files.

You can manipulate text files with the same basic techniques you used to
manipulate numeric files. But because of their multi-record construction,
the programs that operate on text files must be somewhat different than
those that operate on simple byte or word lists. For instance, searching a text
file usually requires you to compare a *part* of each entry (perhaps just the

name field) to the search value, rather than comparing the entire entry. Similarly, bubble-sorting a text file requires you to compare single fields of adjacent entries, but move *entire* entries whenever an exchange is required.

As a simple example of a text file operation, let's look at a program that sorts a list of names and telephone numbers. The first location in the list holds a two-byte count of the name-and-number entries.

Each entry in the list is 42 bytes long, divided into three fields: a 15-byte surname, a 15-byte first name/initial, and a 12-byte phone number. Any unused bytes in a field are assumed to contain ASCII "blank" characters. Hence, a typical entry in the list looks like this:

```
DB    'CORNELL',8 DUP (' ')
DB    'RAY',12 DUP (' ')
DB    '728-732-8437'
```

(Of course, you normally build text files by typing them in from the keyboard, a subject we'll discuss in Section 6. For now, let's just assume the files are already in memory.)

Example 5-13 shows a procedure (PHONE _ NOS) that bubble-sorts a telephone list stored in the extra segment. Its construction is similar to that of the "better bubble sort" procedure in Example 5-5.

After saving affected registers on the stack, the procedure reads the entry count and the address of the first entry into two variables, SAVE _ CNT and FIRST_ ENT. The instructions between NEXT and SWAPEM set up and execute a CMPS operation. Here, DI points to an entry's surname field and SI points to the next entry's surname field, where these fields lie 42 bytes apart in memory.

The loop at SWAPEM exchanges two entries when needed. Since the entries are 42 bytes long, loop counter CX is initialized to 42. The remainder of the procedure is similar to Example 5-5.

Note that PHONE _ NOS does not account for duplicate surnames. Upon finding a duplicate surname, the procedure *should* look at the first name fields of those entries and perform a second, alphabetical sort to put them in order. You might like to modify Example 5-13 to do this.

Example 5-13. Sort a Telephone List

```
;  This procedure sorts a telephone list alphabetically. The
;  list is comprised of a word that holds a count of the
;  entries, followed by the individual entries. Each entry
;  is 42 bytes long, and divided into three fields: a
;  15-byte surname, a 15-byte first name/initial, and a
;  12-byte phone number.
;  The list is in the extra segment, and its starting
;  address (the address of the count word) is in DI.
;
```

```
;  Set up these variables in the data segment.
;
FIRST_ENT    DW   ?
SAVE_CNT     DW   ?
;
;  Here is the main procedure.
;
PHONE_NOS  PROC
             PUSH AX              ;Save scratch registers on
                                  ; stack
             PUSH BX
             PUSH CX
             PUSH BP
             PUSH DI
             PUSH SI
             PUSH DS
             CLD                  ;Set (DF)=0, to move
                                  ; forward
             MOV  CX,ES:[DI]      ;Fetch entry count
             MOV  SAVE_CNT,CX     ; and save this value in
                                  ; memory
             ADD  DI,2            ;Get address of first entry
             MOV  FIRST_ENT,DI    ; and save this address in
                                  ; memory
INIT:        MOV  BX,1            ;Exchange flag (BX)=1
             DEC  SAVE_CNT        ;Get ready for count-1
                                  ; compares
             JZ   SORTED          ;Exit if SAVE_CNT is. 0
             MOV  CX,SAVE_CNT     ;Load compare count into CX
             MOV  BP,FIRST_ENT    ; and first entry addr. into
                                  ; BP
NEXT:        MOV  DI,BP           ;Address one entry with DI
             MOV  SI,BP           ; and the next entry with SI
             ADD  SI,42
             PUSH CX              ;Save current compare count
             MOV  CX,15           ;Compare 15-byte surname
                                  ; fields
                                  ;Is next surname < this
                                  ; surname?
REPE         CMPS ES:BYTE PTR[SI],ES:[DI]
             JAE  CONT            ; No. Go check next pair
             MOV  CX,42           ; Yes. Exchange these
                                  ; entries
SWAPEM:      MOV  AL,ES:[BP]
             XCHG ES:[BP+42],AL
             MOV  ES:[BP],AL
             INC  BP
```

```
           LOOP   SWAPEM
           SUB    BX,BX         ;Set exchange flag=0
CONT:      POP    CX            ;Reload compare count
           ADD    BP,42         ;Point to next entry
           LOOP   NEXT          ; and go compare next two
                                ; names
           CMP    BX,0          ;Were any exchanges made?
           JE     INIT          ;  If so, make another pass
SORTED:    POP    DS            ;  If not, restore registers
           POP    SI
           POP    DI
           POP    BP
           POP    CX
           POP    BX
           POP    AX
           RET                  ;  and exit
PHONE_NOS  ENDP
```

Study Exercises (answers on page 280)

1. The list-processing procedures in this chapter don't check whether the list is empty (it has a count—which contains 0— but no data elements) before conducting an add, delete, or search operation. To rectify the situation, modify Example 5-1 so that AX becomes the first data element in a list if the list is empty. You can then use the modified procedure to build *new* lists as well as to add elements to existing lists.

2. Write a procedure that searches an ordered list for the value in AX and, if the value is found, *replaces* the contents of the matching element with the value in BX.

6

Using the System Resources

The preceding chapters of this book deal mostly with the 8088 microprocessor and, therefore, apply to any 8088-based microcomputer. In this chapter you learn how you can use the built-in resources of your IBM Personal Computer.

By "built-in resources" we primarily mean the software routines that form the computer's main operating program; its *Basic I/O System (BIOS)*. In essence, the BIOS routines maintain the system. Many of these routines are *interrupt service routines*, so you can call them from within your programs by simply executing appropriate INT instructions.

To begin, we'll take a brief look at the overall set-up of memory in the IBM Personal Computer, then discuss each of the useable interrupt service routines within the BIOS.

6.1 System Memory

Figure 6-1 shows how the 8088's one-megabyte address space is allocated in the IBM Personal Computer.

As you can see, the lowest-numbered 64K locations, 00000 through 0FFFF, hold the interrupt vector tables, the BIOS data area, and the Read/Write memory on the System Board. The next 192K bytes are available for add-on memory boards, which lets you expand the R/W memory to 256K bytes. The 384K bytes starting at location 40000 accept additional R/W add-on boards in a future version of the Personal Computer.

Following the future expansion area is a block of 16K locations that IBM reserves for future use. (There is another reserved 16K block at location F0000.) Location A4000 is the start of a 112K block of memory where the PC stores graphics and display data.

197

The 192K bytes starting at location C0000 currently provide ROM memory expansion, but may accept Read/Write memory in a future version of the Personal Computer. The 8K bytes starting at location F4000 are available for a user-provided program ROM chip, which you can plug into a spare socket on the System Board. Finally, the highest-numbered 40K locations, F6000 through FFFFF, hold the Cassette BASIC Interpreter and BIOS ROM chips.

If you have the IBM Small Assembler (ASM), the MACRO Assembler (MASM), or some other relocating assembler, you needn't worry where your programs and data are located in memory. However, you *must* understand the interrupt assignments in the system, so you can use the established interrupts and add others of your own.

Types 0 through 1FH, 20H through 3FH, and 80H through FFH are used by BIOS, DOS, and BASIC, respectively. This leaves 64 interrupts (Types 40H through 7FH) available for your use.

6.2 BIOS Interrupts

The BIOS interrupts give you a way to access the powerful built-in features of the IBM Personal Computer. Table 6-1 summarizes the BIOS interrupt vector assignments. As you can see, BIOS initializes most of these vectors. DOS initializes the rest.

In Table 6-1, the BIOS interrupts fall into five groups:

1. 8088 Interrupt Vectors (Types 0H through 7H)
2. 8259 Interrupt Vectors (Types 8H through 0FH)
3. BIOS Entry Points (Types 10H through 1AH)
4. User-Supplied Routines (Types 1BH and 1CH)
5. BIOS Parameters (Types 1DH, 1EH and 1FH)

In this section we will describe each interrupt group, and emphasize the interrupts you can use in your programs.

8088 Interrupt Vectors

The first five of these interrupts, Types 0 through 4, are required in every 8088- or 8086-based system. The only other initialized interrupt in this group, Type 5, is an interrupt that transmits the screen display to a printer.

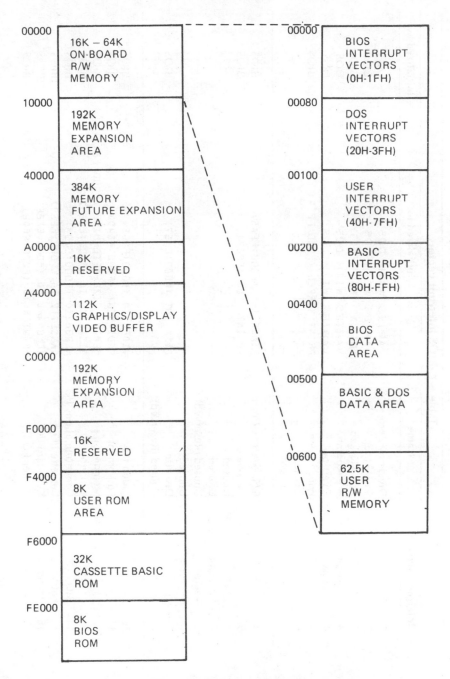

Figure 6-1. System memory map.

Table 6-1. BIOS interrupt vectors.

Interrupt Number		Name	Initialized to:	Initialized by
0		Divide by Zero	VARIES WITH DOS	DOS
1		Single Step	VARIES WITH DOS	DOS
2	8088	Non-Maskable	NMI_INT (F000:E2C3)	BIOS
3	Interrupt	Breakpoint	VARIES WITH DOS	DOS
4	Vectors	Overflow	VARIES WITH DOS	DOS
5		Print Screen	PRINT_SCREEN (F000:FF54)	BIOS
6		Unused	—	—
7		Unused	—	—
8		8253 System Timer	TIMER_INT (F000:FEA5)	BIOS
9		Keyboard	KB_INT (F000:E987)	BIOS
A	8259	Unused	—	—
B	Interrupt	Unused (Reserved)	—	—
C	Vectors	Unused (Reserved)	—	—
D		Unused	—	—
E		Diskette	DISK_INT (F000:EF57)	BIOS
F		Unused (Reserved)	—	—
10		Video I/O	VIDEO_IO (F000:F065)	BIOS
11		Equipment Check	EQUIPMENT (F000:F84D)	BIOS
12		Memory Size	MEMORY_SIZE_DETERMINE (F000:F841)	BIOS
13		Diskette I/O	DISKETTE_IO (F000:EC59)	BIOS
14	BIOS	Communications I/O	RS232_IO (F000:E739)	BIOS
15	Entry	Cassette I/O	CASSETTE_IO (F000:F859)	BIOS
16	Points	Keyboard I/O	KEYBOARD_IO (F000:E82E)	BIOS
17		Printer I/O	PRINTER_IO (F000:EFD2)	BIOS

Table 6-1. BIOS interrupt vectors (continued).

Interrupt Number		Name	Initialized to:	Initialized by
18	BIOS	Cassette BASIC	(F600:0000)	BIOS
19	Entry	Power-on Reset	BOOT_STRAP (F000:E6F2)	BIOS
1A	Points	Time of Day	TIME_OF_DAY (F000:FE6E)	BIOS
1B	User-Supplied	Keyboard Break	VARIES WITH DOS	DOS
1C	Routines	Timer Tick	DUMMY_RETURN (F000:FF53)	BIOS
1D		Video Initialization	VIDEO_PARMS (F000:F0A4)	BIOS
1E	BIOS	Diskette Parameters	DISK_BASE (F000:EFC7)	BIOS
1F	Parameters	Graphics character extension	0:0	BIOS

Type 0, Divide by Zero

This interrupt activates if a divide instruction (DIV or IDIV) produces a quotient that is too large to be contained in the result register (AL or AH). The routine this interrupt initiates aborts your program by simulating a Ctrl-Break. It then displays the message

```
Divide Overflow
```

and returns control to DOS.

Type 1, Single-Step

This interrupt lets you run programs one instruction at a time, so you can debug them. DOS makes this vector point to location 0060:00A4, which contains an Interrupt Return (IRET) instruction. Thus, a Type 1 interrupt simply jumps to the IRET instruction, then returns to the instruction that follows INT 1.

Does this mean you can't single-step through a program? Not at all. It just means you can't use the Type 1 interrupt to single-step. You can single-step with the DEBUG program's Trace (T) command, which executes one or more instructions, starting at the current CS:IP address or at a specified address.

Type 2, Non-Maskable Interrupt

For every interrupt but this one, you can force the processor to ignore interrupt requests. To do this, you set the Interrupt Enable Flag (IF) to 0 with a CLI instruction. The Type 2 interrupt is non-maskable; it *cannot* be "locked out" or disabled. For this reason, the Type 2 interrupt should be activated by some time-critical event, such as imminent loss of power.

In the Personal Computer, memory expansion options use the Non-Maskable Interrupt (NMI, for short) to report storage errors. The service routine this interrupt calls, NMI __ INT (starting address F000:E2C3), displays the error message *Parity Check 1* or *Parity Check 2*. Then it locks out interrupts with a CLI instruction and halts the processor with HLT.

Type 3, Breakpoint

This interrupt lets you execute a program until the 8088 encounters a specified "stop" address, or *breakpoint*. As with the Type 1 (Single Step) interrupt, DOS makes the Type 3 interrupt vector point to an IRET instruction at location 0060:00A4. The Type 3 interrupt is unimplemented because you can get breakpoints as an option with DEBUG's Go (G) command.

Type 4, Overflow

This interrupt performs an operation when the 8088 executes an Interrupt If Overflow (INTO) instruction. As with interrupt Types 1 and 3, DOS makes the Type 4 interrupt vector point to an IRET instruction. DOS doesn't pro-vide an interrupt service routine here because IBM can't anticipate what you wish to do in case of overflow. They leave this decision up to you.

Type 5, Print Screen

The final interrupt in this group, Type 5, is a BIOS feature. The service routine this interrupt calls, PRINT_ SCREEN (F000:FF54), saves the current cursor position, transmits the information on the screen to the printer, then restores the cursor. Hence, the Type 5 interrupt does exactly what the PrtSc key does, but does it under program control instead of from the keyboard.

Memory address 50:0 holds the status of the PRINT_ SCREEN routine, as follows:

- If the print operation is successful, location 50:0 contains 0.
- While the print operation is in progress, location 50:0 contains 1.
- If an error occurs during printing, location 50:0 contains 0FFH.

8259 Interrupt Vectors

The 8259 is an *interrupt controller chip* on the System Board. This chip accepts interrupt request signals (that is, maskable interrupts) from any of eight different devices in the system. Upon receiving an interrupt request, the 8259 passes the request signal and a device identifier code to the 8088.

Presently, only three devices are attached to the 8259: the 8253 system timer, the Keyboard and the 5-1/4" Diskette Drives. Hence, only three of the eight possible interrupt types are in use. IBM reserves two other interrupt types for future versions of the Personal Computer.

Type 8, 8253 System Timer

The 8253 is a chip on the System Board chip that maintains a count of the system clock. You can use this chip to calculate the elapsed time between two events or to generate time delays. The 8253 automatically issues a Type 8 interrupt every 0.0549254 seconds. This means it interrupts the 8088 about 18.2 times per second.

The service routine the Type 8 interrupt calls, TIMER_INT (F000:FEA5), keeps track of the 8253's interrupts while interrupts are enabled (that is, while IF=1), so you can use this count to keep track of the time of day. The time count is a 32-bit value in two 16-bit memory locations, TIMER_LOW (0040:006C) and TIMER_HIGH (0040:006E). The TIMER_INT routine also initiates a Type 1C interrupt at every "timer tick."

BIOS makes the Type 1C interrupt vector point to an IRET instruction, so you have to change the vector if you want the interrupt to do something useful. We'll discuss some possibilities for the Type 1C interrupt under *User-Supplied Routines* in this section. We'll also show you how to set and read the time count when we discuss the Type 1A (Time of Day) interrupt under *BIOS Entry Points.*

Type 9, Keyboard

BIOS activates this interrupt whenever you press a key. For all practical purposes, you should consider the Type 9 interrupt as a system interrupt. We'll discuss a more useful Keyboard interrupt, Type 16, later in this section, under *BIOS Entry Points.*

Type E, Diskette

BIOS uses this interrupt to communicate with attached Diskette Drives. As with Type 9, you should consider Type E as a system interrupt. We'll discuss a more useful Diskette interrupt, Type 13, under BIOS Entry Points.

BIOS Entry Points

Most of these interrupts perform input and output functions; they let you transfer information to or from the peripherals in the system. Other interrupts in this group let you determine the system configuration and the amount of R/W memory installed, and initialize and read the time of day.

Type 10, Video I/O

This interrupt performs any of 16 different I/O operations with the video display, based on a value in AH. The service routine it calls, VIDEO_IO (F000:F065), begins by loading the starting address of the video buffer (a block of memory that holds display characters) into the Extra Segment (ES) register.

If your PC has a Color/Graphics Monitor Adapter card, the video buffer is 16k bytes long and starts at location B8000. If your PC has a Monochrome Display/Printer Adapter card, the video buffer is 4K bytes long and starts at location B0000.

With ES properly initialized, VIDEO _ IO performs the specified I/O operation. Table 6-2 summarizes these operations, and shows you which registers are involved.

The 16 video I/O operations are divided into five groups;

- *CRT Interface Routines* let you set the video mode and the line limits for the cursor, set and read the cursor position, read the light pen position, and manipulate the active display page.
- *Character-Handling Routines* transfer characters to and from the display screen.
- *Graphics Interface Routines* let you transfer graphics dots to and from the screen, and change the colors.
- The *ASCII Teletype Routine* provides a Teletype-like interface to the Video Card. It writes a character to the display, then automatically advances the cursor.
- The *Read Video State Routine* reports the current mode, screen width, and display page.

You probably have questions about certain terms in Table 6-2 (for example, attribute and color value), if not about the service routines themselves. Hold your questions for now. They will (hopefully) be answered when we cover graphics in Chapter 7.

Type 11, Equipment Check

The Type 11 interrupt determines what options are attached to the system, and returns that information in AX. As Figure 6-2 shows, the interrupt service routine, EQUIPMENT (F000:F84D) determines the amount of memory on the System Board, the video mode, the number of disk drives, how many communication (RS-232) cards and printers are installed, and whether anything is connected to the Game I/O port.

This information is irrelevant if you are writing software for your own system because you already know what equipment you have. However, this feature is valuable if you develop general software that can run on anyone's system. Using the contents of AX, you can customize your software to run differently on various systems. To do this, you might use the contents of AX to call one of several system-specific procedures.

Type 12, Memory Size

The Type 12 interrupt determines how many 1K blocks of Read/Write memory are installed on the System Board, and returns this count in AX. Since this interrupt only inventories the System Board, and not add-on memory, it is probably useless for most applications.

Table 6-2. Video I/O operations with Type 10 interrupt.

(AH)	Operation	Additional Input Registers	Result Registers*
CRT Interface Routines			
0	Set video mode	(AL) = 0 40x25 B/W, Alpha (Default)	None
		= 1 40x25 Color, Alpha	
		= 2 80x25 B/W, Alpha	
		= 3 80x25 Color, Alpha	
		= 4 320x200 Color, Graphics	
		= 5 320x200 B/W, Graphics	
		= 6 640x200 B/W, Graphics	
1	Set cursor lines	CH Bits 0-4 = Start line for cursor	None
		CH Bits 5-7 = 0	
		CL Bits 0-4 = End line for cursor	
		CL Bits 5-7 = 0	
2	Set cursor position	(DH,DL) = Row,column (0,0) is upper left	None
		(BH) = Page number (0 for Graphics mode)	
3	Read cursor position	(BH) = Page number (0 for Graphics mode)	(DH,DL) = Row,column of cursor
			(CH,CL) = Current cursor mode
4	Read light pen position	None	(AH) = 0 Light pen switch not down or not triggered
			(AH) = 1 Valid light pen values in registers
			(DH,DL) = Row,column
			(CH) = Raster line (0-199)
			(BX) = Pixel column (0-319,639)

Table 6-2. Video I/O operations with Type 10 interrupt (continued).

(AH)	Operation	Additional Input Registers	Result Registers*
5	Select active display page (Alpha modes)	(AL) = New page value (0-7 for Modes 0 and 1; 0-3 for Modes 2 and 3)	None
6	Scroll active page up	(AL) = Number of lines. Input lines blanked at bottom of window. (AL) = 0 blanks entire window.	None
		(CH,CL) = Row,column of upper left corner of scroll	
		(DH,DL) = Row,column of lower right corner of scroll	
		(BH) = Attribute to be used on blank line	
7	Scroll active page down	(AL) = Number of lines. Input lines blanked at top of window. (AL) = 0 blanks entire window.	None
		(CH,CL) = Row,column of upper left corner of scroll	
		(DH,DL) = Row,column of lower right corner of scroll	
		(BH) = Attribute to be used on blank line	

Table 6-2. Video I/O operations with Type 10 interrupt (continued).

(AH)	Operation	Additional Input Registers	Result Registers*
Character-Handling Routines			
8	Read attribute/ character at current cursor position	(BH) = Display page (Alpha modes)	(AL) = Character read (AH) = Attribute of character read (Alpha modes)
9	Write attribute/ character at current cursor position	(BH) = Display page (Alpha modes) (BL) = Attribute of character (Alpha) 　 = Color of character (Graphics) (CX) = Count of characters to write (AL) = Character to write	None
10	Write character only at current cursor position	(BH) = Display page (Alpha modes) (CX) = Count of characters to write (AL) = Character to write	None
Graphics Interface			
11	Set color palette (320x200 graphics)	(BH) = ID of palette color (0-127) (BL) = Color value to be used with that color ID	None
12	Write dot	(DX) = Row number (CX) = Column number (AL) = Color value If Bit 7 of AL = 1, the color value is exclusive-ORed with the current contents of the dot	None

Table 6-2. Video I/O operations with Type 10 interrupt (continued).

(AH)	Operation	Additional Input Registers	Result Registers*
13	Read dot	(DX) = Row number (CX) = Column number	(AL) = Dot read

ASCII Teletype Routine for Output

(AH)	Operation	Additional Input Registers	Result Registers*
14	Write character to screen, then advance cursor	(AL) = Character to write (BL) = Foreground color (Graphics) (BH) = Display page (Alpha)	None
15	Read current video state	None	(AL) = Current mode — See (AH) = 0 for explanation (AH) = Number of character columns on screen (BH) = Current active display page

*Note: Besides the registers listed here, these routines preserve CS, SS, DS, ES, BX, CX, and DX. All other registers should be considered destroyed.

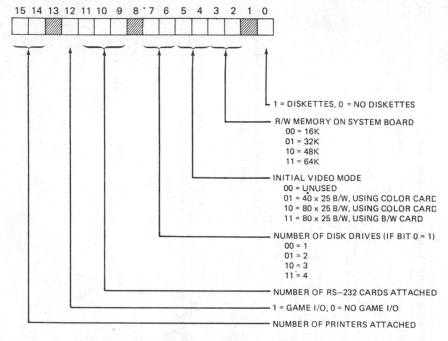

Figure 6-2. Equipment status returned in AX by interrupt 11.

Type 13, Diskette I/O

The DOS commands let you operate on *files* in the system. The Type 13 interrupt gives you a greater degree of control over disk information in that it lets you operate on individual *tracks* or *sectors* in the system.

As Table 6-3 shows, the Type 13 interrupt service routine, DISKETTE __ IO (F000:EC59), provides six different operations, based on a value that has been passed to the routine in AH. The read, write, and verify routines each return a status byte in AL (see Figure 6-3).

To format a track (AH = 5) you need to set up a table of address information in the extra segment. This table must contain 32 bytes; four bytes for each of the eight sectors on the track. The bytes are:

- Track number (0-39)
- Head number (0-1)
- Sector number (1-8)
- Number of bytes per sector
  (0 = 128, 1 = 256, 2 = 512, 3 = 1024)

Table 6-3. Diskette I/O operations with Type 13 interrupt.

(AH)	Operation	Additional Input Registers	Result Registers*
0	Reset diskette system	None	None
1	Read diskette status	None	(AL) = Diskette status (see Figure 6-3)
2	Read sectors into memory	(DL) = Drive number (0-3) (DH) = Head number (0-1) (CH) = Track number (0-39) (CL) = Sector number (1-8) (AL) = Number of sectors (1-8) (ES:BX) = Address of buffer	(AL) = Number of sectors read CF Bit = 0—Successful operation ·(AH) = 0 CF Bit = 1—Failed operation (AH) = Status (see Figure 6-3)
3	Write sectors from memory	Same as Read operation	Same as Read operation
4	Verify sectors	Same as Read operation, except (ES:BX) is not required	Same as Read operation
5	Format a track	(DL) = Drive number (0-3) (DH) = Head number (0-1) (CH) = Track number (ES:BX) = Sector information	Same as Read operation, except AL is not preserved

*Note: These routines preserve DS, BX, CX, DX, DI, SI, and BP.

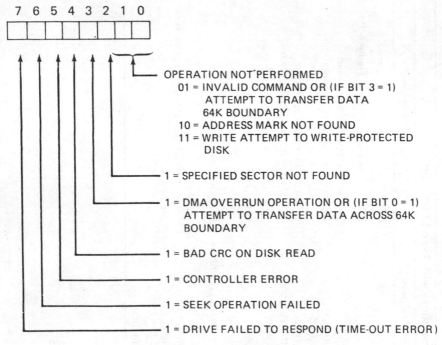

Figure 6-3. Diskette I/O status byte.

Clearly, these operations are not for the faint-hearted. Before attempting them, you'd better know what you're doing! For guidance, consult the IBM *Technical Reference* manual.

Type 14, Communications I/O

This interrupt lets you transmit and receive information through the IBM Personal Computer's communication port. For more information, see the description of the Asynchronous Communications Adapter in Chapter 2 of the IBM *Technical Reference* manual.

Type 15, Cassette I/O

The commands provided in BASIC let you operate on cassette *files* ir the system. The Type 15 interrupt gives you a greater degree of flexibility in that it lets you operate on 256-byte *blocks* of cassette information.

As Table 6-4 shows, the Type 15 interrupt service routine, CASSETTE __ IO (F000:F859), provides operations to turn the cassette motor on or off, and to transfer one or more blocks to or from cassette, as selected by a value in AH. Each block on cassette is comprised of the following fields:

1. An inter-block gap, called a *leader*, consisting of 256 bytes of all ones.
2. A synchronization bit (0), to identify the end of the leader.
3. A synchronization byte with the value 16H.
4. The 256-byte data block.
5. Two Cyclic Redundancy Check (CRC) bytes.
6. A *trailer*, four bytes of all ones.

The CRC bytes help ensure the validity of the data during a read operation. Briefly, as the computer writes a block of data to cassette, each data bit passes through a CRC register, which accumulates the bit values using a polynomial equation. After the 256th bit has been written to cassette, the CRC register contains a 16-bit value that reflects the contents of that particular block. These 16 bits are written onto cassette, as two bytes, immediately after the data block.

Subsequently, when the block is read, the disk controller calculates another CRC value based on the incoming bit values. At the end of the block, this value is compared with the two-byte CRC value read from cassette. If the two CRC's disagree, the cassette read program flags the operation as erroneous.

The *read block routine* turns on the cassette motor, waits until it comes up to speed, then searches for the leader. After sensing at least 64 all-ones bytes, the routine looks for the "sync" byte. If it doesn't find the sync byte, the routine resumes searching for a leader. (This sentence *cries* for a bad joke, but I resisted the temptation.) Otherwise, it reads the data block one bit at a time and assembles these bits into bytes. Each time the routine has accumulated a complete byte, it stores the byte into the data buffer pointed to by ES:BX then increments BX by one.

After reading all blocks, the routine reads the CRC bytes and compares it to the generated CRC value. If the two values do not match, the routine sets CF, loads 1 into AH, turns off the cassette motor, and exits.

The *write block routine* turns on the cassette motor and waits for it to come up to speed, then writes A 256-byte leader of all ones to the cassette. It follows this with a sync bit (0), a sync byte (16H) and the first data block. After this block, the routine writes a two-byte CRC value.

This sequence repeats until the byte count in CX has been satisfied, the data in the last block is less than 256 bytes, the routine "pads" the last block with blanks. With the operation completed, the routine turns off the cassette motor, then exits. Unlike the read routine, the write routine does not generate an error report.

Table 6-4. Cassette I/O operations with the Type 15 interrupt.

(AH)	Operation	Additional Input Registers	Result Registers
0	Turn cassette motor on	None	None
1	Turn cassette motor off	None	None

2	Read one or more 256-byte blocks from cassette	(CX) = Number of bytes to read
		(ES:BX) = Pointer to data buffer
			(DX) = Number of bytes read
			(ES:BX) = Pointer to last byte read +1
			CF Bit = 0—Successful operation
			    (AH) = 0
			CF Bit = 1—Error occurred
			    (AH) = 1 CRC error
			        = 2 Data transitions were lost
			        = 3 Data not found

3	Write one or more 256-byte blocks to cassette	(CX) = Number of bytes to write (ES:BX) = Pointer to data buffer	(CX) = 0 (ES:BX) = Pointer to last byte written +1

Type 16, Keyboard I/O

If your application is typical, you will probably use *this* interrupt more than any other. However, because of the wide range of possibilities it suggests, and the versatility that IBM built into this keyboard I/O system, we will postpone discussing this topic until Section 6.4, where it is given the detailed treatment it deserves.

Type 17, Printer I/O

I his interrupt lets you communicate with any of three printers in the system. With the three operations provided by the Type 17 interrupt service routine, PRINTER_IO (F000:EFD2), you can print a character, initialize the printer port, or read the printer status. These operations are summarized in Table 6-5. All three return a status byte in AH (see Figure 6-4), but affect no other registers.

Type 18, Cassette BASIC

This interrupt calls up cassette BASIC, which is installed in ROM in the IBM Personal Computer.

Type 19, Power-On Reset

This interrupt forces the computer to reinitialize from disk, if a disk drive is installed in the system. If the system does not have a disk drive, or if there is some error in either the drive or the Floppy Disk Controller card, the computer enters Cassette BASIC via the Type 18 interrupt.

Type 1A, Time of Day

Recall that the Type 8 interrupt maintains a count of the system clock, via interrupts from an internal 8253 System Timer. These interrupts occur at a rate of about 18.2 per second.

The Type 1A interrupt allows you to set this "time of day" count (a 32-bit unsigned number), or read its current value, so that you can use this facility to time events in your own programs. For instance, if you set the time count to 0, run a program, then read the time count, the resulting count value tells you how long the 8088 took to execute the program.

As usual, the value in AH selects the interrupt options. *To set the time count,* load 1 into AH and load the high and low 16 bits of the count into CX and DX, respectively. *To read the time count,* load 0 into AH. The high and low 16 bits of the count are returned in CX and DX, respectively. Further, the

Table 6-5. Printer I/O operations with Type 17 interrupt.

(AH)	Operation	Additional Input Registers	Result Registers
0	Print a character	(AL) = Character to be printed (DX) = Printer to be used (0-2)	(AH) = Status of operation (see Figure 6-4)
1	Initialize printer	(DX) = Printer to be used (0-2)	Same as print routine
2	Read printer status	(DX) = Printer to be used (0-2)	Same as print routine

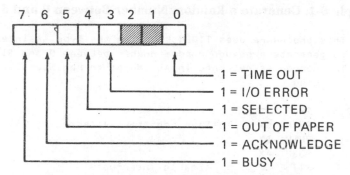

Figure 6-4. Printer I/O status byte.

contents of AL tell you whether 24 hours have passed since you last read the timer. If 24 hours have not passed, AL is zero; otherwise, AL is nonzero. Both options enable interrupts by setting the Interrupt Enable flag (IF) to 1.

As an example, this sequence calculates the execution time of a procedure called MY_PROC:

```
STI               ;Enable interrupts
SUB     CX,CX     ;Set time to zero
SUB     DX,DX
MOV     AH,1
INT     1AH
CALL    MY_PROC   ;Execute the procedure
MOV     AH,0      ;Read the execution time
INT     1AH
```

The execution time of MY_PROC is returned as a 32-bit value in CX and DX. To convert this value to a time in seconds, multiply it by 0.0549254 or divide it by 18.2.

Because the time count locations TIMER_LOW (0040:006C) and TIMER_HIGH (0040:006E) continually change, their contents—particularly those of TIMER_LOW—can be interpreted as a *pseudo random number!* Since the count locations are incremented, rather than changed randomly, they don't provide a true random number. But because the time value is incremented 18.2 times per second, it is "random" enough for most applications.

Being 16 bits long, TIMER_LOW can hold values between 0 and 65,535. To generate a random number between 0 and 51, as you might want to do in a card game program, you could read TIMER_LOW and divide it by 52. This division yields a *remainder* between 0 and 51.

Example 6-1 shows the procedure RAND_51, which returns a value between 0 and 51 in AH. Note that we strip off the high six bits of TIMER_LOW to prevent the division from overflowing.

Example 6-1. Generate a Random Number Between 0 and 51

```
;    This procedure uses TIMER_LOW from the Type 1A interrupt
;    to generate a pseudo-random number between 0 and 51.
;    The number is returned in AH. No other registers are
;    affected.
;
RAND_51   PROC
          PUSH    CX          ;Save registers affected by INT 1AH
          PUSH    DX
          PUSH    AX
          STI                 ;Enable interrupts
          MOV     AH,0        ;Read the timer
          INT     1AH
          MOV     AX,DX       ;Move low count into AX
          AND     AX,3FFH     ; and strip off high 6 bits
          MOV     DL,52       ;Divide low count by 52
          DIV     DL
          POP     DX          ;Restore AL
          MOV     AL,DL
          POP     DX          ;Restore DX and CX,
          POP     CX
          RET                 ; then exit
RAND_51   ENDP
```

User-Supplied Routines

Unlike the preceding interrupt types in this section, these two interrupts—
Type 1B (Keyboard Break) and Type 1C (Timer Tick)—are called by other
interrupt routines, rather than by your programs.

Type 1B, Keyboard Break

This interrupt is invoked whenever you press Ctrl-Break on the keyboard.
BIOS initializes the Type 1B interrupt to point to an IRET instruction, but
DOS re-initializes it to point to the same service routine as the Type 23 (Ctrl
Break Exit Address) interrupt. Type 23, a DOS interrupt, is described in
Section 6.3.

Type 1C, Timer Tick

This interrupt is invoked by TIMER_ INT, the routine that services the Type 8 (8253 System Timer) interrupt. Thus, like the Type 8 interrupt, the Type 1C interrupt executes about 18.2 times per second while interrupts are enabled.

The Type 1C interrupt lets you give the 8088 some additional task to do with each "tick" of the 8253. BIOS makes the Type 1C interrupt vector point to an IRET instruction at location DUMMY_ RETURN (F000:FF53), so the Type 1C interrupt does nothing unless you change this pointer.

What can you do with the Type 1C interrupt? Well, you might have it display the value of the time count in decimal, thereby creating a time of day clock. Or you might have Type 1C's service routine examine the time count, and do something when the time reaches a certain value. You can probably think of other possibilities for this useful interrupt.

BIOS Parameters

Types 1D (Video Initialization) and 1E (Diskette Parameters) are not interrupt vectors at all. They are addresses that point to data tables for the Type 10 and Type 13 interrupts, respectively.

6.3 DOS Interrupts

IBM reserves interrupt Types 20 through 3F for DOS use, but only Types 20 through 27 are currently implemented in the Personal Computer. Table 6-6 summarizes these interrupt assignments.

Most of these interrupts are called from DOS, rather than from your programs, so we won't discuss them here. (See Appendix D of the IBM *Disk Operating System* manual for details.) However, the Type 21 (Function Calls) interrupt has a variety of useful options for interacting with the keyboard, display, printer, disk, and asynchronous communications device. These are well described in Appendix D of the *DOS* manual, but to help you sort them out, Table 6-7 summarizes the various Type 21 function calls.

As a typical example, here is an instruction sequence that uses the Type 21 interrupt's function 9 option to display a character string called MESSAGE_1:

```
STI                     ;Enable interrupts
LEA    DX,MESSAGE_1     ;Put string offset in DX
MOV    AH,9             ;Select string-display option
INT    21H              ;Display the string
```

Table 6-6. DOS interrupts.

Interrupt Number	Name	Initialized to
20	Terminate Program	00B1:0011
21	Function Request	00B1:0015
22	Terminate Address	02F7:01FF
23	Ctrl-Break Exit Address	02F7:0204
24	Critical Error Handler	02B1:019B
25	Absolute Disk Read	0060:0015
26	Absolute Disk Write	0060:0018
27	Terminate, But Stay Resident	02B1:0187
28	Unused (Reserved)	
3F	Unused (Reserved)	

Table 6-7. Function calls with the Type 21 interrupt.

(AH)	Operation	Additional Input Registers	Result Registers
		Console Functions	
1	Wait for keyboard character, then display it (with Ctrl-Break check)	None	(AL) = Keyboard character
2	Display a character	(DL) = Display character	None
5	Print a character	(DL) = Print character	None
6	Read keyboard character (without Ctrl-Break check)	(DL) = 0FFH	(AL) = Keyboard character, if available = 0 if no character is available
6	Display a character	(DL) = Display character (value other than 0FFH)	None
7	Wait for keyboard character, but do not display it (without Ctrl-Break check)	None	(AL) = Keyboard character
8	Same as function 7, but with Ctrl-Break check	None	(AL) = Keyboard character
9	Display a string in memory	(DS:DX) = Address of string	None

Table 6-7. Function calls with the Type 21 interrupt (continued).

(AH)	Operation	Additional Input Registers	Result Registers
A	Read keyboard characters into buffer	(DS:DX) = Address of buffer	None
B	Read keyboard status (with Ctrl-Break check)	None	(AL) = 0FFH if character is available = 0 if no character is available
C	Clear keyboard buffer and call a keyboard input function	(AL) = Keyboard function number (1,6,7,8, or A)	Per keyboard function
Asynchronous Communications Functions			
3	Wait for asynchronous input character	None	(AL) = Asynchronous character
4	Output a character to asynchronous device	(DL) = Output character.	None
Disk Functions			
D	Reset disk	None	None
E	Select default drive	(DL) = Drive number (0 = A, 1 = B)	(AL) = Number of drives in system (2 for single-drive system)
F	Open file	(DS:DX) = Address of unopened file control block (FCB)	(AL) = 0 if file is found = 0FFH if file is not found

Table 6-7. Function calls with the Type 21 interrupt (continued).

(AH)	Operation	Additional Input Registers	Result Registers
11	Search for filename	(DS:DX) = Address of unopened FCB	(AL) = 0 if filename is found = 0FFH if filename is not found
12	Find next occurrence of filename	Same as function 11	Same as function 11
13	Delete file	Same as function 11	Same as function 11
14	Read sequential file	(DS:DX) = Address of opened FCB	(AL) = 0 if transfer successful = 1 if no data in record = 2 if insufficient space = 3 if partial record is read
15	Write sequential file	Same as function 14	(AL) = 0 if transfer successful = 1 if disk is full = 2 if insufficient space
16	Create a file	(DS:DX) = Address of unopened FCB	(AL) = 0 if file is created = 0FFH if no entry is empty
17	Rename a file	(DS:DX) = Address of filename to be re-named (DS:DX+11H) = Address of new filename	(AL) = 0 if rename successful = 0FFH if no match is found
19	Read default drive code	None	(AL) = Code of default drive (0=A, 1=B)
1A	Set disk transfer address	(DS:DX) = Disk transfer address	None

Table 6-7. Function calls with the Type 21 interrupt (continued).

(AH)	Operation	Additional Input Registers	Result Registers
1B	Read allocation table address	None	(DS:DX) = Address of file allocation table (DX) = Number of allocation units (AL) = Records/allocation unit (CX) = Size of physical sector
21	Read random file	(DS:DX) = Address of opened FCB	Same as function 14
22	Write random file	Same as function 21	Same as function 15
23	Set file size	(DS:DX) = Address of unopened FCB	(AL) = 0 if file size is set = 0FFH if no matching entry is found
24	Set random record field	(DS:DX) = Address of opened FCB	None
26	Create a new program segment	(DX) = New segment number	None
27	Read random block	(DS:DX) = Address of opened FCB	(AL) = 0 if transfer successful = 1 if end-of-file = 2 if wrap-around would occur = 3 if last record is a partial record
28	Write random block	Same as function 27	(AL) = 0 if transfer successful = 1 if insufficient space

Table 6-7. Function calls with the Type 21 interrupt (continued).

(AH)	Operation	Additional Input Registers	Result Registers
29	Parse a filename	(DS:SI) = Address of command line to parse (ES:DI) = Address of memory to be filled with an unopened FCB (AL) = 1 to scan off leading separators = 0 no scan-off	(AL) = 0 if parse successful = 1 if filename contains ? or * = 0FFH if drive specifier is invalid
Date and Time Functions			
2A	Get date	None	(CX) = Year (1980-2099) (DH) = Month (1-12) (DL) = Day (1-31)
2B	Set date	(CX) and (DX) = Date, in same format as function 2A	(AL) = 0 if date is valid = 0FFH if date is invalid
2C	Get time	None	(CH) = Hours (0-23) (CL) = Minutes (0-59) (DH) = Seconds (0-59) (DL) = 1/100 Seconds (0-99)
2D	Set time	(CX) and (DX) = Time, in same format as function 2C	(AL) = 0 if time is valid = 0FFH if time is invalid
Miscellaneous Functions			
0	Terminate program	None	None
25	Set interrupt vector	(DS:DX) = Vector address (AL) = Interrupt type	None

6.4   Keyboard I/O

As mentioned in Section 6.2, the Type 16 interrupt lets you communicate with the keyboard. This section covers the Type 16 interrupt operations in detail.

How the Keyboard Works

The keys on the Personal Computer's keyboard are arranged in three groups. In the center are the standard typewriter keys. To the left are ten function keys whose operations are user definable by software. To the right is a numeric keypad.

Most microcomputer keyboards are connected to the computer through an encoder chip, which translates each key depression into an associated eight-bit ASCII code. By contrast, each key you press on the IBM keyboard generates a key identifier (a *scan code*), which the BIOS program converts into a set of codes that IBM calls "Extended ASCII."

Extended ASCII encompasses one-byte ASCII character codes, plus additional codes for certain non-ASCII keyboard functions and functions that are handled within the keyboard routine or through interrupts. Because the IBM keyboard is regulated by software, rather than hardware, you can modify the operation of any or all keys to suit your own purposes.

The BIOS keyboard routine does its own buffering. When you press a key, BIOS puts the key's scan code and character code into a "keyboard buffer" table in memory for subsequent processing. With space for codes from 15 key strokes, the buffer is big enough, and the software fast enough, to keep up with the fastest typists. But if you somehow manage to press a key when the buffer is full, BIOS ignores the new key and beeps the speaker to let you know it has done so.

Character Codes and Scan Codes

Tables 6-8 and 6-9 list the scan codes and characters that are generated by the 83 keys on the keyboard. (These scan codes are listed in hexadecimal, so the keys are numbered 1 through 53 instead of 1 through 83.) We need two separate tables because keys that lie in the key pad area, 47-53 (71-83 in decimal), have meaning only in the base case, Num Lock, Alt, and Ctrl states.

Table 6-8 shows the characters returned by keys 1-46 in the base (unshifted) case and upper (shifted) case, and with the Ctrl or Alt key depressed. In the base case, upper case, and Ctrl state, most keys generate a standard ASCII code. Appendix B lists the codes that correspond to these keys.

Keys that have no ASCII value (such as Alt) return 0 as the character code. The 0 indicates that your program must examine a second code that identifies the actual function; see *Extended Codes* in this section. Other non-ASCII keys produce special operations, such as printing the screen information. These keys are summarized under *Special Key Combinations*. Finally, there are some key combinations that the BIOS keyboard routine does not recognize at all. The table identifies these combinations with the abbreviation N.A., for Not Available.

Extended Codes

As you will see when we discuss *Type 16 Interrupt Operations*, when you read a key value in from the keyboard, its character code and scan code are returned in AL and AH, respectively. Non-ASCII keys return a character code of 0 in AL and an *extended code* in AH. Table 6-10 lists the extended codes and shows which key combinations they represent. Note that extended codes between 3 and 53 correspond to the scan code.

Special Key Combinations

The following combinations of keys produce special effects:

- *Alt Ctrl Del* makes the keyboard routine initiate the equivalent of a system reset/reboot.
- *Ctrl Break* makes the keyboard routine invoke the Type 1B (Keyboard Break) interrupt. This key combination returns AL = 0 and AH = 0.
- *Ctrl Num-Lock* makes the keyboard routine wait for you to press any key but Num-Lock. This gives you a way to suspend an operation (e.g., list or print) temporarily, then resume.
- The keyboard routine treats the following keys as a group, rather than individually: Ctrl, Shift, Num-Lock, Scroll-Lock, Caps-Lock, and Ins. The service routine for the Type 16 (Keyboard I/O) interrupt returns a "shift status" byte that tells you when one of these keys is pressed.
- *Shift PrtSc* makes the keyboard routine invoke the Type 5 (Print Screen) interrupt.

Type 16 Interrupt Operations

The Type 16 (Keyboard I/O) interrupt calls KEY__BOARD IO, which starts at location F000:E82E. This routine lets you select from three different operations, based on a value in AH:

Table 6-8. Keyboard character codes for keys 1-46.

SCAN CODE	BASE CASE	UPPER CASE	CTRL	ALT
1	ESC	ESC	ESC	N.A.
2	1	½	N.A.	Note 1
3	2	@	NUL (Note 1)	Note 1
4	3	#	N.A.	Note 1
5	4	$	N.A.	Note 1
6	5	%	N.A.	Note 1
7	6	<	RS	Note 1
8	7	&	N.A.	Note 1
9	8	*	N.A.	Note 1
A	9	(	N.A.	Note 1
B	0	)	N.A.	Note 1
C	-	_	US	Note 1
D	=	+	N.A.	Note 1
E	Backspace	Backspace	DEL	N.A.
F	→|	|← (Note 1)	N.A.	N.A.
10	q	Q	DC1	Note 1
11	w	W	ETB	Note 1
12	e	E	ENQ	Note 1
13	r	R	DC2	Note 1
14	t	T	DC4	Note 1
15	y	Y	EM	Note 1
16	u	U	NAK	Note 1
17	i	I	HT	Note 1
18	o	O	SI	Note 1
19	p	P	DLE	Note 1
1A	[	{	ESC	N.A.

Table 6-8. Keyboard character codes for keys 1-46 (continued).

SCAN CODE	BASE CASE	UPPER CASE	CTRL	ALT
1B	]	}	GS	N.A.
1C	CR	CR	LF	N.A.
1D CTRL	N.A.	N.A.	N.A.	N.A.
1E	a	A	SOH	Note 1
1F	s	S	DC3	Note 1
20	d	D	EOT	Note 1
21	f	F	ACK	Note 1
22	g	G	BEL	Note 1
23	h	H	BS	Note 1
24	j	J	LF	Note 1
25	k	K	VT	Note 1
26	l	L	FF	Note 1
27	;	:	N.A.	N.A.
28	'	"	N.A.	N.A.
29	`	~	N.A.	N.A.
2A SHIFT	N.A.	N.A.	N.A.	N.A.
2B	\			FS	Note 1
2C	z	Z	SUB	Note 1
2D	x	X	CAN	Note 1
2E	c	C	ETX	Note 1
2F	v	V	SYN	Note 1
30	b	B	STX	Note 1
31	n	N	SO	Note 1
32	m	M	CR	Note 1
33	,	<	N.A.	N.A.
34	.	>	N.A.	N.A.

Table 6-8. Keyboard character codes for keys 1-46 (continued).

SCAN CODE	BASE CASE	UPPER CASE	CTRL	ALT
35	/	?	N.A.	N.A.
36 SHIFT	N.A.	N.A.	N.A.	N.A.
37	*	Note 2	Note 1	N.A.
38 ALT	N.A.	N.A.	N.A.	N.A.
39	SP	SP	SP	SP
3A CAPS LOCK	N.A.	N.A.	N.A.	N.A.
3B F1	NUL (Note 1)	NUL (Note 1)	NUL (Note 1)	NUL (Note 1)
3C F2	NUL (Note 1)	NUL (Note 1)	NUL (Note 1)	NUL (Note 1)
3D F3	NUL (Note 1)	NUL (Note 1)	NUL (Note 1)	NUL (Note 1)
3E F4	NUL (Note 1)	NUL (Note 1)	NUL (Note 1)	NUL (Note 1)
3F F5	NUL (Note 1)	NUL (Note 1)	NUL (Note 1)	NUL (Note 1)
40 F6	NUL (Note 1)	NUL (Note 1)	NUL (Note 1)	NUL (Note 1)
41 F7	NUL (Note 1)	NUL (Note 1)	NUL (Note 1)	NUL (Note 1)
42 F8	NUL (Note 1)	NUL (Note 1)	NUL (Note 1)	NUL (Note 1)
43 F9	NUL (Note 1)	NUL (Note 1)	NUL (Note 1)	NUL (Note 1)
44 F10	NUL (Note 1)	NUL (Note 1)	NUL (Note 1)	NUL (Note 1)
45 NUM LOCK	N.A.	N.A.	Pause (Note 2)	N.A.
46 SCROLL LOCK	N.A.	N.A.	Break (Note 2)	N.A.

Notes: 1. See *Extended Codes* (page 227).
        2. See *Special Key Combinations* (page 227).

Table 6-9. Keyboard character codes for keys 47-53.

SCAN CODE	NUM LOCK	BASE CASE	ALT	CTRL
47	7	Home (Note 1)	Note 1	Clear Screen
48	8	↑ (Note 1)	Note 1	N.A.
49	9	Page Up (Note 1)	Note 1	Top of Text and Home
4A	-	–	N.A.	N.A.
4B	4	← (Note 1)	Note 1	Reverse Word (Note 1)
4C	5	N.A.	Note 1	N.A.
4D	6	→ (Note 1)	Note 1	Adv Word (Note 1)
4E	+	+	Note 1	N.A.
4F	1	End (Note 1)	Note 1	Erase to EOL (Note 1)
50	2	↓ (Note 1)	Note 1	N.A.
51	3	Page Down (Note 1)	Note 1	Erase to EOS (Note 1)
52	0	INS	Note 1	N.A.
53	.	DEL (Notes 1,2)	Note 1	Note 2

Notes: 1. See *Extended Codes* (page 227).
2. See *Special Key Combinations* (page 227).

Table 6-10. Keyboard extended codes.

EXTENDED CODE	FUNCTION
3	NUL Character
F	←
10-19	ALT Q, W, E, R, T, Y, U, I, O, P
1E-26	ALT A, S, D, F, G, H, J, K, L
2C-32	ALT Z, X, C, V, B, N, M
3B-44	F1-F10 Function Keys (Base Case)
47	Home
48	↑
49	Page Up and Home Cursor
4B	←
4D	→
4F	End
50	↓
51	Page Down and Home Cursor
52	INS
53	DEL
54-5D	F11-F20 (Upper Case·F1-F10)
5E-67	F21-F30 (CTRL F1-F10)
68-71	F31-F40 (ALT F1-F10)
72	CTRL PRTSC (Start/Stop Echo to Printer)
73	CTRL ← (Reverse Word)
74	CTRL → (Advance Word)
75	CTRL END (Erase to End of Line)
76	CTRL PG DN (Erase to End of Screen)
77	CTRL HOME (Clear Screen and Home)
78-83	ALT 1, 2, 3, 4, 5, 6, 7, 8, 9, 0, -, = (Top row)
84	CTRL PG UP (Top 25 Lines of Text and Home Cursor)

- If AH = 0, KEYBOARD _ IO reads the scan code of the next key in the buffer into AH and its character code into AL, then advances the buffer pointer. If the buffer is empty, KEYBOARD _ IO waits for a key to be pressed before proceeding.
- If AH = 1, KEYBOARD _IO returns the status of the keyboard buffer in the Zero Flag (ZF). If the buffer is empty, ZF is 1. If any key codes are available for reading, ZF is 0. If ZF is 0, the next available character is in AX and the entry remains in the buffer.
- If AH = 2, KEYBOARD _ IO returns a keyboard status byte in AL. A description of this byte follows.

The KEYBOARD _ IO routine affects only AX and the flags.

The upper half of Figure 6-5 shows the arrangement of the the status byte returned by the AH = 2 option. In this byte (KB _ FLAG in the BIOS listing), the upper four bits tell you whether various keyboard modes are on (1) or off (0) and the lower four bits tell you whether the Alt, Ctrl, and shift keys are depressed.

The lower half of Figure 6-5 shows a companion byte to KB _ FLAG that gives additional keyboard status information. The KEYBOARD _ IO routine uses this second byte, KB _ FLAG _ 1, internally, but provides no way to read it into a register. However, KB _ FLAG _ 1 follows KB _ FLAG in the BIOS, so to find out how KB _ FLAG _ 1 is configured, you read the contents of location 418H (KB _ FLAG is at 417H).

The first KEYBOARD _ IO option, AH = 0, is convenient for setting up *interactive* operations with the computer. In such operations, you essentially tell the computer to wait for an operator to type something at the keyboard before proceeding. Let's take a look at some possible applications.

A Single-Key Read Operation

Suppose your program has displayed a prompt message that tells the operator to press either "Y" or "N" to signify Yes or No. A Y response makes the program jump to a set of instructions labeled YES and an N makes it jump to a set of instructions labeled NO. Any other key makes the program wait until it receives either a Y or an N. This sequence should do the job:

```
          STI              ;Enable interrupts
GET KEY:  MOV   AH,0       ;Read a key
          INT   16H
          CMP   AL,'Y'     ;Is it a Y?
          JE    YES        ; If so, jump to YES
          CMP   AL,'N'     ;Is it an N?
          JE    NO         ; If so, jump to NO
          JNE   GET_KEY    ;If it's neither, wait for Y or N
```

This particular program only accepts an upper-case Y or N. You can accept lower-case responses by adding the instructions CMP AL, 'y' and CMP AL 'n'.

A Multi-Key Read Operation

Quite often you want to read a series of keyboard characters into memory — perhaps a name, a command word, or a number. Example 6-2 shows a procedure that reads key strokes from the keyboard and puts their character codes into a buffer (KEY_CHARS) in the data segment. This procedure, READ_KEYS, continually accepts key strokes until the operator presses Return or enters 30 keys. READ _ KEYS returns the buffer's starting address in BX and the character count in CX.

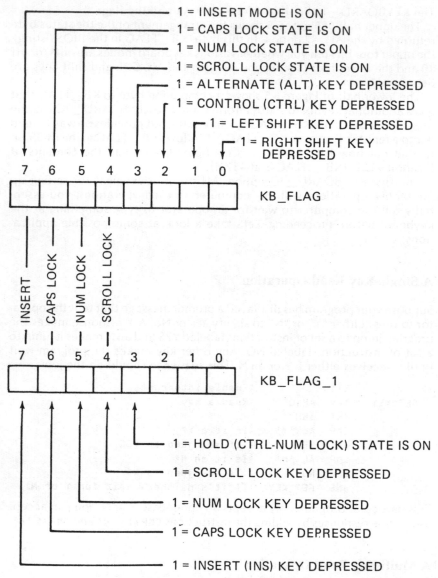

Figure 6-5. Keyboard I/O shift status bytes.

Display Keyboard Characters on the Screen

The READ_KEYS procedure has one glaring deficiency: it doesn't display the characters being entered. To remedy this problem, we can use the Type 10 (Video) interrupt to add a "screen echo" feature to READ_KEYS.

Table 6-2 shows two options that are applicable here: (AH) = 14 writes a character to the screen then advances the cursor, and (AH)=15 returns the number of the active display page in BH—an input required by the previous option. Example 6-3 shows the enhanced, screen-echoing version of READ_KEYS.

6.5 ASCII/Binary Code Conversions

As you now know, characters you enter from the keyboard are coded in ASCII. If these characters represent *numbers*, you must convert them to binary or BCD before the processor can operate on them. Likewise, before you can print a number on the printer or display it on the screen, you must convert that number to its ASCII form.

We address both problems in this section: how to convert an ASCII number to binary and how to convert a binary number to ASCII. (Converting from ASCII to BCD and from BCD to ASCII involves a similar procedure, but as the textbooks say, "That exercise is left to the reader.") To give due credit, the routines presented here are similar to those Ray Duncan developed for an article in Dr. Dobb's Journal (*16-Bit Software Toolbox*, September 1982, pp. 64-65).

Example 6-2. Read Keyboard Characters Into Memory

```
;   This procedure reads keyboard characters into a buffer
;   in memory until the operator presses Return or 30 keys
;   have been entered. Upon return, the buffer's starting
;   address is in BX and the character count is in CX.
;   Only BX and CX are affected.
;   Set up this buffer in the data segment.
;
KEY_CHARS   DB   30 DUP(?)
;
;   Here is the procedure.

READ_KEYS   PROC
            PUSH  AX              ;Save scratch registers
            PUSH  DI
            STI                   ;Enable interrupts
```

```
            MOV     DI,0                ;To start, key count is
                                        ; 0
            MOV     CX,30               ;Get ready for 30 key
                                        ; strokes
GET_KEY:    MOV     AH,0                ;Read the next key
            INT     16H
            CMP     AL,0DH              ;Is it a Carriage Return?
            JE      SAVE_CNT            ; If so, exit
            MOV     KEY_CHARS[DI],AL    ; Otherwise, store the
                                        ; code
            INC     DI                  ;  and update the key
                                        ;  count
            LOOP    GET_KEY             ;Go get next key
SAVE_CNT:   MOV     CX,DI               ;Final key count is in CX
            LEA     BX,KEY_CHARS        ;Buffer address is in BX
            POP     DI                  ;Restore registers
            POP     AX
            RET                         ; and exit
READ_KEYS   ENDP
```

Example 6-3. Read and Display Keyboard Characters

```
;   This procedure reads keyboard characters into a buffer
;   in memory until the operator presses Return or 30 keys
;   have been entered. As the characters are read, they
;   are echoed to the display. Upon return, the buffer's
;    tarting address is in BX and the character count is
;   in CX. Only BX and CX are affected.
;
;   Set up this buffer in the data segment.
;
KEY_CHARS   DB      30 DUP(?)
;
;   Here is the procedure.
;
READ_KEYS   PROC
            PUSH    AX                  ;Save scratch registers
            PUSH    DI
            STI                         ;Enable interrupts
            MOV     AH,15               ;Read display number
                                        ; into BH
            INT     10H
            MOV     DI,0                ;To start, key count is
                                        ; 0
            MOV     CX,30               ;Get ready for 30 key
                                        ; strokes
```

```
GET KEY:    MOV   AH,0              ;Read the next key
            INT   16H
            CMP   AL,0DH            ;Is it a Carriage
                                    ;  Return?
            JE    SAVE_CNT          ;  If so, exit
            MOV   KEY_CHARS[DI],AL  ;  Otherwise, store the
                                    ;  code
            INC   DI                ;  and update the key
                                    ;  count
            MOV   AH,14             ;Display the character
            INT   10H
            LOOP  GET_KEY           ;Go get next key
SAVE_CNT:   MOV   CX,DI             ;Final key count is in.
                                    ;  CX
            LEA   BX,KEY_CHARS      ;Buffer address is in BX
            POP   DI                ;Restore registers
            POP   AX
            RET                     ;  and exit
READ_KEYS   ENDP
```

Converting an ASCII String to Binary

Table 6-11 shows the relationships between the ASCII codes for the decimal digits 0 through 9 and their binary equivalents (shown in hexadecimal). As you can see from this table, the only ASCII values that interest us are those that lie between 30H and 39H. You should also note that the binary equivalent of a decimal digit is nothing more than the four least-significant bits of the ASCII code.

As we've said before, decimal numbers can be expressed as a series of digits multiplied by powers of 10. For example:

$$237 = (7 \times 1) + (3 \times 10) + (2 \times 100)$$

or

$$237 = (7 \times 10^0) + (3 \times 10^1) + (2 \times 10^2)$$

Since you enter digits of a number one at a time, an ASCII based decimal to binary conversion routine must include a multiply-by-10 operation. For instance, if the operator types in 93, the 9 must be multiplied by 10 before the 3 is added. In general, the conversion process proceeds in this order:

- For the first (most-significant) digit, the conversion routine must convert the digit to binary, by stripping off the four high-order bits of the ASCII code, and store the binary value as a partial result.
- For the second digit, and all subsequent digits, the conversion routine must convert the digit to binary, multiply the previous partial result by 10, then add the new digit to the product (thereby updating the partial result).

Table 6-11. The ASCII-based decimal characters.

ASCII Value (Hex.)	Binary Value (Hex.)
30	0
31	1
32	2
33	3
34	4
35	5
36	6
37	7
38	8
39	9

An ASCII-to-Binary Conversion Algorithm

You generally need to convert negative as well as positive numbers, and that number often includes a decimal point, so our conversion program must account for those characters, too. Figure 6-6 is a flowchart for an algorithm to convert an ASCII string in memory into a 2s-complement (signed) binary number. We assume that the number fits into 16 bits, so it's limits are −32768 and +32767.

At the beginning of this algorithm, the result and decimal count (number of digits to the right of the decimal point) are set to zero, and the program scans past any leading blanks. At this point, the program takes either of two paths; one for negative numbers, the other for positive numbers.

Both paths are nearly identical, except that a converted negative number is checked against −32,768 and must be complemented, whereas the converted positive number is checked against 32,767. The actual conversion is made by a procedure called CONV_AB, which is flowcharted in Figure 6-6A.

The CONV_AB procedure begins by checking whether the next string character is a decimal point. If it is, CONV_AB records the remaining character count as the decimal count, then advances the string pointer. If the next character is not a decimal point, CONV_AB checks whether it is a decimal digit. If this character is not a digit, CONV_AB declares it "invalid" and sets an error indicator, then returns to the main program.

Upon finding a valid digit character, CONV_AB multiplies the current partial result by 10, then converts the ASCII character to a digit and adds it to the result. If the addition produces a carry, CONV_AB sets the error indicator and returns. Otherwise it increments the pointer and returns to the decimal point checking instructions. When the entire string has been converted, CONV_AB returns to the main program.

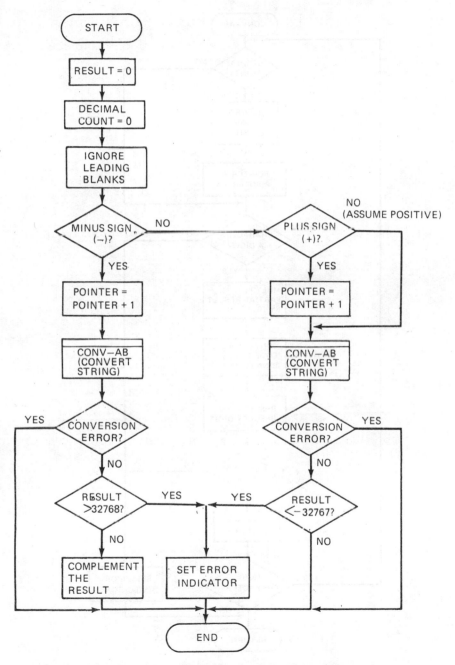

Figure 6-6. Algorithm to convert ASCII string to binary.

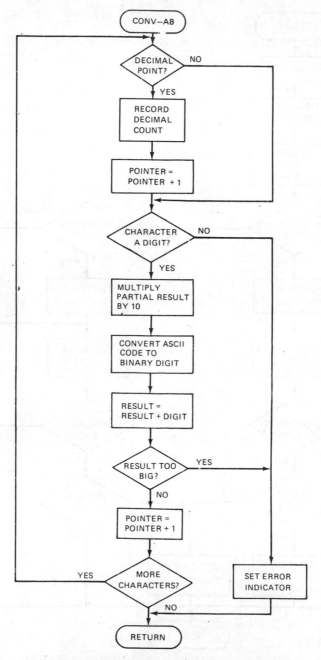

Figure 6-6A. Procedure called by ASCII conversion algorithm.

The ASCII-to-Binary Conversion Program

Example 6-4 shows a procedure that implements the preceding algorithm. This procedure (ASCII_BIN) converts an ASCII string in the data segment — perhaps one entered with the READ_KEYS procedure, Example 6-3 — into a 16-bit signed number.

ASCII_BIN requires the starting address of the string to be in BX and the character count (7 maximum) to be in CX. By no coincidence, these are the parameters returned by READ_KEYS. ASCII_BIN returns the 16-bit value in AX, the number of digits after the decimal point (if any) in DX and the address of the first non-convertible character in DI.

The value in DX indicates the magnitude of the result, and thereby tells you what *scale factor* to apply if you are operating on converted numbers of mixed sizes. The contents of DX can range from 0 (the result is an integer) to 5 (the result is a pure fraction). This means that if AX contains 1000H (decimal 4096) and DX contains 2, your result represents the decimal value 40.96.

If you wish to add this value to a previous result that returned DX equal to 3, you must first divide the previous result by 10. Similarly, if you wish to add 40.96 to a previous result that returned DX equal to 0, you must first divide the new result by 100.

Example 6-4. Convert an ASCII-Based Decimal Number to Binary

```
;   This procedure converts an ASCII string in the data
;   segment to its 16-bit, 2s-complement binary equivalent.
;   Upon entry, the starting address of the string must be
;   in BX and the character count must be in CX.
;   Upon return, the 16-bit value is in AX, a count of the
;   number of digits after the decimal point is in DX, and
;   the address of the first non-convertible character is in
;   DI. If the string contains more than seven characters,
;   or the number is out of range (greater than 32,767 or
;   less than -32,768), or the string contains a non-
;   convertible character, the Carry Flag (CF) is set to 1.
;   If the conversion was made without error, CF is 0 and DI
;   contains 0FFH. The contents of BX and CX are unaffected.
;
ASCII_BIN   PROC
            PUSH    BX              ;Save BX and CX
            PUSH    CX
            SUB     AX,AX           ;To start, result=0,
            SUB     DX,DX           ; decimal count=0,
            MOV     DI,0FFH         ; assume no bad
                                    ; characters
```

```
            CMP   CX,7                 ;String too long?
            JA    NO_GOOD              ; If so, go set CF and
                                       ; exit
BLANKS:     CMP   BYTE PTR [BX],' '    ;Scan past leading
                                       ; blanks
            JNE   CHK_NEG
            INC   BX
            LOOP  BLANKS
CHK_NEG:    CMP   BYTE PTR [BX],'-'    ;Negative number?
            JNE   CHK_POS
            INC   BX                   ; If so, increment
                                       ;  pointer,
            DEC   CX                   ;  decrement the count,
            CALL  CONV_AB              ;  and convert the
                                       ;  string
            JC    THRU
            CMP   AX,32768             ;Is the number too
                                       ;  small?
            JA    NO_GOOD
            NEG   AX                   ; No. Complement the
                                       ;  result
            JS    GOOD
CHK_POS:    CMP   BYTE PTR [BX],'+'    ;Positive number?
            JNE   GO_CONV
            INC   BX                   ; If so, increment
                                       ;  pointer,
            DEC   CX                   ;  decrement the count
GO_CONV:    CALL  CONV_AB              ;  and convert the
                                       ;  string
            JC    THRU
            CMP   AX,32767             ;Is the number too big
            JA    NO_GOOD
GOOD:       CLC
            JNC   THRU
NO_GOOD:    STC                        ; If so, set Carry
                                       ; Flag
THRU:       POP   CX                   ;Restore registers
            POP   BX
            RET                        ; and exit
ASCII_BIN   ENDP
;
;   This procedure performs the actual conversion.
;
CONV_AB     PROC
            PUSH  BP                   ;Save scratch registers
            PUSH  BX
```

```
            PUSH  SI
CHK_PT:     CMP   DX,0                  ;Decimal point already
                                        ; found?
            JNZ   RANGE                 ; If so, skip following
                                        ; check
            CMP   BYTE PTR DS:[BP],'.'  ;Decimal point?
            JNE   RANGE
            DEC   CX                    ; If so, decrement
                                        ;  count,
            MOV   DX,CX                 ;  and record it in DX
            JZ    END_CONV              ;  Exit if CX=0
            INC   BP                    ;  Increment pointer
RANGE:      CMP   BYTE PTR DS:[BP],'0'  ;If the character is
            JB    NON_DIG               ; not a digit...
            CMP   BYTE PTR DS:[BP],'9'
            JBE   DIGIT
NON_DIG:    MOV   DI,BP                 ; put its address in
                                        ;  DI,
            STC                         ; set the Carry Flag,
            JC    END_CONV              ; and exit
DIGIT:      MOV   SI,10                 ;The character is a
                                        ; digit,
            PUSH  DX
            MUL   SI                    ; so multiply AX by 10
            POP   DX
            MOV   BL,DS:[BP]            ; Fetch ASCII code,
            AND   BX,0FH                ; save only high bits,
            ADD   AX,BX                 ; and update partial
                                        ; result
            JC    END_CONV              ; Exit if result is too
                                        ; big
            INC   BP                    ; Otherwise, increment
            LOOP  CHK_PT                ; BP and continue
            CLC                         ;When done, clear Carry
                                        ; Flag
END_CONV:   POP   SI                    ;Restore registers
            POP   BX
            POP   BP
            RET                         ; and return to caller
CON_AB      ENDP
```

The Carry Flag (CF) tells you whether an error occurred during the conversion operation. If CF is 0, the results are valid, but if CF is 1, ASCII_BIN detected one of the following errors:

- If the string was longer than seven characters (CX > 7), AX and DX holds 0 and DI holds 00FFH.

- If an invalid character was found, DI holds its offset value.
- If a number was out-of-range (more negative than –32768 or more positive than 32767), AX is non-zero and DI holds 00FFH.

To check the validity of the answer, you should call ASCII_BIN in this context:

```
         CALL   ASCII_BIN    ;Call the conversion procedure
         JNC    VALID        ;Is the answer valid?
         OR     DI,DI        ; No. Find the error condition
         JNZ    INV_CHAR
         OR     AX,AX
         JNZ    RANGE_ER
         ..                  ; String was too long
         ..
RANGE_ER: ..                 ; Number out-of-range
         ..
INV_CHAR: ..                 ; Invalid character
         ..
VALID:   ..                  ;The answer is valid
         ..
```

Converting a Binary Number to ASCII

If you want to print a result or display it on the screen, you must first convert the result to ASCII. Fortunately, this is easy to do. To convert a 16-bit binary number to ASCII, you need a program that determines how many 1s, 10s, 100s, 1000s, and 10000s the number contains, and converts each of those counts into an ASCII character. You can either output the ASCII characters as they are calculated or store them in memory as a string and output them later with another program.

Example 6-5 shows a procedure (BIN_ASCII) that converts a 16-bit binary number in AX to an ASCII string in memory. To derive the various counts, BIN_ASCII successively divides the contents of AX by 10, then uses the remainder of each divide operation to build the string. BIN_ASCII returns the address of the converted string in BX and the character count in CX.

Example 6-5. Convert a Binary Number to an ASCII String

```
;    This procedure converts a signed binary number to a six-
;    byte ASCII string (sign plus five digits) in the data
;    segment. Upon entry, the number to be converted must be
;    in AX and the starting address of the memory buffer
;    must be in BX. Upon return, BX holds the address of
```

```
;    the converted output string and CX holds the length
;    of the string. Other registers are preserved.
;
BIN_ASCII    PROC
             PUSH   DX              ;Save affected registers
             PUSH   SI
             PUSH   AX              ;Save binary value
             MOV    CX,6            ;Fill buffer with spaces
FILL_BUFF:   MOV    BYTE PTR [BX],' '
             INC    BX
             LOOP   FILL_BUFF
             MOV    SI,10           ;Get ready to divide by 10
             OR     AX,AX           ;If value is negative,
             JNS    CLR_DVD
             NEG    AX              ; make it positive
CLR_DVD:     SUB    DX,DX           ;Clear upper half of dividend
             DIV    SI              ;Divide AX by 10
             ADD    DX,'0'          ;Convert remainder to ASCII
                                    ; digit
             DEC    BX              ;Back up through buffer
             MOV    [BX],DL         ;Store this char. in the string
             INC    CX              ;Count converted character
             OR     AX,AX           ;All done?
             JNZ    CLR_DVD         ; No. Get next digit
             POP    AX              ; Yes. Retrieve original value
             OR     AX,AX           ;Was it negative?
             JNS    NO_MORE
             DEC    BX              ; Yes. Store sign
             MOV    BYTE PTR [BX],'-'
             INC    CX              ;  and increase character count
NO_MORE:     POP    SI              ;Restore registers
             POP    DX
             RET                    ; and exit
BIN_ASCII    ENDP
```

Study Exercises (answers on page 281)

The following procedure is intended to output a string of characters to the display, at the current cursor position. The address of the string buffer is in SI and the character count is in CX. However, as written, the procedure may not work. Why not?

```
DSPLY_BUFF • PROC
             MOV    AH,15           ;Determine display page
             INT    10H
```

```
DISP_NEXT:      MOV     AH,14    ;Output string
                LODSB
                INT     10H
                LOOP    DISP_NEXT
                RET
DSPLY_BUFF      ENDP
```

2. Develop a procedure that uses the Type 1A (Time of Day) interrupt to generate a five-second delay.

3. Develop a procedure that uses the Type 16 (Keyboard I/O) and Type 1A interrupts to calculate the elapsed time between two key depressions.

4. To find out the *minimum* time between key strokes, execute the procedure in Exercise 3 and, when you see the cursor, press a key twice, quickly.

7

Graphics Made Easy

7.1 Display Modes

If you have standard IBM products, your display unit connects to the Personal Computer through either of two adapter cards. The *IBM Monochrome Display and Parallel Printer Adapter* connects to both the IBM Monochrome Display and the IBM 80 CPS Matrix Printer. The *IBM Color/Graphics Monitor Adapter* connects to a TV-frequency monitor, a standard TV set, or the IBM Color/Graphics Monitor.

Monochrome Adapter

The Monochrome Display and Parallel Printer Adapter can only display black and white *alphanumeric* characters—letters, numeric digits, and symbols—and block graphics characters. The adapter derives these characters by translating each of the 256 ASCII character codes into a display character. The adapter displays an 80-column by 25-line character grid on the screen based on the data in an on-card 4K-byte buffer.

Color/Graphics Adapter

The Color/Graphics Monitor Adapter can operate in two modes, Alphanumeric (just discussed) or Graphics, and can display in black and white or color. It provides 16 colors.

In the Alphanumeric mode, the adapter can generate an 80x25 character high-resolution display or a 40x25 character low-resolution display. The adapter card contains 16K bytes of memory, and can store up to four pages of 80x25 screen information or up to eight pages of 40x25 screen information.

In the Graphics mode the adapter divides the screen into a grid of dot-like picture elements, or *pels*, rather like a scoreboard or a time/temperature display. Resolutions of 320x200 pels and 640x200 pels are available. With 320x200 resolution, each pel may have one of four colors and the background may have any of 16 possible colors. The 640x200 resolution mode displays only black and white because the adapter needs the full 16K bytes of on-card storage to define the on or off states of the pels.

Due to the large number of pels and a palette of 16 colors, programming displays in the Graphics mode can be a somewhat complex task. (For more on Graphics mode graphics, refer to the IBM *Technical Reference* manual or to Ray Duncan's article "Graphics on IBM's Personal Computer"; *Dr. Dobb's Journal*; July 1982; pp. 32-43.) For this reason, we limit our discussion to programming in the Alphanumeric mode, using the block graphics characters in the character set. Further, all procedures in this chapter display in black and white on an 80x25 screen grid. You can easily modify them for color and/or the 40x25 grid, however.

7.2 How to Display Characters on the Screen

The Character Set

As mentioned in Section 7.1, when the display adapter is operating in the Alphanumeric mode (as it will be unless you've made a program switch to Graphics mode), it forms characters by converting ASCII codes in its on-card buffer into any of 256 display characters. Table 7-1 shows the relationship between the ASCII codes and the display characters.

As you can see, besides the usual complement of letters, numerals, and symbols, the character set includes letters used with foreign languages, Greek and math symbols, arrows, and a variety of other "goodies." For graphics applications, the characters that interest us most are those in columns 0, 1, A, B, and C. Admittedly, these simple block graphics characters do not let you create complex graphic displays that compete with Disney or George Lucas, but they are convenient for making sales demonstration programs, games, and flashy business programs.

Attributes

Besides an eight-bit code, every character position on the screen also has an eight-bit *attribute*, The attribute specifies the colors of the character and its background, the intensity of the colors, and whether the character is displayed continuously or blinking.

When you turn on power to the computer, the adapter card sets the entire screen to a normal intensity, non-blinking display, with white characters on a black background. However, by specifying new attribute values you can change these settings for any selected position(s) on the screen.

Table 7-2 shows the formats of the attribute byte for displaying characters in black and white. Chapter 2 of the IBM *Technical Reference* manual describes the attribute formats for displaying characters in color.

Display Commands

As mentioned in Section 7.1, all procedures in this chapter display characters on an 80-column by 25-line grid, in black and white. On the 80x25 grid, each character position has a vertical (row, or line) coordinate between 0 and 24, and a horizontal (column) coordinate between 0 and 79. Therefore, if you wish to display a character at the fourth position on the tenth line, you must specify a row coordinate of 3 and a column coordinate of 9. For convenience we can use the notation (3,9). Figure 7-1 shows this grid position.

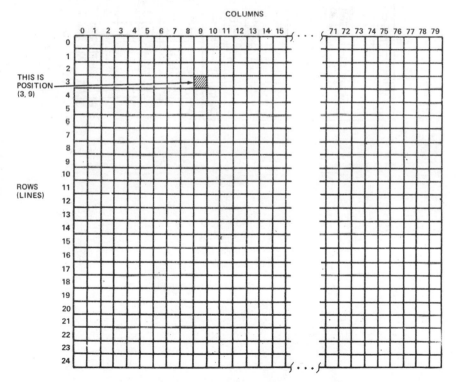

Figure 7-1: The 80x25 alphanumeric screen grid.

250   IBM PC ASSEMBLY LANGUAGE

Table 7-1. ASCII codes for display characters.

DECIMAL VALUE	HEXA DECIMAL VALUE	0	16	32	48	64	80	96	128	144	160	176	192	208	224	240
		0	1	2	3	4	5	6	8	9	A	B	C	D	E	F
0	0	BLANK (NULL)	►	BLANK (SPACE)	0	@	P	`	Ç	É	á	▒	└	╨	∝	≡
1	1	☺	◄	!	1	A	Q	a	ü	Æ	í	▒	┴		β	±
2	2	☻	↕	"	2	B	R	b	é	FE	ó	▒			γ	≥
3	3	♥	‼	#	3	C	S	c	â	ô	ú	│	├	└	π	≤
4	4	♦	¶	$	4	D	T	d	ä	ö	ñ	┤	─	└	Σ	∫
5	5	♣	§	%	5	E	U	e	à	ò	Ñ	╡		╔	σ	
6	6	♠	▬	&	6	F	V	f	å	û	ª	╢		╓	μ	÷
7	7	•	↨	'	7	G	W	g	ç	ù	º	╖	├		τ	≈
8	8	◘	↑	(	8	H	X	h	ê	ÿ	¿	╕			Φ	°
9	9	○	↓	)	9	I	Y	i	ë	Ö	⌐	╣	╔		Θ	•
10	A	◎	→	*	:	J	Z	j	è	Ü	¬	║		╔	Ω	·
11	B	♂	←	+	;	K	[	k	ï	¢	½	╗	╦	▓	δ	√
12	C	♀	∟	,	<	L	\	l	î	£	¼	╝		▓	∞	η
13	D	♪	↔	−	=	M	]	m	ì	¥	¡	╜		▓	Ø	²
14	E	♫	▲	.	>	N	^	n	Ä	Pts	«	╛		▓	∈	■
15	F	☼	▼	/	?	O	_	o	Å	ƒ	»	┐			∩	BLANK 'FF'

Table 7-2. Attribute byte for black and white display.

Video Setting	Bit Position								Character Color	Background Color
	7	6	5	4	3	2	1	0		
Normal	B	0	0	0	1	1	1	1	White	Black
Reverse Video	B	1	1	1	0	0	0	0	Black	White
Non-Display (Black)	B	0	0	0	0	0	0	0	Black	Black
Non-Display (White)	B	1	1	1	1	1	1	1	White	White

I = 0 normal intensity
= 1 high intensity

B = 0 non-blinking
= 1 blinking foreground

How can we communicate with the screen? We've already seen the programs that do this. They are the options provided by the Type 10 (Video I/O) interrupt, which were described in Section 6.2 and summarized in Table 6-2. For your convenience, Table 7-3 shows a subset of Table 6-2 that lists only the options that pertain to 80x25, Alphanumeric, black and white display operations. If you are using a Monochrome Display, which has only one display page and one video mode (80x25, black and white, Alphanumeric), disregard the commands and inputs printed in italic type.

Incidentally, note that Table 7-3 includes two separate write (output) options. Option (AH)=9 outputs a character and an attribute to the cursor location, whereas (AH)=10 outputs just a character and gives it whatever attribute you previously assigned to that grid position. The second option is especially convenient with black and white displays, where you rarely change the attribute.

A Simple Display Operation

With all of the information now at hand, we can begin generating some Alphanumeric graphics. To start, let's display a low-resolution diagonal "line" on the screen. This line starts at the upper left corner of the display and runs diagonally down the screen, advancing one row and one column at a time.

We'll use the "smile face" character (code 02 in Table 7-1) to form the line. Thus, the first face is at screen position (0,0), the next face is at (1,1), and so on.

Example 7-1 shows a procedure (DIAG_LINE) that plots this diagonal line. DIAG_LINE makes use of four options of the Type 10 interrupt. Option (AH)=15 reads the display page number into BH; (AH)=0 selects the 80x25, black and white, and Alphanumeric modes; (AH)=2 positions the cursor; and (AH)=10 sends the character to the screen.

7.3 Basics of Animation

The procedure in Example 7-1 produces a static display, one that does not move. The faces just sit there and smile at you (probably saying, "Have a nice day.") In many applications, however, you'd like to move the shapes around on the screen. That is, you'd like to animate them.

Producing animated affects is not as difficult as you might expect. In fact, it requires only five steps:

1. Plot the shape(s) on the screen.
2. Wait some period of time, so the shape is visible
3. Erase the shape.
4. Change the shape's row and column coordinates.
5. Repeat the process, starting at Step 1.

Table 7-3. Type 10 interrupt options for 80x25, black and white, and Alphanumeric.

(AH)	Operation	Additional Input Registers	Result Registers*
CRT Interface Routines			
0	Set video mode	(AL) = 2 80x25, black and white, and alphanumeric	None
2	Set cursor position	(DH,DL) = Row,column (0-24,0-79) (BH) = Page number (0-4)	None
3	Read cursor position	(BH) = Page number (0-4)	(DH, DL) = Row,column of cursor (CH,CL) = Current cursor mode
5	Select active display page	(AL) = New page value (0-3)	None
6	Scroll active page up	(AL) = Number of lines. Input lines blanked at bottom of window. (AL) = 0 blanks entire window. (CH,CL) = Row,column of upper left corner of scroll (DH,DL) = Row,column of lower right corner of scroll (BH) = Attribute to be used on blank line	None
7	Scroll active page down	Same as above, but input lines are blanked at top of window.	None

Table 7-3. Type 10 interrupt options for 80x25, black and white, and Alphanumeric (continued).

(AH)	Operation	Additional Input Registers	Result Registers*
Character-Handling Routines			
8	Read attribute/ character at current cursor position	(BH) = Display page (0-3)	(AL) = Character read (AH) = Attribute of character read
9	Write attribute/ character at current cursor position	(BH) = Display page (0-3) (BL) = Attribute of character (CX) = Count of characters to write (AL) = Character to write	None
10	Write character only at current cursor position	(BH) = Display page (0-3) (CX) = Count of characters to write (AL) = Character to write	None
ASCII Teletype Routine for Output			
14	Write character to screen, then advance cursor	(AL) = Character to write (BH) = Display page (0-3)	None
15	Read current video state	None	(AL) = Current mode. (See (AH) = 0 for explanation (AH) = Number of character columns on screen (BH) = Active display page

*Note: Besides the registers listed here, these routines preserve CS, SS, DS, ES, BX, CX, and DX. All other registers should be considered destroyed.

Example 7-1. Display a Diagonal Line

```
;   This procedure draws a diagonal line of "smile faces,"
;   starting at the upper left corner of the screen.
;   All registers are preserved.
;
DIAG_LINE   PROC
            PUSH    AX          ;Save registers
            PUSH    BX
            PUSH    CX
            PUSH    DX
            STI                 ;Enable interrupts
            MOV     AH,15       ;Set BH to active display page
            INT     10H
            MOV     AH,0        ;Select 80x25, B/W, Alphanumeric
            INT     10H
            MOV     CX,1        ;Character count=1
            MOV     DX,0        ;Start at row=0, column=0
SET_CRSR:   MOV     AH,2        ;Move cursor to next position
            INT     10H
            MOV     AL,2        ;Display character is smile face
            MOV     AH,10       ;Write character to the screen
            INT     10H
            INC     DH          ;Point to next row
            INC     DL          ; and column position
            CMP     DH,25       ;Bottom of screen?
            JNE     SET_CRSR
            POP     DX          ; Yes. Restore registers
            POP     CX
            POP     BX
            POP     AX
            RET                 ; and exit
DIAG_LINE   ENDP
```

You can generate a time delay (Step 2) by applying a sequence like the one you developed for Exercise 2 at the end of Chapter 6. Of course, instead of a five-second delay, you probably want a much shorter delay; perhaps 1/2 or 3/4 seconds.

To erase a shape from the screen you can either *clear* that portion of the screen, by writing blank (code 0) characters, or *replot* the shape in black. To replot a shape in black, you write a blank character with the (AH)=9 option or give the character a non-display attribute, (BL)=0, with the (AH)=10 option.

The Old Moving-Face Trick

Example 7-2 shows a new line-plotting procedure that "moves" the smile face down the diagonal in half-second spurts. The main procedure (MOVE _ FACE) has only four more instructions than the DIAG _ LINE procedure of Example 7-1. These call a half-second delay procedure (DLY_ HALF) and erase the face by sending a blank (0) code to the screen.

You might like to experiment with the effects of longer or shorter delays Or, to see (or *not see*) the face travel at maximum speed, you can eliminate the delay entirely.

7.4 Create Complex Shapes with Shape Tables

Multi-character shapes are almost as easy to manipulate as single character shapes, like our smile face. But multi-character shapes require multiple write operations; one for each character in the shape.

If a shape is formed from just two or three characters, and only one shape is to be displayed, you can probably program the job with a few successive output operations. However, if a shape contains many characters, or if you wish to display two or more shapes simultaneously, you should consider putting the shape parameters in a *shape table*.

A shape table is a data table that holds the character code, attribute, and row and column offset for each character in a display shape. You already know what the character code and attribute are. The row and column offsets give the vertical and horizontal displacements between the previous character and the current character. In this way, the offsets "tell" the computer how to draw the shape.

To illustrate, Figure 7-2 shows a "car" constructed with seven Alphanumeric characters. Moving left to right, the body consists of the letter R (code 52H), a 1/2-dots-on character (B1), and two solid boxes (DB); the first two characters are in reverse video, the second two are in normal video. The wheels, which are letter Os (4F), and the smile face (02) are in normal video. This shape was designed by my 11-year-old son, Ryan.

The parenthetical numbers in Figure 7-2 are the row and column offsets. The first character we plot is the letter R, so its offsets are (0,0). Next we plot the 1/2-dots-on character. It is on the same row as the R, but one column to the right of the R, so its offsets are (0,1). Similarly, the front characters of the body also have the offsets (0,1).

Example 7-2. Animate a Diagonal Line Display

```
;    This procedure moves a "smile face" diagonally down
;    the screen, starting at the upper left corner, with a
;    1/2-second delay between moves. All registers are
;    preserved.
;
MOVE_FACE   PROC
            PUSH  AX        ;Save registers
            PUSH  BX
            PUSH  CX
            PUSH  DX
            STI             ;Enable interrupts
            MOV   AH,15      ;Set BH to active display page
            INT   10H
            MOV   AH,0       ;Select 80x25, B/W, Alphanumeric
            INT   10H
            MOV   CX,1       ;Character count=1
            MOV   DX,0       ;Start at row=0, column=0
SET_CRSR:   MOV   AH,2       ;Move cursor to next position
            INT   10H
            MOV   AL,2       ;Display character is smile face
            MOV   AH,10      ;Write character to the screen
            INT   10H
            CALL  DLY_HALF   ;Wait a half-second,
            SUB   AL,AL      ; then erase the face
            MOV   AH,10
            INT   10H
            INC   DH         ;Point to next row
            INC   DL         ; and column position
            CMP   DH,25      ;Bottom of screen?
            JNE   SET_CRSR
            POP   DX         ; Yes. Restore registers
            POP   CX
            POP   BX
            POP   AX
            RET              ;  and exit
MOVE_FACE   ENDP
;
;    This procedure generates a one-half second delay.
;
DLY_HALF    PROC
            PUSH  CX        ;Save CX and DX
            PUSH  DX
```

```
            SUB   CX,CX     ;Set time to zero
            SUB   DX,DX
            MOV   AH,1
            INT   1AH
CHK_HALF:   MOV   AH,0      ;Read the time count
            INT   1AH
            CMP   DL,9      ;Has a half-second elapsed?
            JB    CHK_HALF
            POP   DX        ; Yes. Restore registers
            POP   CX
            RET             ;  and return to caller
DLY_HALF    ENDP
```

Next we draw the front wheel, which has offsets of (1,0) from the rightmost character of the body, and then the back wheel, which has offsets of (0,-3) from the front wheel. Finally, the smile face has offsets of (-2,1) from the back wheel.

Each of the shape parameters is a byte value, so the shape table must contain four bytes for each character. If you are operating on more than one shape table, each shape table should also include a byte that contains the character count. Figure 7-3 shows the shape table for the "car" we just described.

A General Display Procedure

Your display program can consist of a routine that loads shape table parameters into the appropriate registers, then issues the output command. You should put this routine in a loop, where it repeatedly executes until every character in the shape table has been output.

Example 7-3 shows a procedure that erases a selected range of lines on the screen, or the entire screen, based on the row limits you enter in CH and DH. To erase the entire screen, as you normally do before displaying shapes, use the values (CH)=0 and (DH)=24.

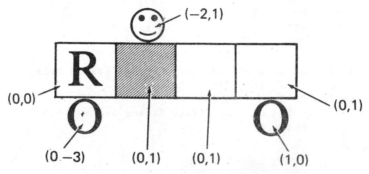

Figure 7-2. Row and column offsets for an alphanumeric "car."

Example 7-3. Clear Lines on the Display Screen

```
;    This procedure clears a portion of the screen, or the
;    entire screen, and gives all affected lines the normal
;    white-on-black attribute.
;    Enter with the upper line number in CH and the lower
;    line number in DH. All registers are preserved.
;
CLEAR_SCREEN  PROC
              PUSH  AX        ;Save-registers
              PUSH  BX
              PUSH  CX
              PUSH  DX
              STI             ;Enable interrupts
              MOV   AH,0       ;Select 80x25, B/W, Alphanumeric
              INT   10H
              MOV   AH,6       ;Clear the screen with the scroll
              MOV   AL,0       ; up option
              MOV   CX,0
              MOV   DH,24
              MOV   DL,79
              MOV   BH,7
              INT   10H
              POP   DX        ;Restore registers
              POP   CX
              POP   BX
              POP   AX
              RET             ; and return
CLEAR_SCREEN  ENDP
```

With the screen erased, you can call the procedure in Example 7-4 to plot a shape on the screen. For instance, this instruction sequence plots our Alphanumeric "car" with the body on line 20:

```
MOV   CH,0           ;Clear the entire screen
MOV   DH,24
CALL  CLEAR_SCREEN
LEA   DI,CAR         ;DI points to car shape table
MOV   DH,20          ;Body is on line 20,
MOV   DL,0           ; starting in column 0
CALL  DSPLY_SHAPE    ;Draw the car.
```

A Mover-and-Shaper

You can animate a complex shape, such as our "car," in the same way you animate a single-character shape. To make a multi-character shape move on the screen, you plot the shape, wait for some time interval to elapse, erase the shape, then redraw it in a new location.

As mentioned earlier, to erase a shape, you can either clear the area of the screen where the shape is displayed or redraw the shape in black. But be aware that if there are several shapes on the screen, you must somehow keep track of where the shape to be erased is located at any given time. This might be a problem if the shape is moving.

```
CAR  DB  7               ;Shape contains seven characters

     DB  52H,70H,0,0     ;Rear character of body

     DB  0B1H,70H,0,1    ;Driver's compartment

     DB  0DBH,7,0,1      ;Next character of body

     DB  0DBH,7,0,1      ;Front character of body

     DB  4FH,7,1,0       ;Front wheel

     DB  4FH,7,0,-3      ;Rear wheel

     DB  2,7,-2,1        ;Smile face
```

Figure 7-3. Shape table for alphanumeric "car."

Example 7-4. Construct a Shape From a Shape Table

```
;    This procedure constructs a shape on the screen based on
;    the data in a shape table in the data segment.
;    Upon entry, DI holds the address of the shape table, and
;    DH and DL hold the row and column coordinates of the
;    first character in the shape.
;    The shape table is assumed to hold a character count
;    byte, followed by a code, attribute, row offset and
;    column offset byte for each character in the shape.
;    No registers are affected.
;
DSPLY_SHAPE  PROC
             PUSH    AX            ;Save registers
             PUSH    BX
             PUSH    CX
             PUSH    DX
             PUSH    DI
             STI                   ;Enable interrupts
             MOV     AH,15         ;Set BH to active display page
             INT     10H
             SUB     CH,CH         ;Clear high byte of count
             MOV     CL,[DI]       ;CL holds char. count
             INC     DI            ;DI points to first char.
NEXT_CHAR:   ADD     DH,[DI+2]     ;Update row pointer
             ADD     DL,[DI+3]     ; and column pointer
             MOV     AH,2          ;Move cursor
             INT     10H
             MOV     AL,[DI]       ;Fetch char. value
             MOV     BL.[DI+1]     ; and attribute
             PUSH    CX            ;Save character count
             MOV     CX,1          ;Write character to screen
             MOV     AH,9
             INT     10H
             POP     CX            ;Restore character count
             ADD     DI,4          ;DI points to next character
                                   ; block
             LOOP    NEXT_CHAR     ;When all characters are
                                   ; displayed,
             POP     DI            ; restore registers
             POP     DX
             POP     CX
             POP     BX
             POP     AX
             RET                   ; and exit
DSPLY_SHAPE  ENDP
```

Example 7-5 shows a procedure that moves a shape from left to right across the screen. The main procedure, MOVE _ SHAPE, plots the shape on the screen using the same general approach as DSPLY_ SHAPE. The delay period (1/4-second, in this case) and the screen erase function are provided by two additional procedures: DLY_ QRTR and ERASE,

Here, ERASE erases the shape by replotting it with an attribute of zero. This produces a black-on-black display (that is, a *non-display*). ERASE also increments the column number — the variable COL _ NO in the data segment — at the end of the erase operation. Since the rightmost column on the screen is Column 79, MOVE _ SHAPE terminates when any character in the shape has a column number greater than or equal to 80.

Although this particular procedure only moves a shape horizontally, you can easily modify it to move a shape vertically or diagonally. Just change the row coordinate (rather than the column coordinate) or both the row and the column coordinates after each display-delay-erase sequence.

Example 7-5. Animate a Multi-Character Shape

```
;    This procedure moves a shape horizontally across the
;    screen, with a 1/4-second delay between moves.
;    Upon entry, DI holds the address of the shape table, and
;    DH and DL hold the row and column coordinates of the
;    first character in the shape.
;    No registers are affected.
;
;    Set up these temporary storage locs. in the data
;    segment.
;
CHAR CNT    DW  ?
POINTER     DW  ?
LINE NO     DB  ?
COL NO -    DB  ?


;    This is the main procedure.

MOVE_SHAPE  PROC
            PUSH   AX          ;Save registers
            PUSH   BX
            PUSH   CX
            PUSH   DX
            PUSH   DI
            STI                ;Enable interrupts
            MOV    AH,15       ;Set BH to active display
            INT    10H         ; page
            SUB    CH,CH       ;Clear high byte of count
```

```
              MOV    CL,[DI]      ;CL holds char. count
              INC    DI           ;DI points to first char.
              MOV    CHAR_CNT,CX  ;Save character count,
              MOV    POINTER,DI   ; shape table pointer
              MOV    LINE_NO,DH   ; and coordinates
              MOV    COL_NO,DL
;
;    These instructions plot the shape on the screen.
;
PLOT_NEXT:    ADD    DH,[DI+2]    ;Update row pointer
              ADD    DL,[DI+3]    ; and column pointer
              CMP    DL,80        ;Is this char. off the screen?
              JB     MOV_CRSR
              CALL   ERASE        ; If so, erase the shape and
                                  ;  exit
              POP    DI
              POP    DX
              POP    CX
              POP    BX
              POP    AX
              RET
MOV_CRSR:     MOV    AH,2         ; Otherwise, move cursor
              INT    10H
              MOV    AL,[DI]      ;Fetch char. value
              MOV    BL,[DI+1]    ; and attribute
              PUSH   CX           ;Save character count
              MOV    CX,1         ;Write character to screen
              MOV    AH,9
              INT    10H
              POP    CX           ;Restore character count
              ADD    DI,4         ;DI points to next character
                                  ; block
              LOOP   PLOT_NEXT    ;When all characters are
              CALL   DLY_QRTR     ; displayed, wait a
              CALL   ERASE        ; quarter-second then
                                  ; erase the shape
              JMP    SHORT PLOT_NEXT
MOVE_SHAPE    ENDP
;
;    This procedure erases a shape by replotting it with
;    attribute=0.
;
ERASE         PROC
              MOV    CX,CHAR_CNT  ;Reload character count,
              MOV    DI,POINTER   ; shape table pointer,
              MOV    DH,LINE_NO   ; line number,
              MOV    DL,COL_NO    ; and column number
```

```
ERASE_NEXT:    ADD     DH,[DI+2]
               ADD     DL,[DI+3]
               MOV     AH,2
               INT     10H
               MOV     AL,[DI]         ;To erase a character, use
               MOV     BL,0            ; an attribute of 0
               PUSH    CX
               MOV     CX,1
               MOV     AH,9
               INT     10H
               POP     CX
               ADD     DI,4
               LOOP    ERASE_NEXT
               MOV     CX,CHAR_CNT     ;Reload character count,
               MOV     DI,POINTER      ; shape table pointer,
               MOV     DH,LINE_NO      ; and line number
               INC     COL_NO          ;Point to next column
               MOV     DL,COL_NO
               RET                     ; and return to caller
ERASE          ENDP
;
;    This procedure generates a one-quarter second delay.
;
;DLY_QRTR      PROC
               PUSH    CX              ;Push CX and DX
               PUSH    DX
               SUB     CX,CX           ;Set time to zero
               DUB     DX,DX
               MOV     AH,1
               INT     1AH
CHK_QRTR:      MOV     AH,0            ;Read the time count
               INT     1AH
               CMP     DL,5            ;Has a quarter-second
                                       ; elapsed?
               JB      CHK_QRTR
               POP     DX              ; Yes. Restore registers
               POP     CX
               RET                     ;  and return to caller
DLY_QRTR       ENDP
```

Study Exercises (answers on page 282)

In addition to moving a shape on the screen, you can introduce another element of animation by having the shape *change* as it moves. To discover how to do this, develop a procedure that moves a "bird" across the screen, and changes the bird's shape from a lower-case "v" character (code 76H in Table 7-1 to a "dash" character (code 0C4H), or vice-versa, with each new column. Start the bird at row 20, column 0, and display it for two "ticks" of the 8253 Timer.

2. Game programs often use random numbers to move shapes around on the screen. To introduce yourself to this topic, you are to develop a program that displays a "smile face" (character code 2) at column 0 of a randomly-derived line number, then move the face across the screen.

The face should always advance one column at a time, but may move one line lower or one line higher, depending on whether a random number generator produces the value 0 (down one line), 1 (up one line) or 2 (same line).

The display operation should end when the face crosses line 0, line 24, or column 79. Use the Type (Time of Day) 1A interrupt to derive both the initial line number and the up/down/same indicator; see Example 6-1 in Section 6.2.

8

Let There Be Sound!

All three BASICs for the Personal Computer—Cassette BASIC, Disk BASIC and Advanced BASIC—provide a statement that lets you generate sound through the internal speaker. This statement, *SOUND*, takes two operands: a frequency and a duration. The frequency can range from 37 Hertz (cycles/ second) to 32767 Hertz. The duration can range from 0 to 65535 "clock ticks," the 8253 Timer interrupts we discussed in Chapter 6. You will recall that these interrupts occur about 18.2 times a second.

In this chapter we develop an assembly language counterpart of SOUND, and use it to play music through the speaker. However, our assembly language procedure is somewhat more flexible, in that it lets you enter the duration in increments of 1/100 of a second instead of the 1/20-second increments BASIC's SOUND statement provides.

8.1 How the Speaker Works

Most I/O operations in the IBM Personal Computer are regulated by an *8255 Programmable Peripheral Interface (PPI)* chip on the System Board. The PPI contains three 8-bit registers; two registers dedicated to input functions, the third register dedicated to output functions. The input registers are assigned I/O port numbers 60H and 62H and the output register is assigned I/O port number 61H.

As Figure 8-1 shows, either or both of two sources can drive the speaker, as selected by two bits in the PPI's output register. If Bit 0 is 1, the 8253 Timer chip drives the speaker. When Bit 1 is 1, the speaker goes on, and stays on until Bit 1 becomes 0. The programs in this chapter use the timer technique.

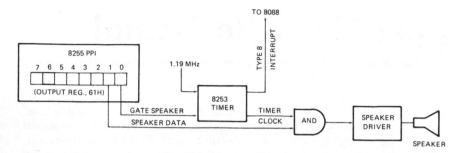

Figure 8-1. Speaker drive system.

8.2 Programming the Speaker

To avoid "reinventing the wheel," we modeled our sound procedure after a procedure that the BIOS uses to beep the speaker if its power-up reliability tests find a hardware error in the system. This BIOS procedure, called BEEP, is listed in Appendix A of the IBM *Technical Reference* manual as lines 1259 through 1277.

The BIOS "Beep" Procedure

BEEP generates a 1000-Hz tone for one or more 500-millisecond intervals, based on an interval count in BX. The interval count (1 for a "short beep," 6 for a "long beep") is set by the calling procedure, ERROR_ BEEP (lines 1225 through 1255).

BEEP configures the 8253 Timer to generate a frequency output, then sends a "divisor" value of 533H to the 8253's Timer 2. This value selects a frequency of 1000 Hz. After that, BEEP forces Bits 0 and 1 of AL to be 1 and outputs AL to the 8255's output register (I/O port 61H), which turns on the speaker. A subsequent loop keeps the speaker on for one or more 500-millisecond intervals, based on the value in BX.

A More General Sound Generator

Although BEEP is a good model for a general sound-generating procedure, we need to change two aspects of its design. First, BEEP can only produce 1000-Hz tones; we want a procedure that can produce tones of any frequency. Second, BEEP's durations are multiples of 500 milliseconds; we want a procedure whose durations are multiples of 10 milliseconds.

The BEEP procedure shows us that sending a value of 533H (decimal 1331) to Timer 2 makes it generate a 1000-Hz tone. Therefore, to generate a tone of any other frequency we just multiply 1331 by 1000/Frequency. If our sound procedure accepts a frequency in DI, the following instructions produce the correct value for Timer 2 in AX:

```
MOV   DX,14H    ;Timer divisor=
MOV   AX,4F38H  ; 1331000/Frequency
DIV   DI
```

You can generate a 10-millisecond delay with a two-instruction sequence of the general form

```
          MOV   CX,n
SPKR_ON:  LOOP  SPKR_ON
```

where n is the immediate value that makes the two instructions execute in 10 milliseconds.

From Appendix C we know that the MOV instruction executes in four clock cycles and the LOOP instruction executes in either 17 clock cycles (if the transfer takes place) or five clock cycles (if the transfer doesn't take place). Since the transfer takes place until CX is 1 — that is, (n–1) times — the general equation is:

$$[17(n-1)+5+4]\ [210 \times 10^{-9}] = 0.01$$

which solves to n = 2801. Hence, the instruction pair that generates a 10-millisecond delay is:

```
          MOV   CX,2801
SPKR_ON:  LOOP  SPKR_ON
```

By making these changes to BEEP, we can write a general purpose procedure that creates sounds of any frequency (as specified by DI) and any duration, in increments of 0.01 seconds (as specified by BX). Example 8-1 shows this assembly language SOUND procedure.

Example 8-1. A Speaker-Beeper Procedure

```
;  This procedure produces a tone of a specified frequency
;  and duration on the speaker.
;  Enter with the frequency, in Hertz, in DI (21 to 65535
;  Hz) and the duration, in hundredths of a second, in BX
;  (0 to 65535).
;  All registers are preserved.
;
SOUND      PROC
           PUSH  AX          ;Save registers
           PUSH  BX
           PUSH  CX
           PUSH  DX
           PUSH  DI
           MOV   AL,0B6H     ;Write timer mode register
           OUT   43H,AL
           MOV   DX,14H      ;Timer divisor=
           MOV   AX,4F38H    ; 1331000/Frequency
           DIV   DI
           OUT   42H,AL      ;Write Timer 2 count low byte
           MOV   AL,AH
           OUT   42H,AH      ;Write Timer 2 count high byte
           IN    AL,61H      ;Get current Port B setting
           MOV   AH,AL       ; and save it in AH
           OR    AL,3        ;Turn speaker on
           OUT   61H,AL
WAIT:      MOV   CX,2801     ;Wait 10 milliseconds
SPKR_ON:   LOOP  SPKR_ON
           DEC   BX          ;Speaker-on count expired?
           JNZ   WAIT        ; If not, keep speaker on
           MOV   AL,AH       ; Otherwise, recover value of port
           OUT   61H,AL
           POP   DI          ;Restore registers
           POP   DX
           POP   CX
           POP   BX
           POP   AX
           RET               ; and exit
SOUND      ENDP
```

As noted in the prelude to this procedure, SOUND can generate tones between 21 Hz and 65535 Hz. (The lower limit, 21 Hz, is the smallest value of DI that divides into 1,331,000 without producing an overflow.) The upper limit is, of course, superfluous, since human hearing only extends to about 20000 Hz. Still, these limits better the BASIC SOUND statement's range of 37 Hz to 32767 Hz.

Further, you can give SOUND duration values between 0 and 65535. Because BX gets decremented before it is tested for zero, the 0 input produces a duration of 256. Hence, SOUND can produce durations from 0.01 seconds (BX = 1) to 655.36 seconds (BX = 0).

8.3 Music, Music, Music

Now that we have a general-purpose sound procedure, we can build upon it to play tunes through the speaker. To do this, however, we must know how frequencies relate musical notes.

Figure 8-2 shows a portion of a piano keyboard that spans two *octaves* (octave = eight notes). The lower octave runs from low C to middle C and the upper octave runs from middle C to high C.

This drawing labels each key with its standard note name. The white keys (A through G) play the *natural* notes. The black keys play the *accidentals*, the sharped and flatted notes. Black keys produce tones one-half note higher (sharp) or one-half note lower (flat) than the white keys beside them. Figure 8-2 also shows the frequency of each note in Hertz.

We now have all the necessary data to develop a music-playing program. What should this program do? It should look up a series of frequencies and durations in two tables and make repeated calls to SOUND to "play" these notes through the built-in speaker.

The frequencies are, of course, obtained from Figure 8-2. The durations depend on what tempo you want and how many beats the note should be sustained. In 4/4 time, which has four beats to a measure, you sustain a *whole note* for four beats, a *half* note for two beats, a *quarter note* for one beat, an *eighth note* for 1/2-beat, and so on.

As a simple illustration, Figure 8-3 shows the music for "Mary Had a Little Lamb," along with its frequency and duration tables. Most of these notes are quarter notes, but the second and fourth bars end with half notes (E and G, respectively) and the final bar consists of a whole note (C).

To build the duration table, we arbitrarily give a whole note a duration of one second, which means a half note lasts a half-second and a quarter note lasts a quarter-second. The final value in the frequency table, 0FFFFH, is not a note at all. It is a terminator that tells the note-playing procedure when to stop.

A Music-Playing Procedure

Now that we have the SOUND procedure and have defined the frequency and duration tables, we must develop a procedure that accesses the tables and calls SOUND to "play" the tune. Example 8-2 lists a procedure that does this. This procedure, PLAY, assumes that the data segment addresses of the frequency and duration tables are in SI and BP, respectively.

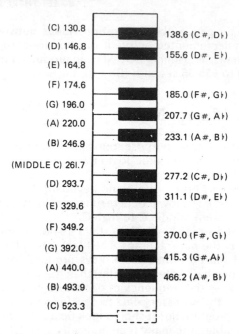

Figure 8-2. Two octaves on a piano keyboard.

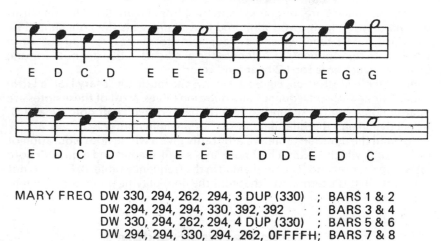

MARY FREQ	DW 330, 294, 262, 294, 3 DUP (330)	; BARS 1 & 2
	DW 294, 294, 294, 330, 392, 392	; BARS 3 & 4
	DW 330, 294, 262, 294, 4 DUP (330)	; BARS 5 & 6
	DW 294, 294, 330, 294, 262, 0FFFFH;	BARS 7 & 8
MARY TIME	DW 6 DUP (25), 50	; BARS 1 & 2
	DW 2 DUP (25, 25, 50)	; BARS 3 & 4
	DW 12 DUP (25), 100	; BARS 5 – 8

Figure 8-3. Mary Had a Little Lamb.

The Tune Module

Of course, we need one other module that defines the frequency and duration tables for the tune we want to play, puts their addresses in SI and DI, and then calls PLAY. Example 8-3 shows this module for "Mary Had a Little Lamb." Just for fun, we've also included the data tables for the lively old standard "Turkey In the Straw" (Example 8-4).

Example 8-2. A Music-Playing Procedure

```
;  This procedure "plays" a tune through the internal
;  speaker, based on two tables in the data segment.
;  Upon entry, the address of the frequency table is in SI
;  and the address of the duration table is in BP.
;  The frequency table must end with the value 0FFFFH.
;  This procedure calls SOUND (Example 8-1).
;  All registers are preserved.
;
EXTRN       SOUND:FAR           ;SOUND is an external procedure
PLAY        PROC  FAR
            PUBLIC  PLAY
            PUSH  BX            ;Save registers
            PUSH  DI
            PUSH  SI
            PUSH  BP
FREQ:       MOV   DI,[SI]       ;Fetch a frequency
            CMP   DI,0FFFFH     ;End of tune?
            JE    END_PLAY      ; If so, exit
            MOV   BX,DS:[BP]    ; Otherwise, fetch the duration
            CALL  SOUND         ;"Play" the note
            ADD   SI,2          ;Update the table pointers
            ADD   BP,2
            JNZ   FREQ          ;Go process next note
END_PLAY:   POP   BP            ;Restore registers
            POP   SI
            POP   DI
            POP   BX
            RET                 ; and exit
PLAY        ENDP
```

Example 8-3. Data Module Needed to Play a Tune

```
;  This module sets up the data tables for the tune "Mary
;  Had a Little Lamb," and puts the frequency table
;  address in SI and the duration table address in BP.
;
;  This is the stack segment.
;
EXTRN          PLAY:FAR
MARY_STACK     SEGMENT   PARA STACK 'STACK'
               DB        64 DUP('STACK    ')
MARY_STACK     ENDS
;
;  This is the data segment.
;
MARY_DATA     SEGMENT  PARA 'DATA'
MARY_FREQ     DW   330,294,262,294,3 DUP(303)          ;Bars 1 & 2
              DW   294,294,294,330,392,392             ;Bars 3 & 4
              DW   330,294,262,294,4 DUP(330)          ;Bars 5 & 6
              DW   294,294,330,294,262,0FFFFH          ;Bars 7 & 8
;
MARY_TIME     DW   6 DUP(25),50                        ;Bars 1 & 2
              DW   2 DUP(25,25,50)                     ;Bars 3 & 4
              DW   12 DUP(25),100                      ;Bars 5-8
MARY_DATA     ENDS
;
;  This is the code segment.
;
MARY_CODE     SEGMENT  PARA 'CODE'
MARY_PROC     PROC     FAR
              ASSUME   CS:MARY_CODE,DS:MARY_DATA,SS:MARY_STACK
;
;  Set up the stack to contain the proper values so this
;  procedure can return to DOS.
;
              PUSH     DS         ;Put return seg. addr. on
              SUB      AX,AX      ; stack.  Clear a register
              PUSH     AX         ;Put zero return addr. on
                                  ; stack
;
;  Initialize the data segment address.
;
              MOV      AX,SEG MARY_DATA
              MOV      DS,AX
;
;  Initialize SI and BP, then call PLAY.
```

```
        LEA     SI,MARY_FREQ
        LEA     BP,DS:MARY_TIME
        CALL    PLAY
        RET
MARY_PROC  ENDP
MARY_CODE  ENDS
        END     MARY_PROC
```

Example 8-4. Data Tables for "Turkey In the Straw"

```
TRKY_FREQ  DW   294,262,233,233,262,233,175,147,156    ;Line 1
           DW   175,196,175,147,175,233,262,294,294    ;Line 2
           DW   294,262,233,262
           DW   294,262,262,294,262,233,233,262        ;Line 3
           DW   233,175,147,156
           DW   175,196,175,147,175,233,262,294,349    ;Line 4
           DW   349,294,233,262
           DW   294,262,233,294,349,294,349,349        ;Line 5
           DW   294,349,294,349 311,392,311,392,392    ;Line 6
           DW   311,392,311,392,466,466,349,349        ;Line 7
           DW   294,294,262,233,262,294,349,392        ;Line 8
           DW   349,294,233,262,294,262,233 0FFFFH

TRKY_TIME  DW   2 DUP(12),25,6 DUP(12)                 ;Line 1
           DW   4 DUP(12),25,2 DUP(12),2 DUP(25)       ;Line 2
           DW   4 DUP(12)
           DW   3 DUP(25),2 DUP(12),25,6 DUP(12)       ;Line 3
           DW   4 DUP(12),25,2 DUP(12),2 DUP(25)       ;Line 4
           DW   4 DUP(12)
           DW   2 DUP(25),50,12,25,12,2 DUP(25)        ,Line 5
           DW   12,25,12,50,2 DUP(12,25),25            ;Line 6
           DW   12,25,12,50,4 DUP(25)                  ;Line 7
           DW   3 DUP(25),3 DUP(12),25,5 DUP(12)       ;Line 8
           DW   3 DUP(25)
```

Answers to Study Exercises

Chapter 0. A Crash Course in Computer Numbering Systems (page 8)

1. (a) 1100 (b) 10001 (c) 101101 (d) 1001000

2. (a) 8 (b) 21 (c) 31

3. (a) 8 (b) 15 (c) 1F

4. The hexadecimal value DB can represent the unsigned number 216 or the signed number -40. The signed number is derived by converting the hexadecimal value to binary (11011000), then reversing each bit (which gives 00100111) and adding 1 (which gives 00101000, or decimal 40).

Chapter 1. Introduction to Assembly Language Programming (page 21)

1. There is *no* difference between the instruction set of the 8088 and that of the 8086 — they are identical.

2. When calculating a physical address, the 8088 automatically appends four zeroes to the segment number to form the *segment address*. Therefore, 4000H is used as 40000H and the physical address is calculated as

    Physical address = 2H + 40000H = 40002H

3. If the AX register contains 1A2BH, AL (the low-order byte of AX) contains 2BH.

4. Variables are usually stored in the data segment, so the Data Segment (DS) register is normally used to access these variables.

5   Bit 7, the Sign Flag (SF), is set to 1 if a subtraction gives a negative result.

Chapter 2. Using an Assembler (page 78)

1. The assembler allocates one byte for VAR1, ten bytes (five words = ten bytes) for VAR2, and ten bytes for VAR3, for a total of *21* bytes.

2. The assembler doesn't put any value into VAR1. The ? operand tells the assembler to simply *reserve* one byte for VAR1. Your program must put something into VAR1.
    Note that the assembler only puts a value into one location here; it puts 20 into the fifth word of VAR2. All other locations are "undefined."

3. The = statement can be redefined later in the program, the EQU statement cannot.

4. CONST is a *byte* variable, and cannot hold values greater than 255.

5. Every procedure starts with PROC and ends with ENDP.

6. You can only call a NEAR procedure from within the segment in which it is defined. You can call a FAR procedure from any segment in the program.

7. The END pseudo-op must appear at the end of every source program, so that the assembler knows when to stop assembling.

8. The Linker program generates a *relocatable run module* that DOS can store at any convenient place in memory. This relieves you of the task of deciding where to store a program in memory. The Linker also combines two or more object modules.

Chapter 3. The 8088 Instruction Set (page 148)

1. The instruction is MOV ES:SAVE _ AX,AX.

2. The sequence shown stores 0 into the first location of the data segment (addressed by BX) and the stack segment (addressed by BP).

3. a. *Invalid.* A constant cannot be a destination.
    b. *Valid,* but since TEMP has not been initialized, you will get "garbage" in AL.
    c. *Invalid.* You can't move a word value into a byte variable.
    d. *Invalid.* The MOV instruction cannot be used to make a direct memory-to-memory transfer.
    e. *Invalid.* The assembler does not recognize the addressing form [BX][BP]. See Table 3-1 for valid operand formats.

4. These instructions clear the AX register:

   ```
   SUB  AX,AX
   MOV  AX,0
   ```

5. These instructions are identical. Both load the offset of location TABLE + 4 into BX. However, LEA is both shorter and more explicit.

6. This loop subtracts V2 from V1:

   ```
            MOV   CX,3       ;Word count=3
            MOV   BX,0       ;Offset=0
            CLC              ;Clear Carry (CF)
   NEXT:    MOV   DX,V2[BX]  ;Subtract words
            SBB   V1[BX],DX
            INC   BX         ; and address next word
            INC   BX
            LOOP  NEXT
   ```

   Note that BX is increased by 2 after each subtraction because words lie two bytes apart in memory. We use two INCs rather than one ADD so as not to affect the Carry Flag (CF), which is included in the SBB operation.

7. This MUL instruction generates an error. You cannot multiply by an immediate value.

8. The results are as follows:

   a. (AX) = 0220H
   b. (AX) = 9335H
   c. (AX) = 9115H
   d. (AX) = 0EDCBH
   e. (AX) = 1234H (Because TEST affects only the flags)

9. The sequence to normalize AX is:

   ```
            TEST  AX,0FFFFH
            JZ    NORM       ;Exit if (AX)=0
            MOV   CX,15      ;Get set for 15 shifts
   NEXT_BIT: JS   NORM       ;Exit if Bit 15=1
            SHL   AX,1       ;Otherwise shift AX left by
                             ; one
            LOOP  NEXT_BIT
   NORM:    ..
            ..
   ```

10. If you said the sequence subtracts 30 from AX, look again. LOOP decrements CX, then jumps to START if CX is zero. However, the MOV instruction continually reinitializes CX to 3, so CX will *never* reach zero. This kind of endless loop is a common programming error. Watch out for it.

Chapter 4. High-Precision Mathematics (page 163)

1. This procedure extracts a square root by subtracting successively higher odd numbers:

```
SR32    PROC
        PUSH    AX      ;Save original number
        PUSH    DX
        PUSH    CX      ; and CX on the stack
        MOV     BX,1    ;To start, (BX)=1
        SUB     CX,CX   ; and ((CX)=0
AGAIN:  SUB     AX,BX   ;Subtract next odd number
        SBB     DX,0    ; from AX and DX
        JC      DONE    ;Did this subtraction
                        ; create a borrow?
        INC     CX      ; No. Increase the square
        ADD     BX,2    ;  root by 1, calculate
        JMP     AGAIN   ;  the next odd number,
                        ;  then go make the next
                        ;  subtraction
DONE:   MOV     BX,CX   ; Yes.  Transfer result to
        POP     CX      ;  BX,and restore the
        POP     DX      ;  registers
        POP     AX
        RET
SR32    ENDP
```

Chapter 5. Operating on Data Structures (page 196)

1. This modified version of Example 5-1 can be used to build a list from scratch, as well as add a new element to an existing list:

```
ADD_TO_UL  PROC
           PUSH    DI          ;Save starting address
           MOV     CX,ES:[DI]  ;Fetch word count
           ADD     DI,2        ;Make DI point to 1st
                               ; element
           CMP     CX,0        ;Is the list null?
           JE      ADD_IT      ; Yes.  Value is 1st
                               ; element
           CLD                 ; No.  Set DF=0
REPNE      SCASW               ;Value already in the
                               ; list?
           JNE     ADD_IT
           POP     DI          ; Yes.  Restore starting
           RET                 ; addr. and exit
```

```
ADD_IT:      STOSW                    ; No.  Add it to end of
             POP    DI                ; list then update
                                      ; element count
             INC    WORD PTR ES:[DI]
             RET
ADD_TO_UL    ENDP
```

2. Here is the find-and-replace procedure:

```
; This procedure searches an ordered list in the extra
; segment for the word value contained in AX. If a
; matching element is found, its contents are replaced
; with the value in BX.
; AX and BX are unaffected.
;
REPLACE  PROC
         CALL   B_SEARCH     ;Is the search value in the
                             ; list?
         JC     QUIT         ; If not, exit
         MOV    ES:[SI],BX   ; If so, replace it with BX
QUIT:    RET
REPLACE  ENDP
```

Chapter 6. Using the System Resources (page 245)

1. This display procedure will not work unless interrupts have been previously enabled. To make sure that happens, you should insert an STI instruction at the beginning of the procedure.

2. Since the 8253 Timer increments the time count about 18.2 times per second, a five-second delay program must wait for the count to be incremented 91 times. The following procedure will do the job.

```
FIVE_SECS  PROC
           PUSH  AX          ;Save registers
           PUSH  CX
           PUSH  DX
           STI               ;Enable interrupts
           SUB   CX,CX       ;Set time to zero
           SUB   DX,DX
           MOV   AH,1
           INT   1AH
CHK_TIME:  MOV   AH,0        ;Read the time count
           INT   1AH
           CMP   DL,91       ;Have five seconds elapsed?
           JB    CHK_TIME
           POP   DX          ; Yes.  Restore registers
```

```
                    POP    CX
                    POP    AX
                    RET              ; and exit.
         FIVE_SECS  ENDP
```

3. The following procedure measures the elapsed time between two key depressions, and returns that time count as a 32-bit number in CX (high 16 bits) and DX (low 16 bits). No other registers are affected. To convert this count to "real time," divide it by 18.2.

```
         TIME_KEYS  PROC
                    PUSH   AX       ;Save AX
                    STI             ;Enable interrupts
                    MOV    AH,0     ;When the first key is pressed
                    INT    16H
                    SUB    CX,CX    ; set time count to zero
                    SUB    DX,DX
                    MOV    AH,1
                    INT    1AH
                    MOV    AH,0     ;When another key is pressed,
                    INT    16H
                    MOV    AH,1     ; read the count
                    INT    1AH
                    POP    AX       ;Restore AX
                    RET             ; and exit
         TIME_KEYS  ENDP
```

4. The author got a minimum count of DX = 3, which translates to about 0.165 seconds. However, many years of wine, women and song (not to mention computer programming) have taken their toll. Perhaps you can get a smaller count value. At any rate, this test shows how much slower humans are than computers. The processor can execute *thousands* of instructions in the same time it takes you to press a key twice!

Chapter 7. Graphics Made Easy (page 264)

1. This procedure moves a "bird" across the screen, on line 20:

```
         MOVE_BIRD  PROC
                    PUSH   AX       ;Save registers
                    PUSH   BX
                    PUSH   CX
                    PUSH   DX
                    STI             ;Enable interrupts
                    MOV    AH,15    ;Set BH to active display
                    INT    10H      ; page
                    MOV    AH,0     ;Select 80x25, B/W, Alpha-
```

```
                INT     10H         ; numeric
                MOV     CX,1        ;Character count=1
                MOV     DH,20       ;Start at row 20,
                MOV     DL,0        ; column 0
DSPLY_V:        MOV     BL,'v'      ;Display a "v"
                CALL    NEXT_BIRD
                CMP     DL,80       ;Done?
                JE      BIRD_DONE
                MOV     BL,0C4H     ; No.  Display a "dash"
                CALL    NEXT_BIRD
                CMP     DL,80       ;Done?
                JNE     DSPLY_V     ; If not, begin again
BIRD_DONE:      PUSH    DX          ; Otherwise, restore regis-
                PUSH    CX          ;  ters
                PUSH    BX
                PUSH    AX
                RET                 ; and exit
MOVE_BIRD       ENDP
;
; This procedure displays the bird (either "v" or
; "dash") for two time ticks, then erases it and
; advances DL to the next column.
;
NEXT_BIRD       PROC
                MOV     AH,2        ;Move cursor to next
                                    ; position
                INT     10H
                MOV     AH,10       ;Write character to the
                                    ; screen
                MOV     AL,BL
                INT     10H
                CALL    DLY_TWO     ;Wait two ticks
                SUB     AL,AL       ; then erase the bird
                MOV     AH,10
                INT     10H
                INC     DL          ;Point to next column
                RET                 ; and return to caller
NEXT_BIRD       ENDP
;
; This procedure generates a two-tick delay.
;
DLY_TWO         PROC
                PUSH    CX          ;Save CX and DX
                PUSH    DX
```

```
                SUB     CX,CX       ;Set time to zero
                SUB     DX,DX
                MOV     AH,1
                INT     1AH
CHK_TWO:        MOV     AH,0        ;Read the time count
                INT     1AH
                CMP     DL,2        ;Two Timer ticks?
                JB      CHK_TWO
                POP     DX          ; Yes. Restore registers
                POP     CX
                RET                 ; and return to caller
DLY_TWO         ENDP
```

Admittedly, the display this program produces doesn't look very much like a bird, but that's the price we pay with block graphics rather than true graphics. If you come up with a better program that moves and changes a shape, the author would like to hear about it.

2. The following procedure, which moves a smile face randomly, is a combination of Examples 6-1 and 7-2. The face is displayed for a quarter-second between moves.

```
RAND_FACE   PROC
            PUSH    AX          ;Save registers
            PUSH    BX
            PUSH    CX
            PUSH    DX
            STI                 ;Enable interrupts
            MOV     AH,15       ;Set BH to active display
            INT     10H         ; page
            MOV     AH,0        ;Select 80x25, B/W, Alpha-
            INT     10H         ; numeric
            MOV     CX,1        ;Character count=1
INIT_LINE:  CALL    RAND_8      ;Get a random line number
            AND     DL,1FH
            CMP     DL,24       ; between 0 and 24,
            JA      INIT_LINE
            MOV     DH,DL       ; and put it in DH
            MOV     DL,0        ;Start at column 0
NEXT_FACE:  MOV     AH,2        ;Move cursor to next
            INT     10H         ; position
            MOV     AL,2        ;Display smile face
            MOV     AH,10
            INT     10H
            CALL    DLY_QRTR    ;Wait a quarter-second
            SUB     AL,AL       ; then erase the face
            MOV     AH,10
            INT     10H
            MOV     AX,DX       ;Save row, column in AX
```

```
LINE_IND:   CALL    RAND_8      ;Get a number between 0
            AND     DL,3        ; and 2
            CMP     DL,2
            JNE     CHK_3
            MOV     DX,AX       ;It's a 2.   Do nothing
            JE      INC_COL
CHK_3:      JA      LINE_IND
            CMP     DL,1
            JNE     ITS_0
            MOV     DX,AX       ;It's a 1.   Increment row
            INC     DH
            CMP     DH,25       ; and make sure row < 25
            JE      EXIT_FACE
            JNE     INC_COL
ITS_0:      MOV     DX,AX       ;It's a 0.   Decrement row
            DEC     DH
            JS      EXIT_FACE   ; and make sure row is
                                ; positive
INC_COL:    INC     DL          ;Point to next column
            CMP     DL,80       ; and exit if it's 80
            JNE     NEXT_FACE
EXIT_FACE:  POP     DX          ;Restore registers
            POP     CX
            POP     BX
            POP     AX
            RET                 ; and exit
RAND_FACE   ENDP
;
;   This procedure generates a quarter-second delay.
;
DLY_QRTR    PROC
            PUSH    BX          ;Save registers
            PUSH    CX
            PUSH    DX
            MOV     AH,0        ;Read the time count
            INT     1AH
            MOV     BL,DL       ; and save low byte in BL
CHK_QRTR:   MOV     AH,0        ;Read the time count again
            INT     1AH
            SUB     DL,BL
            CMP     DL,5        ;Has a quarter-second
            JB      CHK_QRTR    ; elapsed?
            POP     DX          ; Yes.   Restore registers
            POP     CX
            POP     BX
            RET                 ;    and return to caller
```

```
DLY_QRTR   ENDP
;
; This procedure returns a 16-bit random number in DX,
; but the caller, RAND_FACE, only uses the value
; in DL.
;
RAND_8     PROC
           PUSH   AX        ;Save AX And CX
           PUSH   CX
           MOV    AH,0      ;Read the timer
           INT    1AH
           POP    CX        ; and exit
           POP    AX
           RET
RAND_8     ENDP
```

Appendix A

Hexadecimal/Decimal Conversion

HEXADECIMAL COLUMNS											
6		**5**		**4**		**3**		**2**		**1**	
HEX	DEC	HEX	DEC	HEX	DEC	HEX	DEC	HEX	DEC	HEX	DEC
0	0	0	0	0	0	0	0	0	0	0	0
1	1,048,576	1	65,536	1	4,096	1	256	1	16	1	1
2	2,097,152	2	131,072	2	8,192	2	512	2	32	2	2
3	3,145,728	3	196,608	3	12,288	3	768	3	48	3	3
4	4,194,304	4	262,144	4	16,384	4	1,024	4	64	4	4
5	5,242,880	5	327,680	5	20,480	5	1,280	5	80	5	5
6	6,291,456	6	393,216	6	24,576	6	1,536	6	96	6	6
7	7,340,032	7	458,752	7	28,672	7	1,792	7	112	7	7
8	8,388,608	8	524,288	8	32,768	8	2,048	8	128	8	8
9	9,437,184	9	589,824	9	36,864	9	2,304	9	144	9	9
A	10,485,760	A	655,360	A	40,960	A	2,560	A	160	A	10
B	11,534,336	B	720,896	B	45,056	B	2,816	B	176	B	11
C	12,582,912	C	786,432	C	49,152	C	3,072	C	192	C	12
D	13,631,488	D	851,968	D	53,248	D	3,328	D	208	D	13
E	14,680,064	E	917,504	E	57,344	E	3,584	E	224	E	14
F	15,728,640	F	983,040	F	61,440	F	3,840	F	240	F	15
7654		3210		7654		3210		7654		3210	
Byte				Byte				Byte			

POWERS OF 2

2^n	n
256	8
512	9
1 024	10
2 048	11
4 096	12
8 192	13
16 384	14
32 768	15
65 536	16
131 072	17
262 144	18
524 288	19
1 048 576	20
2 097 152	21
4 194 304	22
8 388 608	23
16 777 216	24

2^0	$= 16^0$
2^4	$= 16^1$
2^8	$= 16^2$
2^{12}	$= 16^3$
2^{16}	$= 16^4$
2^{20}	$= 16^5$
2^{24}	$= 16^6$
2^{28}	$= 16^7$
2^{32}	$= 16^8$
2^{36}	$= 16^9$
2^{40}	$= 16^{10}$
2^{44}	$= 16^{11}$
2^{48}	$= 16^{12}$
2^{52}	$= 16^{13}$
2^{56}	$= 16^{14}$
2^{60}	$= 16^{15}$

POWERS OF 16

16^n	n
1	0
16	1
256	2
4 096	3
65 536	4
1 048 576	5
16 777 216	6
268 435 456	7
4 294 967 296	8
68 719 476 736	9
1 099 511 627 776	10
17 592 186 044 416	11
281 474 976 710 656	12
4 503 599 627 370 496	13
72 057 594 037 927 936	14
1 152 921 504 606 846 976	15

Appendix B

The IBM PC ASCII Character Set

DECIMAL VALUE →		0	16	32	48	64	80	96	128	144	160	176	192	208	224	240
↓	HEXADECIMAL VALUE	0	1	·2	3	4	5	6	8	9	A	B	C	D	E	F
0	0	BLANK (NULL)	►	BLANK (SPACE)	0	@	P	‘	Ç	É	á	▨	└	╨	∝	≡
1	1	☺	◄	!	1	A	Q	a	ü	Æ	í	▒	┴	╤	β	±
2	2	☻	↕	"	2	B	R	b	é	FE	ó	▓	┬	╥	γ	≥
3	3	♥	‼	#	3	C	S	c	â	ô	ú	│	├	╙	π	≤
4	4	♦	¶	$	4	D	T	d	ä	ö	ñ	┤	─	└	Σ	∫
5	5	♣	§	%	5	E	U	e	à	ò	Ñ	╡	┼	╒	σ	
6	6	♠	▬	&	6	F	V	f	å	û	ª	╢	╞	╓	μ	÷
7	7	•	↨	'	7	G	W	g	ç	ù	º	╖	╟	╫	τ	≈
8	8	◘	↑	(	8	H	X	h	ê	ÿ	¿	╕	╚	╪	Φ	°
9	9	○	↓	)	9	I	Y	i	ë	Ö	⌐	╣	╔	┘	Θ	•
10	A	◎	→	*	:	J	Z	j	è	Ü	¬	║	╩	┌	Ω	•
11	B	♂	←	+	;	K	[	k	ï	¢	½	╗	╦	█	δ	√
12	C	♀	∟	,	<	L	\	l	î	£	¼	╝	╠	▄	∞	η
13	D	♪	↔	−	=	M	]	m	ì	¥	¡	╜	═	▌	∅	²
14	E	♫	▲	.	>	N	^	n	Ä	Pts	«	╛	╬	▐	∈	■
15	F	☼	▼	/	?	O	_	o	Å	ƒ	»	┐	╧	▀	∩	BLANK 'FF'

288

Appendix C

8088 Instruction Times

You can use the two tables in this appendix to calculate how long the IBM Personal Computer's 8088 microprocessor will take to execute instructions in your program. These tables give execution times in *clock cycles*. To convert clock cycles to nanoseconds, you multiply by 210.

Table C-1 lists execution time increments for operand addressing modes that reference memory. You should add these increments to the execution times in Table C-2 that include "EA".

For each instruction in the 8088 instruction set, Table C-2 lists the number of *clocks* the instruction takes to execute and the number of *bytes* it occupies in memory. When using Table C-2, note the following:

1. Some instructions take more time to execute if their operands are word values, rather than byte values. For these instructions, execution times are listed in the form *b(w)*, where *b* denotes the number of clock cycles for byte operands and *w* denotes the number of clock cycles for word operands.

2. Most instructions that reference memory have the abbreviation EA in the Clocks column. This abbreviation tells you that additional clock cycles are required to calculate the Effective Address; these incremental times are listed in Table C-1.

3. The execution time of conditional jump instructions and loop instructions depends on whether the transfer is made. If the transfer *is* made, use the larger number in the Clocks column. Otherwise, if execution "drops through" to the next instruction, use the smaller number.

For instance, suppose you want to find the execution time of the instruction

ADD SS:[BX],DX

This instruction has the general form *ADD memory, register*, so its execution time is given by the equation

16(24)+EA

Since this particular ADD instruction operates on word values, you use the 24 instead of the 16. Because the equation contains EA, you must add an address calculation time from Table C-1. The destination operand has the form [BX], which tells you to add 5 additional clock cycles. However, because this operand has a segment override, you must add 2 more clock cycles. Combining these three values gives a total execution time of 31 clock cycles (24 + 5 + 2).

Table C-1. Effective Address Calculation Time.

EA Components	Operand Formats	Clocks*
Displacement Only	disp label	6
Base or Index Only	[BX] [BP] [DI] [SI]	5
Displacement + Base or Index	[BX] + disp [BP] + disp [DI] + disp [SI] + disp	9
Base + Index	[BX][SI] [BX][DI] [BP][SI] [BP][DI]	7 8
Displacement + Base + Index	[BX][SI] + disp [BX][DI] + disp [BP][SI] + disp [BP][DI] + disp	11 12

*Add 2 clocks for segment override.

Table C-2. Instruction Times.

Instruction		Clocks	Bytes
AAA		4	1
AAD		60	2
AAM		83	1
AAS		4	1
ADC	register,register	3	2
ADC	register,memory	9(13)+EA	2-4
ADC	memory,register	16(24)+EA	2-4
ADC	register,immediate	4	3-4
ADC	memory,immediate	17(25)+EA	3-6
ADC	accumulator,immediate	4	2-3
ADD	register,register	3	2
ADD	register,memory	9(13)+EA	2-4
ADD	memory,register	16(24)+EA	2-4
ADD	register,immediate	4	3-4
ADD	memory,immediate	17(25)+EA	3-6
ADD	accumulator,immediate	4	2-3
AND	register,register	3	2
AND	register,memory	9(13)+EA	2-4
AND	memory,register	16(24)+EA	2-4
AND	register,immediate	4	3-4
AND	memory,immediate	17(15)+EA	3-6
AND	accumulator,immediate	4	2-3
CALL	near-proc	23	3
CALL	far-proc	36	5
CALL	memptr16	29+EA	2-4
CALL	regptr16	24	2
CALL	memptr32	57+EA	2-4
CBW		2	1
CLC		2	1
CLD		2	1
CLI		2	1
CMC		2	1
CMP	register,register	3	2
CMP	register,memory	9(13)+EA	2-4
CMP	memory,register	9(13)+EA	2-4

Table C-2. Instruction Times (continued).

	Instruction	Clocks	Bytes
CMP	register, immediate	4	3-4
CMP	memory,immediate	10(14)+EA	3-6
CMP	accumulator,immediate	4	2-3
CMPS	dest-string, source-string	22(30)	1
CMPS	(repeat) dest-string, source-string	9+22(30)/rep	1
CWD		5	1
DAA		4	1
DAS		4	1
DEC	reg16	2	1
DEC	reg8	3	2
DEC	memory	15(23)+EA	2-4
DIV	reg8	80-90	2
DIV	reg16	144-162	2
DIV	mem8	(86-96)+EA	2-4
DIV	mem16	(154-172)+EA	2-4
ESC	immediate,memory	8(12)+EA	2-4
ESC	immediate,register	2	2
HLT		2	1
IDIV	reg8	101-112	2
IDIV	reg16	165-184	2
IDIV	mem8	(107-118)+EA	2-4
IDIV	mem16	(175-194)+EA	2-4
IMUL	reg8	80-98	2
IMUL	reg16	128-154	2
IMUL	mem8	(86-104)+EA	2-4
IMUL	mem16	(138-164)+EA	2-4
IN	accumulator,immed8	10(14)	2
IN	accumulator,DX	8(12)	1
INC	reg16	2	1
INC	reg8	3	2
INC	memory	15(23)+EA	2-4
INT	3	52	1
INT	immed8 (not type 3)	51	2
INTO		53 or 4	1
IRET		32	1

Table C-2. Instruction Times (continued).

Instruction		Clocks	Bytes
All conditional jump instructions except JCXZ:			
Jccc	short-label	16 or 4	2
JCXZ	short-label	18 or 6	2
JMP	short-label	15	2
JMP	near-label	15	3
JMP	far-label	15	5
JMP	memptr16	18 + EA	2-4
JMP	regptr16	11	2
JMP	memptr32	24 + EA	2-4
LAHF		4	1
LDS	reg16,mem32	24 + EA	2-4
LEA	reg16,mem16	2 + EA	2-4
LES	reg16,mem32	24 + EA	2-4
LOCK		2	1
LODS	source-string	12(16)	1
LODS	(repeat) source-string	9 + 13(17)/rep	1
LOOP	short-label	17 or 5	2
LOOPE/ LOOPZ	short-label	18 or 6	2
LOOPNE/ LOOPNZ	short-label	19 or 5	2
MOV	memory,accumulator	10(14)	3
MOV	accumulator,memory	10(14)	3
MOV	register,register	2	2
MOV	register,memory	8(12) + EA	2-4
MOV	memory,register	9(13) + EA	2-4
MOV	register,immediate	4	2-3
MOV	memory,immediate	10(14) + EA	3-6
MOV	seg-reg,reg16	2	2
MOV	seg-reg,mem16	8(12) + EA	2-4
MOV	reg16,seg-reg	2	2
MOV	memory,seg-reg	9(13) + EA	2-4
MOVS	dest-string, source-string	18(26)	1
MOVS	(repeat) dest-string, source-string	9 + 17(25)/rep	1

Table C-2. Instruction Times (continued).

Instruction		Clocks	Bytes
MUL	reg8	70-77	2
MUL	reg16	118-133	2
MUL	mem8	(76-83)+EA	2-4
MUL	mem16	(128-143)+EA	2-4
NEG	register	3	2
NEG	memory	16(24)+EA	2-4
NOP		3	1
NOT	register	3	2
NOT	memory	16(24)+EA	2-4
OR	register,register	3	2
OR	register,memory	9(13)+EA	2-4
OR	memory,register	16(24)+EA	2-4
OR	register,immediate	4	3-4
OR	memory,immediate	17(15)+EA	3-6
OR	accumulator,immediate	4	2-3
OUT	immed8,accumulator	10(14)	2
OUT	DX,accumulator	8(12)	1
POP	register	12	1
POP	seg-reg (CS illegal)	12	1
POP	memory	25+EA	2-4
POPF		12	1
PUSH	register	15	1
PUSH	seg-reg (CS legal)	14	1
PUSH	memory	24+EA	2-4
PUSHF		14	1
RCL	register,1	2	2
RCL	register,CL	8+4/bit	2
RCL	memory,1	15(23)+EA	2-4
RCL	memory,CL	20(28)+EA+4/bit	2-4
RCR	register,1	2	2
RCR	register,CL	8+4/bit	2
RCR	memory,1	15(23)+EA	2-4
RCR	memory,CL	20(28)+EA+4/bit	2-4
REP		2	1
REPE/REPZ		2	1
REPNE/REPNZ		2	1

Table C-2. Instruction Times (continued).

Instruction		Clocks	Bytes
RET	(intra-seg, no pop)	20	1
RET	(intra-seg, pop)	24	3
RET	(inter-seg, no pop)	32	1
RET	(inter-seg, pop)	31	3
ROL	register,1	2	2
ROL	register,CL	8+4/bit	2
ROL	memory,1	15(23)+EA	2-4
ROL	memory,CL	20(28)+EA+4/bit	2-4
ROR	register,1	2	2
ROR	register,CL	8+4/bit	2
ROR	memory,1	15(23)+EA	2-4
ROR	memory,CL	20(28)+EA+4/bit	2-4
SAHF		4	1
SAL/SHL	register,1	2	2
SAL/SHL	register,CL	8+4/bit	2
SAL/SHL	memory,1	15(23)+EA	2-4
SAL/SHL	memory,CL	20(28)+EA+4/bit	2-4
SAR	register,1	2	2
SAR	register,CL	8+4/bit	2
SAR	memory,1	15(23)+EA	2-4
SAR	memory,CL	20(28)+EA+4/bit	2-4
SBB	register,register	3	2
SBB	register,memory	9(13)+EA	2-4
SBB	memory,register	16(24)+EA	2-4
SBB	register,immediate	4	3-4
SBB	memory,immediate	17(25)+EA	3-6
SBB	accumulator,immediate	4	2-3
SCAS	dest-string	15(19)	1
SCAS	(repeat) dest-string	9+15(19)/rep	1
SHR	register,1	2	2
SHR	register,CL	8+4/bit	2
SHR	memory,1	15(23)+EA	2-4
SHR	memory,CL	20(28)+EA+4/bit	2-4
STC		2	1
STD		2	1
STI		2	1

Table C-2. Instruction Times (continued).

Instruction		Clocks	Bytes
STOS	dest-string	11(15)	1
STOS	(repeat) dest-string	9 + 10(14)/rep	1
SUB	register,register	3	2
SUB	register,memory	9(13) + EA	2-4
SUB	memory,register	16(24) + EA	2-4
SUB	register,immediate	4	3-4
SUB	memory,immediate	17(25) + EA	3-6
SUB	accumulator,immediate	4	2-3
TEST	register,register	3	2
TEST	register,memory	9(13) + EA	2-4
TEST	register,immediate	5	3-4
TEST	memory,immediate	11 + EA	3-6
TEST	accumulator,immediate	4	2-3
WAIT		3 + 5n	1
XCHG	accumulator,reg16	3	1
XCHG	memory,register	17(25) + EA	2-4
XCHG	register,register	4	2
XLAT	source-table	11	1
XOR	register,register	3	2
XOR	register,memory	9(13) + EA	2-4
XOR	memory,register	16(24) + EA	2-4
XOR	register,immediate	4	3-4
XOR	memory,immediate	17(15) + EA	3-6
XOR	accumulator,immediate	4	2-3

Appendix D

8088 Instruction Set Summary

Table D-1 summarizes the 8088 instruction set in alphabetical order. For each instruction, it shows the general assembler format and which flags are affected. In the *Flags* column, – means unchanged, * means may have changed, and ? means undefined.

Table D-1. The 8088 Instruction Set.

Mnemonic	Assembler Format	OF	DF	IF	TF	SF	ZF	AF	PF	CF
AAA		?	–	–	–	?	?	*	?	*
AAD		?	–	–	–	*	*	?	*	?
AAM		?	–	–	–	*	*	?	*	?
AAS		?	–	–	–	?	?	*	?	*
ADC	destination,source	*	–	–	–	*	*	*	*	*
ADD	destination,source	*	–	–	–	*	*	?	*	*
AND	destination,source	0	–	–	–	*	*	?	*	0
CALL	target	–	–	–	–	–	–	–	–	–
CBW		–	–	–	–	–	–	–	–	–
CLC		–	–	–	–	–	–	–	–	0
CLD		–	0	–	–	–	–	–	–	–

Table D-1. The 8088 Instruction Set (continued).

Mnemonic	Assembler Format	Flags								
		OF	DF	IF	TF	SF	ZF	AF	PF	CF
CLI		–	–	0	–	–	–	–	–	–
CMC		–	–	–	–	–	–	–	–	*
CMP	destination,source	*	–	–	–	*	*	*	*	*
CMPS	dest-string,source-string	*	–	–	–	*	*	*	*	*
CMPSB		*	–	–	–	*	*	*	*	*
CMPSW		*	–	–	–	*	*	*	*	*
CWD		–	–	–	–	–	–	–	–	–
DAA		?	–	–	–	*	*	*	*	*
DAS		?	–	–	–	*	*	*	*	*
DEC	destination	*	–	–	–	*	*	*	*	–
DIV	source	?	–	–	–	?	?	?	?	?
ESC	ext-opcode,source	–	–	–	–	–	–	–	–	–
HLT		–	–	–	–	–	–	–	–	–
IDIV	source	?	–	–	–	?	?	?	?	?
IMUL	source	*	–	–	–	?	?	?	?	*
IN	accumulator,port	–	–	–	–	–	–	–	–	–
INC	destination	*	–	–	–	*	*	*	*	–
INT	interrupt-type	–	–	0	0	–	–	–	–	–
INTO		–	–	0	0	–	–	–	–	–
IRET		*	*	*	*	*	*	*	*	*
JA/JNBE	short-label	–	–	–	–	–	–	–	–	–
JAE/JNB	short-label	–	–	–	–	–	–	–	–	–

Table D-1. The 8088 Instruction Set (continued).

Mnemonic	Assembler Format		OF	DF	IF	TF	SF	ZF	AF	PF	CF
JB/JNAE/JC	JB	short-label	–	–	–	–	–	–	–	–	–
JBE/JNA	JBE	short-label	–	–	–	–	–	–	–	–	–
JCXZ	JCXZ	short-label	–	–	–	–	–	–	–	–	–
JE/JZ	JE/JZ	short-label	–	–	–	–	–	–	–	–	–
JG/JNLE	JG	short-label	–	–	–	–	–	–	–	–	–
JGE/JNL	JGE	short-label	–	–	–	–	–	–	–	–	–
JL/JNGE	JL	short-label	–	–	–	–	–	–	–	–	–
JLE/JNG	JLE	short-label	–	–	–	–	–	–	–	–	–
JMP	JMP	target	–	–	–	–	–	–	–	–	–
JNC	JNC	short-label	–	–	–	–	–	–	–	–	–
JNE/JNZ	JNE	short-label	–	–	–	–	–	–	–	–	–
JNO	JNO	short-label	–	–	–	–	–	–	–	–	–
JNP/JPO	JNP	short-label	–	–	–	–	–	–	–	–	–
JNS	JNS	short-label	–	–	–	–	–	–	–	–	–
JO	JO	short-label	–	–	–	–	–	–	–	–	–
JP/JPE	JP	short-label	–	–	–	–	–	–	–	–	–
JS	JS	short-label	–	–	–	–	–	–	–	–	–
LAHF	LAHF		–	–	–	–	–	–	–	–	–
LDS	LDS	reg16,mem32	–	–	–	–	–	–	–	–	–
LEA	LEA	reg16,mem16	–	–	–	–	–	–	–	–	–
LES	LES	reg16,mem32	–	–	–	–	–	–	–	–	–
LOCK	LOCK		–	–	–	–	–	–	–	–	–
LODS	LODS	source-string	–	–	–	–	–	–	–	–	–

Table D-1. The 8088 Instruction Set (continued).

Mnemonic	Assembler Format	OF	DF	IF	TF	SF	ZF	AF	PF	CF
LODSB		–	–	–	–	–	–	–	–	–
LODSW		–	–	–	–	–	–	–	–	–
LOOP	short-label	–	–	–	–	–	–	–	–	–
LOOPE/ LOOPZ	short-label	–	–	–	–	–	–	–	–	–
LOOPNE/ LOOPNZ	short-label	–	–	–	–	–	–	–	–	–
MOV	destination,source	–	–	–	–	–	–	–	–	–
MOVS	dest-string,source-string	–	–	–	–	–	–	–	–	–
MOVSB		–	–	–	–	–	–	–	–	–
MOVSW		–	–	–	–	–	–	–	–	–
MUL	source	*	–	–	–	?	?	?	?	*
NEG	destination	*	–	–	–	*	*	*	*	*
NOP		–	–	–	–	–	–	–	–	–
NOT	destination	–	–	–	–	–	–	–	–	–
OR	destination,source	0	–	–	–	*	*	?	*	0
OUT	port,accumulator	–	–	–	–	–	–	–	–	–
POP	destination	–	–	–	–	–	–	–	–	–
POPF		*	*	*	*	*	*	*	*	*
PUSH	source	–	–	–	–	–	–	–	–	–
PUSHF		–	–	–	–	–	–	–	–	–

Table D-1. The 8088 Instruction Set (continued).

Mnemonic	Assembler Format	OF	DF	IF	TF	SF	ZF	AF	PF	CF
RCL	destination,count	*	–	–	–	–	–	–	–	*
RCR	destination,count	*	–	–	–	–	–	–	–	*
REP		–	–	–	–	–	–	–	–	–
REPE/REPZ		–	–	–	–	–	–	–	–	–
REPNE/REPNZ		–	–	–	–	–	–	–	–	–
RET	[pop-value]	–	–	–	–	–	–	–	–	–
ROL	destination,count	*	–	–	–	–	–	–	–	*
ROR	destination,count	*	–	–	–	–	–	–	–	*
SAHF		–	–	–	–	*	*	*	*	*
SAL/SHL	destination,count	*	–	–	–	*	*	?	*	*
SAR	destination,count	*	–	–	–	*	*	?	*	*
SBB	destination,source	*	–	–	–	*	*	*	*	*
SCAS	dest-string	*	–	–	–	*	*	*	*	*
SCASB		*	–	–	–	*	*	*	*	*
SCASW		*	–	–	–	*	*	*	*	*
SHR	destination,count	*	–	–	–	0	*	?	*	*
STC		–	–	–	–	–	–	–	–	1
STD		–	1	–	–	–	–	–	–	–
STI		–	–	1	–	–	–	–	–	–
STOS	dest-string	–	–	–	–	–	–	–	–	–
STOSB		–	–	–	–	–	–	–	–	–
STOSW		–	–	–	–	–	–	–	–	–
SUB	destination,source	*	–	–	–	*	*	*	*	*

Table D-1. The 8088 Instruction Set (continued).

Mnemonic	Assembler Format	Flags								
		OF	DF	IF	TF	SF	ZF	AF	PF	CF
TEST	destination,source	0	-	-	-	*	*	?	*	0
WAIT		-	-	-	-	-	-	-	-	-
XCHG	destination,source	-	-	-	-	-	-	-	-	-
XLAT	source-table	-	-	-	-	-	-	-	-	-
XOR	destination,source	0	-	-	-	*	*	?	*	0

Disk User's Guide

The optional disk holds 40 programs from the book. One side of the disk has the *source programs,* the other side has the assembled *object programs.* Having the source programs allows you to change a program if you wish to do so. Having the object programs allows you to link and run the programs without assembling them.

What the Disk File Names Mean

The names of the files on the disk refer to the program listings in the book. Disk files whose names start with the "EX" hold programs listed as Examples. For example, file EX513.ASM holds the source program for Example 5-13, while EX513.OBJ holds the object program for Example 5-13. Disk files whose names start with "ANS" are solutions to programming problems posed in the end-of-chapter exercises. For example, files ANS52.ASM and ANS52.OBJ are the source and object programs that solve Exercise problem 2 at the end of Chapter 5.

Programs You May Execute From DOS

Some programs in the book are intended to be used by themselves, rather than with a calling program. For these programs, listed in Table 1, the disk provides a *run file* in addition to the source and object file. Run files, which have the suffix EXE, are stored on the side of the disk that has the object programs.

With the DOS prompt (A>) on the screen, you can run any of these programs by simply entering its name. For instance, to play "Turkey In the Straw," enter

```
A>ex84.exe
```

The disk also contains the source and object files for EX_PROG, the example program in Chapter 2, but not its run file. *You* create that file using the procedure we describe in the book.

Files You Must Link

The remaining disk files are general-purpose procedures you can use in your programs. To do so, however, you must first create a *calling program,* assemble the calling program, then link the two object (OBJ) files to form a run (EXE) file. Table 2 summarizes the information you need to use these files.

Incidentally, some procedures in the book call other procedures. For your convenience, the programs on the disk *include* any procedures they call. For

Table 1.   Programs That Have Run Files.

File Name	Description
EX71	Display a Diagonal Line
EX72	Animate a Diagonal Line Display
ANS71	Move a "Bird" Across the Screen
ANS72	Move a "Smile Face" Across the Screen, Randomly
EX83	Play "Mary Had a Little Lamb"
EX84	Play "Turkey In the Straw"
EX85	Play Music From the Keyboard

example, the MULS32 procedure in Example 4-2 calls the MULU32 procedure in Example 4-1. The file that holds MULS32, EX42, includes the instructions for MULU32. This means you never need to link more than two object files: your calling program and the disk program you wish to use.

How to Create a Calling Program

A calling program is a procedure that executes one or more other procedures, then returns control to DOS or DEBUG. Every calling program must contain a code segment, a stack segment, and an EXTRN pseudo-op.

The code segment holds instructions that return control to DOS, plus the CALL instruction (for example, CALL MULU32) and, often, instructions that initialize registers and memory locations the called program expects to receive. The stack segment allocates memory for return addresses. The EXTRN pseudo-op tells the assembler that the procedure CALLed in the code segment is in another object file on disk. For example, EXTRN MULU32:FAR tells the assembler that the procedure MULU32 is in an object file you will link to this file *and* (via the FAR suffix) that MULU32 is in a different code segment.

Some calling programs also need a data segment and/or an extra segment, if the called procedure requires you to supply data in them.

Figure 1 lists a program that calls MULU32, the 32-bit X 32-bit unsigned multiply procedure from Example 4-1. Once you've entered your calling program into the PC (it's named MULU32C.ASM in Figure 1), you assemble it, then link the two object modules (MULU32C.OBJ and EX41.OBJ here). The Linker creates a run module (MULU32C.EXE), which you run under DEBUG.

The program in Figure 1 is general-purpose, so it doesn't tell MULU32 which numbers to multiply. After you've entered DEBUG, you must supply these numbers in CX and BX (multiplier) and in DX and AX (multiplicand).

Table 2.   Files You Must Link.

Link This Object Module	Call Procedure With This Name	Description
EX41	MULU32	32-Bit X 32-Bit Unsigned Multiply
EX42	MULS32	32-Bit X 32-Bit Signed Multiply
EX43	AVERAGE	Average Unsigned Words
EX44	DIVUO	Divide, Account for Overflow
EX45	SQRT32	Square Root of 32-Bit Number
ANS41	SR32	Square Root by Subtracting
EX51	ADD_TO_UL	Add Element to Unordered List
EX52	DEL_UL	Delete Element From Unord. List
EX53	MINMAX	Max & Min Value in Unord. List
EX55	BUBBLE	Bubble Sort an Unord. List
EX56	B_SEARCH	Search Ordered List
EX57	ADD_TO_OL	Add Element to Ordered List
EX58	DEL_OL	Delete Element From Ordered List
FX59	FIND_SINE	Sine of an Angle
EX510	FIND_COS	Cosine of an Angle
EX511	CONV_HEX	Hex to ASCII, BCD, and EBCDIC
EX513	PHONE_NOS	Sort a Telephone List
ANS51	ADD_TO_UL	Create an Unordered List
ANS52	REPLACE	Replace Element in Ordered List
EX61	RAND_51	Random Number Between 0 and 51
EX62	READ_KEYS	Read Keys Without Display
EX63	READ_KEYS	Read Keys With Display
EX64	ASCII_BIN	ASCII String to Binary Number
EX65	BIN_ASCII	Binary Number to ASCII String
ANS62	FIVE_SECS	Five-Second Delay
ANS63	TIME_KEYS	Time Between Key Depressions
EX73	CLEAR_SCREEN	Clear Lines on the Screen
EX74	DSPLY_SHAPE	Construct Shape From Shape Table
EX75	MOV_SHAPE	Move a Shape Across the Screen
EX81	SOUND	Generate a Sound
EX82	PLAY	Play a Tune

Since MULU32C doesn't give visual results, the best way to run it is to execute down to the RET instruction, then examine the registers. If you assemble MULU32C and examine the list file (MULU32C.LST), you discover that the RET instruction has an offset of 000A. Hence, you run the program with the DEBUG command *ga*.

You will find the MULU32C.ASM file on the disk. Feel free to use it as "boilerplate" to create your own calling programs.

```
TITLE     MULU32 Caller (MULU32C.ASM)
          PAGE      ,132
          EXTRN     MULU32:FAR   ;MULU32 is an external
                                 ; procedure
;
; Set up the stack segment.
;
STACK     SEGMENT   PARA STACK 'STACK'
          DB        64 DUP('STACK   ')
STACK     ENDS
;
; Here is the code for the calling program.
;
CODE      SEGMENT   PARA 'CODE'
CALLER    PROC      FAR
          ASSUME    CS:CODE,SS:STACK
;
; Set up the stack so this program returns to DEBUG.
;
          PUSH      DS           ;Put return seg. addr. on
                                 ; stack
          MOV       DI,0         ;Clear a register
          PUSH      DI           ;Put zero return addr. on
                                 ; stack
;
; Call MULU32
;
          CALL      MULU32
          RET                    ;Return to DEBUG
CALLER    ENDP
CODE      ENDS
          END       CALLER
```

Figure 1.   A Program That Calls MULU32.

Index